Ecological Thought

ECOLOGICAL THOUGHT

An Introduction

Tim Hayward

Polity Press

The right of Tim Hayward to be identified as author of this work has been asserted in accordance with the Copyright, Designs and Patents Act 1988.

First published in 1995 by Polity Press in association with Blackwell Publishers Ltd.

Editorial office:
Polity Press
65 Bridge Street
Cambridge CB2 1UR, UK

Marketing and production:
Blackwell Publishers Ltd
108 Cowley Road
Oxford OX4 1JF, UK

Blackwell Publishers Inc.
238 Main Street
Cambridge, MA 02142, USA

ISBN 0 7456 1319 5
ISBN 0 7456 1320 9 (pbk)

A CIP catalogue record for this book is available from the British Library and the Library of Congress.

Typeset in 11 on 12½ pt Times
by Photoprint
Printed in Great Britain by T.J. Press, Padstow, Cornwall

This book is printed on acid-free paper.

To Mum and Dad

Contents

Preface

This book began with a conviction – one which I know is shared by a growing number of people throughout the world – that the devastation which humans are wreaking with increasing intensity upon their environment and upon other species, as well as upon their own kind, requires a radical response; and if ecologically and socially deleterious practices are to be transformed, this cannot occur without a radical transformation of the attitudes and values which sustain and are sustained by them.

Yet this conviction was tempered by a perplexity, which can be summed up in the question of whether what were previously taken as emancipatory and enlightened values are really part of the problem, or may not yet be part of a solution. In writing this book I have tried to work through this perplexity – which has essentially meant appreciating how, in various ways, they are both. In doing so, I hope to have shown how constructive debate is possible: between, for instance, those concerned with making a better life for humans and those concerned with the good of beings other than humans; or between those who believe in a gradual reform of existing practices and those who seek their radical transformation. Thus in surveying a diversity of views I have also sought out grounds for unity and pointed up common problems.

This book has been written at an interesting time for ecological social and political theory. Not so long ago, the main problem was to get these questions on to the agenda at all. But since the first wave of now classic ecological writings of the 1960s and 1970s things have changed quite considerably, and the problem today is rather different: with the value of 'ecology' now ranking alongside other concepts like 'freedom' and 'democracy' as an unquestionable good, it is subject, like them, to various and sometimes contradictory interpretations. Ecology has become, in short, an essentially contested concept. Recognized as such, it is now the subject of more probing theoretical inquiry. Accordingly, the book takes stock of a range of views on the most significant questions in this area, attempting to set them out as dispassionately as possible. In doing so, however, I have also evaluated them. My evaluations are made from a position which has also been developed in the course of writing the book – and regarding this, I must leave it to the reader to be dispassionate.

Acknowledgements

Because my interest in the questions examined here goes back many years, the development of this book will have been influenced by more friends, colleagues, teachers and students than I can single out by name, but I hope that those who have tried to set me straight on various points down the years will find here some evidence of success and accept that as a sufficiently sincere form of gratitude. There are also more identifiable dues. Parts of an early draft were read at seminars and conferences at Cardiff, Oxford, Kent, Lancaster and London from 1990 to 1991, and I have benefited from the helpful suggestions and criticisms made by the participants on each occasion. Sections 2.3 and 3.3 are revised versions of articles which previously appeared in *Radical Philosophy*, and permission to use the material is gratefully acknowledged. Some of the questions dealt with in this book were also discussed with students of my Green Political Thought and Environmental Debate courses at the University of Glamorgan between 1991 and 1994: I count myself particularly lucky to have had the chance to share their enthusiasm and insights. I am also particularly grateful to a number of people who read and commented on parts of an earlier draft: Robin Attfield, Bob Baker, Ted Benton, Peter Dickens, Andy Dobson, Sharif Gemie, Angelika Krebs, Sue Lamb and John O'Neill. Robert Goodin and an anonymous reader made constructive criticisms of the first draft; Brian Goodale made sensitive suggestions for improving the final text. I could not have wished for a more efficient or considerate publishing team, and would like to thank all at Polity, especially David Held for his constant encouragement. Finally, my biggest and most special thanks go to Annamaria Jatta for her support and patience throughout; she has helped me keep a sense of perspective on the important things, as, in his own way, has our son David.

Introduction
Environmental Values in Social and Political Thought

One of the most urgent intellectual tasks of our time is to understand the implications of ecology for social and political thought. In view of how environmental degradation is increasingly undermining the biological, and in some ways also the psychological, basis of human life, it is evident that no social or political theory can now proceed ignoring or abstracting from the natural conditions of its existence and reproduction. One cannot ignore the relationship between ecological devastation and the deteriorating quality of human life; nor should one overlook its incidence – that is, how it hits hardest at those who already suffer the greatest social and economic disadvantage. Now, perhaps more than ever, the exploitation of nature goes hand in hand with the exploitation of some humans by others. Moreover, it is also pertinent to point out that humans are not the only species on this planet, and as their power to influence its destiny increases, so does their responsibility.

However, in much of the literature which attempts to apply ecological insights to social and political concerns, one finds intuitive responses, which, although in themselves appropriate, have not always been brought under adequate concepts. This means that resistance to ecological thinking, on the part of the unconverted, has remained too easy. That is, what is deemed reasonable in ecological thought can be coopted into existing paradigms of thought and value, with whatever is more challenging or inconvenient dismissed as implausible.

A central aim of this book, therefore, is to show how ecological concerns can and must be given an important place in mainstream social and political thought. It aims, thereby, to transform controversy into constructive dialogue.

Radicalism versus Reformism, and Beyond

One controversy which suffuses virtually all debate in this field concerns
the general question of whether there is a need for a change in people's
attitudes and values – and, if so, how radical and what sort of a change.
In contemporary debates, answers tend to polarize. For some people,
especially optimists and those with an interest in continuing 'business as
usual', what is needed is to modify present practices – for example, by
introducing lead-free petrol and ozone-friendly aerosols – but without
questioning the need for the products, let alone the underlying values of
the resultant green consumerism or green capitalism. This *reformist*
approach was supported by authoritative reports during the 1970s and
1980s. Thus Brundtland, for instance, tended to affirm that modern economic development could become greener and more equitable without
radically changing its character.[1] Today, however, a more *radical*
response is called for, not only by green activists but also by a growing
number of theorists who argue that a whole new trajectory of development must be sought: one where economy and technology are
ecologically sensitive, one whose values and attitudes are 'ecocentric',
whose politics are 'ecologistic' and whose view of ecology itself is deep
rather than shallow. In short, they claim, a fundamental change in attitudes is required.

The various dimensions of the debate between what I am calling
reformist and radical approaches to matters of environmental concern
will be examined in the following chapters. At this stage I shall just
broadly illustrate the contrast between them.

Common to reformist positions in general, whatever their other differences from one another may be, is the view that concern with the
environment can appropriately and adequately be taken up within prevailing modes of thought and action. This view has been succinctly
stated by a group of eminent scientists who launched an appeal to those
assembled at the Rio Summit in 1992. These scientists affirm a commitment to 'the preservation of our common heritage, the Earth', but express
their concern at 'the emergence of an irrational ideology which is
opposed to scientific and industrial progress, and impedes economic and
social development'. They say that natural resources must be taken stock
of, monitored and preserved, but insist this must be carried out according
to scientific criteria. They claim that 'many essential human activities
are carried out either by manipulating hazardous substances or in their
proximity, and that progress and development have always involved

increasing control over hostile forces, to the benefit of mankind'. Hence they conclude:

> The greatest evils which stalk our Earth are ignorance and oppression, and not Science, Technology and Industry whose instruments, when adequately managed, are indispensable tools of a future shaped by Humanity, by itself and for itself, overcoming major problems like over-population, starving and world-wide diseases.[2]

In essence, what they proclaim is that the causes of problems of the environment and of social justice are to be found not in science, but in ill-informed and irresponsible applications of it. The fundamental problem, as these scientists see it, therefore, is not that people's present attempts to 'master nature' in pursuit of development are wrong in principle, but that in practice they are *not yet sufficiently enlightened.*

A markedly contrasting view has been captured in the words of Vandana Shiva:

> The Age of Enlightenment, and the theory of progress to which it gave rise, was centred on the sacredness of two categories: modern scientific knowledge and economic development. Somewhere along the way, the unbridled pursuit of progress, guided by science and development, began to destroy life without any assessment of how fast and how much of the diversity of life on this planet is disappearing. The act of living and of celebrating and conserving life in all its diversity – seems to have been sacrificed to progress, and the sanctity of life been substituted by the sanctity of science and development.[3]

Shiva speaks of a new questioning growing throughout the world, rooted in the experience of those for whom the spread of enlightenment has been the spread of darkness, of the extinction of life and life-enhancing processes. This new questioning represents a challenge to the environmentalism of the Heidelberg scientists, which appears to be based on an essentially unreconstructed Enlightenment rationality. This is what Shiva, in common with other radical ecologists, challenges on the grounds that it is precisely the application of apparent advances in human reason which lies at the root of the increasing irrationality of the human relation with nature. Thus, not only have the results of human attempts to control nature got out of control – with each new solution becoming part of a new problem – but it appears that the very objective of a rational domination of nature is in principle self-defeating.

Underlying specific controversies, then, are markedly contrasting worldviews. An important contrast concerns the status of science, and rationality more generally. For their part, the signatories of the Heidelberg Appeal claim a strength of their approach to be that it is based on established principles of rationality, and abjures irrational and mythologizing modes of thought. In this respect the scientists feel themselves to be on strong ground in asserting the superiority of their reformist position over the idealizing and backward-looking ideologies that have been put forward by some green radicals over the years as alternatives to the prevailing scientific rationality. Nevertheless, this does not altogether dispose of radical criticisms which point to serious shortcomings and weaknesses in the very scientific rationality appealed to; and if some ways of formulating the objections can be scathingly dismissed by the scientists, this does not mean they are altogether without foundation. The most effective opposition, of the sort Shiva has in mind, does not resort to irrationalism, but seeks to challenge the very notion of rationality being appealed to:

> 'Rational' man of the modern West is exposed today as a bundle of irrationalities, threatening the very survival of humankind. When we find that those who claimed to carry the light have led us into darkness and those who were declared to be inhabiting the dark recesses of ignorance were actually enlightened, it is but rational to redefine categories and meanings.[4]

There is a challenge, then, to the very rationality and values of enlightenment. But what is especially noteworthy is that the grounds of the objection to enlightenment rationality, as stated by Shiva, are that it is precisely not *rational*, that it is not *enlightened*.

This is a key point which will be returned to in different contexts throughout the book. It is enlightenment itself which often provides the standards in terms of which enlightenment is criticized. This apparent paradox permits us to break through the stalemate between reformism and radicalism. Unreconstructed enlightenment, quite simply, is to be challenged whenever it proves unable fully to live up to its own professed goals. In each chapter which follows, therefore, the first strategy is to see how far a specific enlightenment value can, if consistently pursued, be pressed into the service of ecological ends. This strategy will usually take us some way to breaking down the opposition between enlightenment and ecology, reformism and radicalism; it will not take us all the way, though, for ecology and enlightenment do still imply different substantive commitments which, even if not immutable or implacably opposed to one another, need to be reckoned with in their own terms. Ecology brings new concerns which are not to be found in enlightenment thought: hence the end result will be not to efface differences but to investigate whether there is any basis for a higher synthesis.

The general procedure to be followed can be illustrated by reference to the very idea of environmental values. On a view which is consistent with the rationality and worldview of enlightenment, the environment can be understood as the context of human activities and as an object of rational scientific enquiry; it is thereby considered as existing quite separately from humans. The environment is nevertheless of value to humans because they depend on it and it answers to their needs: it is therefore in humans' own best interest to take good care of the environment. At the root of the enlightenment view of environmental concern is the idea of human self-interest. Taking an ecological view, by contrast, there are important respects in which this first sort of account is inadequate or objectionable. In fact, it can be argued that the very use of the term 'environment' betrays a worldview based on certain problematic assumptions. To speak at all of humans on the one hand and their environment on the other, as if they were two discrete and externally related entities, is fundamentally to misconceive the nature of reality: humans are a part of the natural world, not something separate from it; individually and collectively, humans themselves are also the environment for other beings. On the basis of such misconceptions about the nature of reality, moreover, contestable values are generated, values which promote an unwarranted privileging of human concerns. Ecological values, by contrast, would be based on the insight that humans are not completely autonomous of nature, and that their interests are not the only, or even the most important, locus of value in the world.

Between the enlightenment view and the ecological view there are thus dramatic contrasts; there are also strong grounds for an ecological critique of enlightenment values. Nevertheless, the opposition is not so simple or clear-cut as some theorists have attempted to portray it. A marked tendency in the literature dealing with ecological ideas in social and political thought has been to set up all-embracing conceptual distinctions between two worldviews whose rationality and values are mutually exclusive. This was very common in the classic texts of political ecology of the 1970s which were rightly concerned to set out a new political agenda, and it has persisted in more recent works aiming at a more sophisticated elaboration of the theoretical basis of that agenda. For example, a recent book by Robyn Eckersley takes as its organizing principle a distinction between ecocentrism and anthropocentrism.[5] This distinction captures certain aspects of the contrast between ecological and enlightenment perspectives – for instance how the worldview and values of the former are oriented to ecosystems as opposed to humans only – but cannot capture all of it. For instance, it has to disregard how the ascendancy of enlightenment rationality was in large measure precisely due to *purging* anthropocentric assumptions and methods from science. In this regard, therefore, it is interesting to note that the earlier use of ecocentrism in the seminal work of environmental scientist T. O'Riordan was in contrast not to anthropocentrism but to 'technocentrism'.[6] Although the spirit of the distinction is in some ways similar, its scope and purchase is different in ways which make a difference – since some of the things which Eckersley criticizes for their anthropocentrism are the result, precisely, of excising anthropocentrism in the first place.

What emerges more generally, as the inquiry of the present book progresses, is that the implications of ecology for social and political thought are more complex than often acknowledged by those who have sought to establish their *importance*. Thanks to earlier, now classic works, which drew attention to ecological problems, we are at a new stage – one of theoretical consolidation. It is important at this stage, I believe, that a sense of practical urgency should not lead to intellectual impatience. For it is necessary to reassess some of the more sweeping claims which have been made in the past. The implications of ecology, as often elaborated within green movements and by their intellectual sympathizers, present a challenge to the most fundamental values we have inherited from the historical Enlightenment, for it is they, above all, which have underpinned the practices leading to ecological crisis. This book argues that the radical challenge needs to be taken very seriously, but that it is a mistake to see the values of ecology and enlightenment as mutually exclusive. Hence the aim of the book is to move beyond polemic to seek *clarification* of the real aspects of opposition between values of ecology and enlightenment, and thereby to foster *communication* between their respective proponents. We may then even find there is some basis for a synthesis of the values of ecology and enlightenment.

Overview of Chapters

Chapter 1 explains what is meant by 'ecology' and 'enlightenment' as used in this book. Although both are contested terms, I argue that claims for ecology as a critical science do make sense, and that precisely this commitment to criticism promises an ecological renewal, rather than abandonment, of the enlightenment project. The emphasis of this chapter is on questions to do with humans' cognitive relation to nature. Chapter 2 then investigates the ethical aspects of humans' conceptions of themselves and their relation to nature. I focus on the ambiguous legacy of Enlightenment humanism, where an emancipatory respect for human dignity is accompanied by an exalted view of humans as set over and above the rest of nature: I argue that the contemporary ecological criticisms of anthropocentrism can nevertheless be accommodated by a humanism which takes the interests of non-humans seriously; ecological considerations lead us to qualify, but not abandon, an enquiry guided by human values.

The question then to be addressed in chapter 3 is whether the values of an ecological humanism can hold sway in the real world, in view of the powerful economic interests which oppose them. I argue that success depends on demonstrating how ecological concern coincides with economic interest: this reformist strategy, though, requires a radical critique of existing economic assumptions, and can benefit from feminist insights into the relation between production and various kinds of reproduction. In focusing on the practical relation of humans to nature as a basis for a redefinition of what constitutes a good life, this chapter is primarily concerned with aggregative goods. The related but conceptually distinct question of distributive goods is taken up in chapter 4, which focuses on questions of justice and rights. This chapter inquires, in particular, whether a concern for human rights is consistent with ecological objectives, by asking: what about the rights of non-human beings? What about limits to human rights in view of population increases? What about human *duties*? In reply is proposed a conception of human rights which is consistent with ecological responsibilities.

Having thus examined the relation of humans to nature, human values and needs, conceptions of the good and the right, it remains to be asked how the values articulated may be instantiated. Hence chapter 5 is guided by the underlying question: what is to be done? It asks whether there is or needs to be a distinctively green political philosophy, or whether ecological concerns can adequately be pursued as part of, say, a liberal or socialist programme. It is argued that because both ecological concerns and the concerns of social justice are equally and irreducibly important, we should be seeking out new bases for alliance, rather than dwelling on old oppositions. This will mean, I claim, a firm commitment to the values of radical democracy.

1
Ecology and Enlightenment

> Enlightenment, in the most general sense of progressive thought, has always
> aimed at liberating people from fear and establishing their mastery. Yet the
> fully enlightened earth radiates disaster triumphant.
>
> Max Horkheimer and Theodor Adorno, *Dialectic of Enlightenment*

What is ecological thought? For reasons which will soon become clear, this question does not admit of a simple direct answer. Conceived narrowly, ecology can be described as a scientific discipline of interest 'only to a relatively small number of academic biologists and applied biologists, range managers, foresters, and fishery and game managers'.[1] The uptake of ecological ideas in social and political thought, however, has led to a much broader understanding whereby ecology is claimed to be an intrinsically critical science with subversive and revolutionary potentialities such as to overturn old worldviews and inspire new values. Clearly, the conception of ecological thought implied by the broader understanding will not necessarily be supported by the narrower view without further arguments – if at all. In due course, we shall have to examine what relation, if any, there might be between them.

One thing about ecological thought which can be said with confidence, though, is that it has risen to prominence as part of a response to the problems with the human relation to nature that have become so evident in recent years. Hence many writers on the subject have found it relatively easy to explain what ecological thought is *not*. For instance, it does not accept that organisms in general, and human beings in particular, can be understood in isolation from their environments; accordingly, it does not see nature in mechanistic terms, or take a dualistic view of the world whereby mind is opposed to matter or society to nature; it does not see humans and their interests as the only loci of value in the world; it is therefore not anthropocentric, and it is not committed to the 'domination of nature'. In all these respects ecological thought can be claimed to stand in opposition to the values and rationality of *enlightenment*.

This claim is made so frequently and in so many contexts that it warrants taking seriously. In the first section of this chapter, though, I shall indicate why the claim is in fact more problematic and more complex than often acknowledged by those who make it. Certainly, there are precedents for taking 'enlightenment' to stand for a whole worldview embodying questionable assumptions about the relation of humans to nature. Indeed, the lines quoted in the epigraph to this chapter, although written more than 50 years ago, anticipate exactly the charge ecological critics level at enlightenment in the general sense – that 'the fully enlightened earth radiates disaster triumphant'.[2] Yet the authors of those lines, Horkheimer and Adorno, stressed how the problem concerns the *dialectic* of enlightenment. That is to say, enlightenment is essentially contradictory; it is not solely and simply pernicious or wrongheaded, for it aims, first and foremost, at *liberating* people – from superstition and arbitrary authority – and enabling them to realize their autonomy as free, mature and responsible beings. The problems arise in pursuit of those very aims. A major question for ecological thought, therefore, is whether it requires us to abandon the emancipatory aims of enlightenment. That might be one way of avoiding the errors of enlightenment, but to do so may not only be undesirable – since it would mean being prepared to relinquish major ethical values like democracy, freedom and equal rights – it may in fact not even have much prospect of success, since the abandonment of enlightenment values is perfectly compatible with the most unecological exploitation of nature. But if emancipatory values – at least *ceteris paribus* – are to be ecological values too, the question is how they are to be preserved without a commitment to the domination of nature.

The problem, in terms of which ecological thought is to be defined, even only negatively, already appears more complex. Whilst the characterization of it as the antithesis of enlightenment may have had some programmatic usefulness – in establishing ecological thinking against active opponents or hard-nosed sceptics – such a one-sided view becomes counterproductive when the shorthand name 'enlightenment' becomes mistaken for the reality. Hence in the first section of this chapter I seek to offer a more balanced view, not for the sake of defending enlightenment in itself – which would be of little direct interest for our present purposes – but to get clear exactly what is at stake, and why, ultimately, significant parts of the enlightenment project are important to ecological thought too. I ask what is enlightenment and what is unecological about it. I point out that not all that is unecological is attributable to enlightenment rationality and values, and moreover that some antidotes to it *are* to be found in enlightenment thinking. This account focuses on the concept of rational mastery of nature: I examine criticisms and defences of this project and identify a conception of enlightenment – as critique – which presents a challenge for ecologists who wish to make claims for the critical purchase of ecology.

Having sketched out what, according to most of its advocates, ecological thought is not, in the second section I then turn to the more difficult question of what it *is*. The attempt to elaborate an affirmative account is difficult because the meaning of ecology is as contested and open to contrasting interpretations as the meaning of enlightenment. On the minimum and least controversial definition of it, ecology is the science of interrelationships between living organisms and between organisms and their environments. Yet the implications of its field of study are so vast and momentous that the term 'ecology' has come to mean more than the object or practice of the science of that name. With growing perceptions of environmental crisis, 'ecology' has become a watchword in political circles too; and because it deals with phenomena which touch humans deeply and directly in spheres such as aesthetics, ethics and economics, it has been taken as a source of values and a guide to action. Yet, as McIntosh notes, the hard-won knowledge gained by ecological scientists has often hereby been 'bypassed, or even distorted, to support ill-founded "ecological" panaceas'.[3] It is helpful therefore to draw a threefold distinction between ecology as a professional science, ecology as a political movement or philosophy, and ecology as the relation of any organism to the environment (i.e. its ecology).[4] Observing these distinctions will help avoid many elementary confusions. It should not be expected to resolve every controversy surrounding ecology, though, for these permeate each aspect of ecological thought. Thus, even *within* the science, for instance, there are disputes, such as between those urging a 'hard-science', reductionist approach and those arguing for a holistic, organismic approach. Scientists can have good reasons for subscribing to and promoting a broader view of ecology, just as those who bring ecology to bear on their philosophy and politics may do so in an intellectually impeccable manner.

In the third section of this chapter, accordingly, I seek to sketch the epistemological and ontological assumptions of an account of ecological thought which is both rigorous and broad enough to make talk about ecological values intelligible and useful. This will be to complete the philosophical preliminaries to the chapters which follow. The basic premise here is that when it comes to thinking about social values one must be prepared to learn from ecology but also to recognize that it does not supply all the answers. Thus although enlightenment thinking is sometimes criticized for arrogance, in its best and most critical forms it also emphasizes the *limits* to possible knowledge. Heeding these limits not only makes for a necessary form of humility – a complement of heeding ecological limits – but also helps guard against taking deceptively easy, but fundamentally spurious, lessons from ecology. For, as we shall see, the dialectic of enlightenment is in many respects a dialectic of ecology too.

1.1   Enlightenment and the Rational Domination of Nature

In this section I begin by explaining what 'enlightenment' means in the context of our present concerns; I then review one account of why it appears to be a problem from an ecological point of view – namely, because it seeks the rational mastery of nature. I show that this particular problem can perhaps be resolved in enlightenment's own terms if 'mastery' is understood not as dominating or riding roughshod over nature, but as heeding and following nature's own ways. Then, however, I identify a deeper problem which touches on fundamental assumptions of metaphysics and ontology: namely, the suggestion that a more rational *and* harmonious relation to nature may not be possible even with a more enlightened attitude, for what is wrong with our present relation to nature is not a contingent lack of wisdom or virtue, but is something intrinsic to the very notion of rationality; this rationality, moreover, underpins a value system in which only humans count. In reply to this I suggest that by distinguishing dogmatic from critical aspects of enlightenment one can take much of the sting out of such criticisms: for whereas the dogmatic aspect of a dualistic metaphysics and value system which privilege humans over the rest of nature can rightly be objected to, the critical aspect which seeks to discern the limits of human knowledge enables one better to appreciate when the limits of human concern for non-humans are or are not potentially surmountable. This might allow one to accept that some enlightenment values may be worth trying to hold onto while also granting that they need to be made more ecologically sensitive.

The enlightenment project

The first thing to clarify is what is meant by the term 'enlightenment'. In its everyday sense, to be enlightened means to become aware of something about which one was previously in the dark – or, in other words, to become a bit wiser. Sometimes it can mean, more specifically, the gaining of *spiritual* insight: this is a form of wisdom which is particularly emphasized in some, particularly Eastern, cultures, and is what 'enlightenment' means for Buddhists, for example. In modern Western culture, however, the idea has rather different associations: those stamped by the broad movement of philosophers, scientists and other intellectuals who, in the eighteenth century, proclaimed the Age of Enlightenment.[5]

The Enlightenment was seen by its proponents as a kind of cultural coming of age, a generalized conquest of wisdom on the part of European civilization. The epoch certainly saw a growth in knowledge and in the power to manipulate the natural world. It was a period of indisputable advances in science, and these advances could be considered both cause and effect of a shift in the balance of power, apparently, in favour of humans against nature – through technological applications. A central theme of enlightenment was that of emancipation from the various fetters which had hitherto bound humanity in subjection and darkness: on the one hand, advances in scientific knowledge promoted liberation from prejudice and superstition, and, via their technological application, from helpless subjection to forces of nature; on the other, the increasingly confident assertion of human autonomy was reinforced in the political and ethical spheres through the overthrow of traditional, and arbitrary, seats of authority and the ascendance of inalienable human rights.

However, such advances were only achieved, as ecological critics now emphasize, at a price. Having witnessed the kind of devastation which can be wrought by technologically embodied science, there is considerable room for doubt as to how wise this has all been. Particularly with ecological crises in view, therefore, the proclamation of an Age of Enlightenment is liable to appear at best premature and at worst arrogant nonsense. Certainly, no serious thinker could take it to be an unalloyed success story. In each area of enlightenment a dark underside could also be identified: for example, growth in wealth and cultural refinement for some only meant intensified exploitation, misery and even slavery for many others; advances in scientific rationality could also mean spiritual impoverishment; development of technology could be used for destructive as well as productive purposes, for coercive as well as liberatory ends; the rationalization of social relations could spell the breaking of traditional bonds of community, with human rights being honoured more in form than in substance.

Notwithstanding these points, however, a significant line of argument which can be mustered in defence of the enlightenment project is that the gains associated with it would eventually outweigh the losses; hence the best hope would lie in furthering the process rather than reversing, arresting, or radically altering its course. In this way defenders of the Enlightenment might accept their critics' points, but without thereby relinquishing their underlying project. For they may argue that the problems arise precisely where enlightenment is deficient or incomplete, and that the solution, therefore, would be to seek *more* enlightenment.

This is a case which might be made with relative ease as regards the questions which bear on human freedom and social justice. For deficits in these spheres can be recognized as such in the enlightenment's own terms. For example, when the Founding Fathers proclaimed the inalienable rights of all men, those men and women who were still held in slavery did not thereby become free, but their struggle for freedom did then become also a struggle to hold the enlightenment to its own promise. Of course, the argument cannot quite so readily be used as a defence against ecological critics. For whilst the enlightenment is not explicitly committed to the domination of humans by humans, it does appear to be committed to the rational domination of nature: and this might be considered a threat to be avoided rather than a promise to be fulfilled. Nevertheless, its defenders can still adapt the argument by claiming, with the Heidelberg appellants mentioned in the introduction, that if the problem is simply that scientific achievements sometimes find harmful technological employment through miscalculation, misunderstanding or even mischief, then an increment of wisdom, care or goodwill would perhaps suffice to sort it out. Thus there could be reason to think that there is nothing *intrinsically* wrong with the project of mastering nature.

In what follows I shall briefly show how an argument to this effect constitutes a first line of defence against ecological criticisms. I shall then examine a deeper objection which may yet undermine that defence.

If the ideal of mastery of nature is defended and even celebrated this is because it is considered *emancipatory*: achieving it would mean no longer being at the mercy of external nature or held in thrall by dogma or instinct, but becoming fully autonomous. To see how it can be defended, it will be helpful to distinguish the three main contexts in which it appears. These are, firstly, the theoretical (scientific) mastery of nature which facilitates, secondly, a material (technological) mastery of external nature as well as, thirdly, the practical (ethical) mastery of internal nature. I shall comment on these in turn. It can plausibly be claimed, to start with, that the idea of *theoretical* mastery does not automatically imply any untoward consequences for nature. If theoretical mastery is the mastering in thought of the facts and rules of a situation, like the mastering by a scholar of her subject for instance, then it would seem to be perfectly consistent with respect, or reverence even, for nature and all its ways. (As we know, some of the greatest scientists have been among the greatest reverers of nature.) If this is so, then the blame might be claimed to lie not with science as such but with technology, since technology, as we've noted, can have unfortunate or even disastrous consequences. Thus it could be proposed to emphasize the difference between theoretical or scientific mastery on the one hand, and technological or material mastery on the other – seeing the former as neutral and the latter as malign. For example, theoretical physics might be seen as a disinterested pursuit of truth, but its application in the construction of nuclear weapons as intrinsically bad. Yet if the defence of theoretical mastery works, then technological mastery might well be absolved of responsibility in a similar way. For, to put it simply, there can be appropriate and inappropriate, ecologically sensitive and ecologically insensitive, forms and uses of technology: so unless one is prepared to say that any intervention whatsoever in the natural world is wrong, then one has to admit that not technology *per se*, but only 'bad' technology, is the problem. The blame then, it would appear, must ultimately come to rest with humans themselves – who are, perhaps, just too ignorant, evil or stupid. There is, after all, nothing intrinsically wrong even with nuclear reactions: it is humans who sometimes use them in a bad way or in an inappropriate context. And yet, to the extent that humans do manifest various such deficiencies, what it could still be argued to come down to, once again, is precisely a lack or insufficiency of mastery – this time by humans (or rational beings) of their selves and their powers (or the non-rational parts of their nature) – with part of the problem being that humans are insufficiently enlightened as to their own best interests. Mastery, in short, continues to appear not as the problem but as the solution.

This is, I think, a robust line of argument; and ecological critics would not altogether reject it. Indeed, its robustness is in large part due to the compelling claim that science, technology and human knowledge and capacities cannot so easily be separated one from another; and this is a claim to which ecologists themselves are committed, to the extent that they emphasize the need to take a holistic view of the world and the humans within it. Nevertheless, they would strongly disagree with the conclusion that more human mastery is the solution to ecological crises. Indeed, they would incline more to the diametrically opposed conclusion that technology is not innocent, and nor are the human aims which seek it or the science which produces it. The scientific mastery of nature involves a theoretical reduction which goes hand in hand with the practical devaluation of nature; the two dimensions are combined in a single world-view which, therefore, needs wholesale transformation. On this view, the ideal of mastering nature remains the problem, not a solution.

Given, then, that from the same line of argument opposed conclusions can be drawn, this must be due to contrasting underlying assumptions. There is, therefore, a deeper objection to unearth.

To focus this objection we should note that, on the enlightenment account, when things go awry it is, more or less by definition, a case of inadequate mastery: hence there may be contingent misapplications of reason in the actual domination of nature, but the root of the problem lies with imperfect, though potentially perfectible, human beings. One notable feature of this view is its optimism: it depends not only on seeing human beings as perfectible, but also on the process occurring with opportune timing. Ecologists would be disinclined to accept either of these assumptions. The first is a speculation which it would be impossible to prove or disprove in the here and now; but the second seems wholly unwarranted, going against all the evidence which tends to show that while enlightenment has been proceeding apace, the problems have gone from bad to worse, with all the indications suggesting that this is an unremitting trend. Hence enlightenment optimism is at best complacent and at worst catastrophic. Implicit in the enlightenment view is the idea that, in principle, human reason is capable of solving all problems, that mastery ultimately knows no bounds. This is the kind of hubris which critics see as the source not of solutions but of the problem.

So the deeper problem, for critics, lies not with humans failing to achieve full mastery, but with them thinking they are capable of achieving it. In this respect, ecological critics make common cause with contemporary postmodernists and earlier generations of liberal thinkers who have questioned some of the central assumptions of enlightened thought. These assumptions·have been summed up, in another context by Isaiah Berlin:

> first, that all men have one true purpose . . . that of rational self-direction; second, that the ends of all rational beings must of necessity fit into a single universal, harmonious pattern, which some men may be able to discern more clearly than others; third, that all conflict, and consequently all tragedy, is due solely to the clash of reason with the irrational or the insufficiently rational . . . and that such clashes are, in principle, avoidable . . . finally, that when all men have been made rational, they will obey the rational law of their own natures, which are one and the same in them all, and so be at once wholly law-abiding and wholly free.[6]

The deeper objection questions these assumptions and the worldview in which they are embedded. If they are not true, then perhaps a radically different conception of the human place in the world will be required – even a new paradigm.

The deeper objection can be construed as a claim that ecologically harmful practices arise not simply as a contingent misuse or misapplication of an intrinsically neutral science in technology, but because there is something amiss with the scientific view itself. Modern science is criticized both for its methods and for its metaphysics – which implies that, ultimately, its very definition of rationality is faulty, as indeed are the values produced by and informing that rationality. More precisely, the claim as usually expressed is, firstly, that modern science works with an analytic method which is reductionist and thereby reduces the natural world in various ways which undermine its integrity, wholeness and interconnectedness; secondly, that its metaphysics is dualist, so that whereas humans are seen as not just physical but also mental and spiritual beings, the rest of nature is seen in purely mechanistic terms; and finally, that this justifies a disregard for nature. In the remainder of this section I shall consider these claims in turn.

Modern science

The methods to which modern science owes its success were already established in their essentials by notable forerunners of the Enlightenment such as Bacon and Descartes.[7] Despite their differences both from one another and from eighteenth-century thinkers, what these thinkers shared was a commitment to the *analytic* method – that is, the view that the appropriate approach to any scientific problem is to break it down into a set of subproblems, and arrange these in their logical order. But although this analytic method of reasoning has contributed to the impressive power of modern science, it has also led, as Capra has observed, not only to a fragmentation in our general thinking and our academic disciplines, but also to the widespread attitude of reductionism in science – that is, 'the belief that all aspects of complex phenomena can be understood by reducing them to their constituent parts'.[8] What is of particular concern about the analytic method, therefore, is the way it fosters a particular view of the reality of the world: for if analysis works, the inference is, this is because the world itself is composed of discrete and largely independent atomistic entities. Ecologists raise forceful objections against this view of the world. For however convenient it may be, for certain purposes, to see the world in terms of independently given and mechanistically related atoms, this does not adequately capture the way it actually is. So the analytic method, at least in its Cartesian formulation, entails a metaphysics which ecologists find unacceptable.

The metaphysics objected to is dualist. Because the Cartesian method involves systematic doubt, which means that the enquirer accepts as true and indubitable knowledge only that of which it is possible to form 'clear and distinct ideas', as a consequence mind attains a certainty of itself which does not hold for matter; and this leads Descartes to posit a fundamental – ontological – difference between the two: 'there is nothing included in the concept of body that belongs to the mind; and nothing in that of mind that belongs to body.'[9] This dualism itself has had a profound effect on modern Western perceptions of the natural world. For Descartes, the material world could be viewed as a machine, with nature working according to mechanical laws governing matter in motion. This mechanistic view applied to living beings, plants and animals, too: 'I do not recognize any difference', wrote Descartes, 'between the machines made by craftsmen and the various bodies that nature alone composes.'[10] The problem is, as Capra points out, 'that scientists, encouraged by their success in treating living organisms as machines, tend to believe that they are *nothing but* machines'.[11] He also notes that the Cartesian view of the universe provided a scientific sanction for the manipulation and exploitation of nature, reaffirming Bacon's view, now so entrenched in Western culture, that the aim of scientific knowledge is to 'render ourselves the masters and possessors of nature'.[12]

Hence the metaphysics, in turn, seems to imply a particular value system in which, to put it bluntly, only humans count. And here we come to the heart of ecological criticisms. The supposedly disinterested pursuit of knowledge proclaimed by enlightenment thinkers is in fact a highly interested enterprise: that is, it pursues the interests of human beings. That may not be objectionable in itself, but when humans benefit at the expense of other parts of nature, when they see nothing wrong in doing so, and do not even recognize interests other than theirs, then their view is decidedly unecological.

From what has so far been said, the deeper objection to the enlightenment worldview appears to be very powerful. Indeed, if enlightenment rationality were nothing more than an elaboration of Cartesianism, then there would be little to synthesize with ecology, and ecologists would have a case for simply rejecting that too. However, it is important to raise the question of whether the Enlightenment proper – both historically and, more importantly, intellectually – is not better represented by thinkers who in fact criticized Cartesian metaphysics. Hume, for example, is one such thinker; but, more especially, there is Kant. What I want now to suggest is that the Kantian critique of metaphysics is doubly significant in the context of our enquiry: not only does it expose the dogmas of previous metaphysics and theories of knowledge, it also represents an implicit challenge to any alternative metaphysics that an opponent, rejecting Cartesianism, might be inclined to propose.

We have observed that ecologists have reasons for objecting to Descartes regarding his method, his metaphysics, and his underlying value commitments. It is another matter whether these objections apply to Kant too. For it may be that the analytic employment of reason can be differently understood, and need not imply a Cartesian dualism or spe- ciesist value system. Whereas Descartes's method was based on systematic doubt, in Kant the place of doubt is taken by *criticism*.[13] For Kant, the analytic employment of reason is addressed to conditions of possibility of experience; this involves an analysis of those operations of mind which are *constitutive* of experience; but operations of mind do not furnish the *content* of knowledge; hence the idea that matter is one kind of substance and mind, or soul, another is to make a pronouncement which is really unintelligible.[14] So although Kant is also, in a sense, a dualist – in that he sees a radical difference between rational beings and the rest of nature – there is also the quite radical difference that this is not a dogmatic metaphysical dualism of mind and body, but a critical dis- tinction marking the bounds of possible knowledge. Moreover, Kant recognizes that nature cannot be adequately comprehended on analogy with a machine. So although Kant sees reason as the contrary of nature, his conception of reason is not exhausted in *theoretical* reason, which can only grasp nature in mechanistic terms, and there remains for him an inescapable place for the 'teleological estimate' which takes organic nature to be much what ecologists insist, against Cartesianism, that it is.[15] So it is arguable that Kant, and the kind of enlightenment thought he represents, escapes at least some of the strictures ecologists make against an enlightenment characterized in chiefly Cartesian terms. Indeed, as we shall further see in due course, Kant presents an implicit challenge to those who, in emphasizing ecological limits to human thought and action, attempt to formulate an alternative metaphysics without giving adequate heed to limits of knowledge.

If the analytic employment of reason need not imply Cartesian meta- physics, more important still, in the context of the present inquiry, is the question of whether it implies arbitrarily human-centred values.

Emancipatory values

There does appear to be some ambivalence at the heart of enlightenment values, as manifest in the tension between the twin ideals of mastery and criticism: while criticism promises an open and emancipatory atmosphere from which beings other than humans might in principle benefit, this benign promise seems permanently threatened by the ideal of mastery, with its connotations of human domination. This impression is reinforced by the consideration that criticism itself is a function of reason, and reason, as typically celebrated by representatives of the enlightenment, is considered a peculiarly human faculty to be contrasted quite decisively with phenomena of nature. In what follows, I shall examine some reasons for drawing this contrast, and show why doing so need not imply a straightforward glorification of reason; this in turn will mean that rationally grounded values are not necessarily ecologically malign.

Once again, the arguments can be well stated by reference to the philosophy of Kant, which arguably marks the culmination of Enlightenment thought.[16] For Kant, the idea of rational mastery of nature appears in a moral context, firstly, as a mastery of internal nature. A central theme in Kant's philosophy is that humans are not merely beings of adaptation and survival, but beings of choice and purpose – free, rational and moral. The sphere of rational moral freedom is other than that of nature, Kant believes, for reasons he straightforwardly states:

> Suppose now that for a being possessed of reason and a will the real purpose of nature were his *preservation*, his *welfare*, or in a word his *happiness*. In that case nature would have hit on a very bad arrangement by choosing reason in the creature to carry out this purpose. For all the actions he has to perform . . . would have been mapped out for him far more accurately by instinct . . . Nature would herself have taken over the choice, not only of ends, but also of means, and would with wise precaution have entrusted both to instinct alone.[17]

Moral values, then, cannot be learnt from nature, but only from reason. Reason has an imperative, therefore, to gain knowledge not only of external nature but of human nature too.

But it is not only over nature that reason must seek mastery. There are also other factors whose influence a moral agent must reckon with, other 'heteronomous determinations of the will' as Kant calls them, which are by no means less serious challenges to reason in the ethical sphere. In fact, his very definition of enlightenment makes reference to these rather than to nature, for he describes it as the emergence of free rational beings from their self-imposed tutelage. The attainment of *Mündigkeit*, mature autonomy, means the freedom to take responsibility for one's own life, self-governed and guided by the lights of reason alone. On this definition, enlightenment refers, first and foremost, to emancipation not so much from nature as from arbitrary traditional authority. Kant clearly has the autonomy of individuals in mind, and the imperative of overcoming *self-imposed* tutelage is summed up in a motto – 'dare to know!'– which clearly implies self-responsibility. But the concept of enlightenment is not exhausted in an interpretation which focuses on its meaning for an individual. The tutelage which keeps individuals in a state of immaturity is not simply imposed on themselves by each and every individual, but, more importantly, is reinforced by the cultural, social and political conditions of life in which they find themselves. As Kant observes:

> The guardians who have so benevolently taken over the supervision of men have carefully seen to it that the far greatest part of them (including the entire fair sex) regard taking the step to maturity as very dangerous, not to mention difficult.[18]

So emergence from immaturity would seldom be achieved simply by individuals struggling alone in isolation. The prospects of any individual attaining rational autonomy depend on transindividual conditions, or, as Kant puts it:

> The development in a rational being of an aptitude for any ends whatever of his own choosing, consequently of being able to use his freedom, is *culture*.[19]

Thus whereas it is difficult for individuals to work themselves out of the immaturity that has all but become their nature, writes Kant, 'that the public should enlighten itself is more likely; indeed, if it is only allowed freedom, enlightenment is almost inevitable.' He emphasizes that it is the *public* use of one's reason which must always be free, and which alone can bring about enlightenment among humankind.

I think it is important to note this emphasis on the *public* use of reason: for this helps one appreciate that just as enlightenment is not a narrowly individualistic affair, nor does it simply imply an unqualified glorification of the power of reason. As Peter Gay has pointed out, the age in which Kant was writing is frequently referred to by historians of ideas as the Age of Reason, but he suggests a very significant correction of that view, seeing the Enlightenment not as an age of reason but as a revolt against rationalism. This revolt involved rejecting the belief, in particular, that all mysteries in the world can be penetrated by inquiry. Thus he writes:

> The claim for the omnicompetence of criticism was in no way a claim for the omnipotence of reason. It was a political demand for the right to question everything, rather than the assertion that all could be known or mastered by rationality.[20]

The view of the claims of enlightenment as 'a political demand for the right to question everything' is, I believe, quite consonant with Kant's definition of enlightenment as *Mündigkeit*, and also enables us to understand Kant's own verdict on the intellectual and political character of his time:

> If it is now asked, 'Do we presently live in an *enlightened* age?' the answer is, 'No, but we do live in an age of *enlightenment*.'[21]

That is to say, Kant was under no illusion that the claims of the Enlightenment had yet been achieved, but nor did he underestimate the significance of the fact that they were now, so to speak, on the agenda – an agenda which has still, perhaps, to be fully worked through.

Perhaps the most important value to gain currency in the Enlightenment was the idea that human beings are born free and equal in rights and dignity. By contrast with inherited hierarchy and inequality, the men of the eighteenth century could see the rights of man as eternal, unchanging and self-evident.[22] In giving philosophical grounding to this idea, Kant's philosophy can also be seen as an expression of certain fundamental tenets of liberalism: in particular, the idea of universal values and individualism. These values have exerted a tremendous influence in the development of modern culture, and provided a benchmark for criticizing it too: so that, for example, if human rights are universal, they must apply to men *and* women, Europeans and non-Europeans, and societies or governments which allow discrimination are in default of their own professed values. Of course, these ideas themselves are not unassailable: universalism can be criticized for disregarding particularity; individualism can be criticized for disregarding the claims of collectives; progress can be criticized as an ideological illusion at both descriptive and evaluative levels. And yet such criticisms do not necessarily require the abandonment of those values: after all, it is arguably universality and the principle of equality at its heart which makes respect for particular differences possible. Regarding individualism, what is sought is the full

development of the faculties and capacities of each individual, not necessarily in opposition to the good of collectivities; hence, for example,
Marx could be seen as in continuity with the Enlightenment in this
respect. In short, there are values here which, other things being equal,
there are good reasons to hold on to.

As regards ecological criticisms, it can be argued that if enlightenment
ideals include the mastery of nature, and if this can only be achieved by
following and obeying nature, then that means being aware of human–
natural interdependence and of the limits to which nature can be forced
to meet human ends. So the mastery of nature need not be so malign as
might at first sight be supposed. Indeed, if enlightenment is taken not as
a glorification of reason but as the pursuit of critique, whose objective is
to identify the *limits* of the powers of human reason, then some of the
more swingeing objections levelled at it by ecologists do not necessarily
find their mark. This, of course, may just mean that critics have to be
more precise in their aim. The arguments considered show enlightenment
values and rationality to be quite resilient, but they do not put them
beyond criticism. In particular, if critique reveals the limits of possible
human knowledge, this could yet be used as an alibi for limited consideration of non-human beings. Therefore substantive worries about the
human relationship to nature are not necessarily assuaged, and at this
stage it is appropriate to examine alternative, more determinedly ecological, conceptions of that relationship.

1.2 Ecological Thought: Epistemology, Ontology and Values

In this section I want to ask: what is ecology, and in what way does it
represent a challenge to enlightenment? As already noted in the introduction to this chapter, the meaning of the term 'ecology' varies depending
on whether one understands by it the scientific discipline which goes by
that name, the reality which the science studies, or the wider penumbra
of ideas with an evaluative aspect which have come to be invoked in the
context of social and political thought. Given the present interest in how
ecology can legitimately be understood in this broader sense, this means
understanding how ecological thought can be related to ecological science. It could be argued that the one thing appropriately called
'ecological thought' is the cognitive activity of an ecological scientist.
Ecological thought would thus name a type of epistemology and/or methodology. What will emerge in the first part of this section, though, in

attempting to identify what is distinctive about the methods and epistemology of ecological scientists, is that there are markedly contrasting accounts of them even *within* the science. Not only does each new paradigm of ecological science admit of different interpretations, but each attempt to purge unscientific elements seems to readmit new ones. In particular, there is something of a running debate about the potentially normative idea of a balance of nature which some see as central to the science of ecology and others as extraneous to it.

Given that a clear and uncontested distinction between what is and is not rigorously scientific appears to be unavailable, this could mean that the broader penumbra is as ecological as the narrower science; alternatively, though, it could mean that there is really no such thing as ecological thought. At this point, therefore, a different approach to the question is in order, and I shall turn to consider the possibility that what makes thought ecological is not its epistemology or methods but its object, that is the reality of ecology. It may be that there is more to the reality of ecology than is grasped by the science narrowly understood, so that ecological thought in a broader sense can be grounded in ecological reality. Support for this suggestion comes from recent developments in various sciences which undermine the old criteria of scientificity and imply an ontology which has more in common with many ideas of the wider penumbra than what was previously considered rigorous science. Although this conclusion cannot be definitive, I shall suggest it is plausible at least to hold *that* there is an ecological ontology which can be distinguished in certain key respects from the ontology presupposed by earlier conceptions of science. For the purposes of this section, the meaning of ecology will have been sufficiently defined once it allows the formulation of the ecological challenge to enlightenment rationality and values. Ecological thought, on the account which emerges and which is at least compatible with the findings of contemporary science and possibly also in important respects supported by them, is opposed to enlightenment rationality and values in these ways: its methods and epistemology are not reductionist, its ontology is not dualistic, and its ethics are not atomistic. In each respect, ecological thought is *holistic*. Given that holism can be considered the antithesis of each of reductionism, dualism and atomism, then if there is any one characteristic of ecological thought it ought to be this. Of course, whether holism is a sufficient criterion of ecological thought, and what exactly 'holism' means, in different contexts and to different people, are questions which will require a good deal of further consideration. In the third part of this section I will offer some preliminary discussion of these questions in relation to values

– what ecological values are, whether they are necessarily holistic, and how these values relate to ecological epistemology and ontology.

Ecology as a new scientific paradigm

If 'ecology' is defined as what scientists of ecology do, then ecological thought might be characterized in terms of the methods and epistemology they employ in doing it. The problem is, though, that there are different views, even amongst its practitioners, of the scope, methods and epistemological commitments of the science. In asking whether ecology represents a new scientific paradigm, therefore, one has first to ask whether the different views can be unified.

A major split between different conceptions of ecology can be identified by reference to the idea of a balance of nature. On one conception, ecology is a rigorous science which can and should have nothing to do with the sort of teleological cosmology which seems to be implied by such ideas; on another, however, this idea is taken as absolutely central. It may be that if ecology is to be claimed to have a distinctive epistemology at all, it will have to do justice to both conceptions.

From the perspective of a narrowly focused history of the science of ecology it has decidedly inconspicuous and recent origins, first emerging in the nineteenth century, as a biological subdiscipline, from the field of plant geography. Robert P. McIntosh notes that ecology grew from a complex interaction of natural history and physiology.[23] While initially focused on the environment of plants it developed novel methods and concepts which subsequently found application in relation to animals too. But even though its best practitioners were introducing methodological novelty into the science already in the nineteenth century, according to McIntosh, the methods which made of ecology a science were, at least initially, those of conventional science. For instance, it could for some time be understood as a variety of biometrics, focusing on food chains and statistical studies of animal populations. The history of ecology in the first half of the twentieth century is that of the successful creation of concepts, such as form of growth, succession, and ecological niche, relating living entities to their environments, but without a theory to unify them. It is worth noting, then, that to the extent that we are talking about a rigorous science here, we are talking about a science which by and large uses methods of conventional sciences. McIntosh offers a snapshot of the state of ecology as it entered the second half of the twentieth century:

It had a large and unwieldy body of physiological and life history information, environmental analysis and community description. It had a few general, but not neatly circumscribed entities, such as population, community, habitat and environment and a number of key processes especially competition, predation and succession. It had developed an increasingly quantitative and statistical methodology for sampling and analysis and at least an incipient mathematical theory of single species populations and two species interactions.[24]

But in spite of having this growing stock of knowledge, what is significant in the context of our present enquiry is that ecology lacked, even on the admission of its own adherents, a broad theoretical base.

A broad theoretical base is just what is claimed to be offered by those who see the balance of nature as a constitutive idea of ecological thought. This idea has ancient origins, but in more specifically modern versions is presented in terms of the economy of nature. Thus one of the first natural historians held by many to occupy a significant place in the development of ecology is Linnaeus, the eighteenth-century botanist who wrote the widely acclaimed work *The Oeconomy of Nature*. For some historians of ecology this work articulated the theoretical axis of what was to become the science of ecology: Worster, for instance, has described it as 'the single most important summary of an ecological point of view still in its infancy'.[25] The concept 'economy of nature' as used by Linnaeus denoted 'the grand organisation and government of life on earth: the rational ordering of all material resources in an interacting whole'. Under the auspices of 'the Supreme Economist', God, 'each species serves to support others as it earns its own living'. There are no scarcities in nature and nothing superfluous is in abundance: 'By assigning to all species their unique kinds of food and by "putting limits to their appetites", Linnaeus maintains, God has set up an enduring community of peaceful coexistence.'[26]

Although few would now deny to Linnaeus a place in the history of ecology, it is also generally recognized that, judged by the standards of twentieth-century science, his work could not today be said to be fully ecological. The idea of an essentially benign balance of nature may have been useful for reconciling the growth of natural science with the claims of religion, but it did not exactly encourage effective research into material causes since the final cause and the intermediate ends are already known. Everything is there as testimony to the glory of God. Because Linnaeus never considers the relations between living creatures and their environment in terms other than those of equilibrium, a providential balance, his thought remains at the level of simple affirmation.

So an important question is whether the idea of a balance, or economy, of nature is compatible with or useful to the science of ecology at all. Historians of ecology who believe it is point to continuities between the two conceptions we have outlined. They can note, for instance, that when Haeckel coined the very term 'ecology' he considered it a synonym of 'nature's economy'. Thus, according to his definition of 1868 the field of ecology is

> the totality of relations of organisms with the external world in general, with the organic and inorganic conditions of existence; what we have called the economy of nature, the mutual relations of all the organisms which live in a single location, their adaptation to the environment around them, the transformations produced by their struggle for existence.[27]

This is noteworthy because the idea of nature's economy here appears alongside Darwinian concepts of struggle and adaptation which played such a significant role in overthrowing teleological accounts of causality in nature. This encourages some to see a conception of nature's economy as being compatible with the nascent science of ecology as more strictly and narrowly understood. Others, however, who emphasize that the science of ecology has developed from the painstaking observation of empirical relationships at a local level between organisms and their environment, are sceptical whether it is particularly relevant or helpful to ask if this research really fits into the paradigm of nature's economy. This ancient idea includes so much of a general speculative account of the human relation to nature, they argue, that it would expand the idea of ecology beyond anything useful:[28] not just any concern with human – nature relations can be considered 'ecological' if the term is to have a distinctive meaning.

There is thus disagreement among ecological theorists on the question of whether advances in ecological knowledge will tend to yield a convergence with balance-of-nature holism or, on the contrary, a decisive move, or paradigm shift, away from it. Although there are reasons for wanting to avoid the idea, it also seems to be the case that with each significant conceptual advance of the science it continues to crop up. To illustrate this I shall very briefly trace some of the ways that the idea of the balance of nature has permeated twentieth-century ecological science.

The first major uptake of the idea comes with Frederic Clements's concept of the 'superorganismic' community. First propounded in 1905 and developed in subsequent years, the crux of this highly influential concept 'was that single species populations in nature are integrated into well-defined, organic entities'.[29] In other words, communities, particularly of plants in Clements's original formulation, are the basic units with which ecology has to deal. A community is considered as an integrated and evolving entity with its own homeostatic properties. Clements developed this concept in relation to another key idea, that of ecological succession: communities change and develop through time, and there is a succession of plant groupings that occupy a site for a while and then give way to others. For Clements, succession takes a definite evolutionary direction through a series of developmental stages that 'begins with a primitive, inherently unbalanced plant assemblage and ends with a complex formation in relatively permanent equilibrium with the surrounding conditions, capable of perpetuating itself forever'.[30] This culminating stage, the 'climax community', is viewed by Clements quite literally as the adult form towards which the less mature forms were striving. He thus takes a holistic view which has an element of teleology and is arguably a direct descendant of the economy-of-nature and balance-of-nature tradition.[31] For his critics, though, this constitutes a ground for objection. Simberloff, for instance, sees the Clementsian conception as appealing in its tidiness, but poor as a description of reality because, he claims, there are just no objective criteria for determining membership and boundaries of communities: the superorganism is a fictitious construct, not grounded in observation, but offered *a priori*, thereby betraying a deeper commitment to old and unscientific beliefs about the world.[32] Simberloff sees the direction of a revolutionary paradigm shift *away* from the balance-of-nature idea.

Certainly the next major conceptual shift in twentieth-century ecological theory appeared to be in this direction. This came with Arthur Tansley's rejection of Clements's superorganicist theory, claiming that Clements's superorganic wholes 'are *in analysis* nothing but the synthesized actions of the components in associations'.[33] In their place, Tansley introduced the concept of the ecosystem, arguing that although organisms do live in closely integrated units, these are best studied not as organic wholes but as physical systems: 'all relations among organisms can be described in terms of the purely material exchange of energy and of such chemical substances as water, phosphorus, nitrogen, and other nutrients.'[34] Taking the ecosystem approach, some therefore thought, ecology 'would gradually cease to be set off as a kind of comprehensive biology, and would instead be increasingly absorbed into the physics of energy systems'.[35] But if this view emphasizes how reductive is ecosystems theory, others argue that it is actually holistic. Eugene Odum, for instance, sees ecology as *essentially* holistic because new systems properties emerge in the course of ecological development and these emergent properties cannot be grasped reductively.[36] Moreover, Worster has observed that, paradoxical as it may seem, the ecosystems approach is actually more inclusive than the community idea: for whereas the latter suggests a sharp disjunction between living and non-living entities, the ecosystem includes all aspects of nature – rocks and gases as well as biota.[37]

Still, scope for dispute about the nature and the status of the ecosystem paradigm remains. Some, like Odum, claim that systems ecology has revolutionized the field of ecology, turning it into an integrative science; they emphasize that the dynamic and complex nature of ecosystems renders reductionist approaches inadequate. Others, like Simberloff, argue that to the extent there is a continuity of ecosystems theory with the organismic tradition and the idea of balance of nature, the materialist revolution is simply incomplete. This view appears to be supported by McIntosh when he writes:

> For a long time (and still in some quarters) the view has prevailed that the ecosystems of nature are too complex for understanding . . . This was the view of some biochemists in the 30's about the structure of proteins – yet great leaps of understanding were made by those who were prepared to simplify the complexity and, *as an act of faith*, assume that the complex whole is no more than the sum of the components and their interactions.[38]

In reproducing these criticisms of holism I have underlined the frank admission that an *act of faith* may be required. If the objection to the holistic, balance-of-nature tradition of ecological thought is that its propositions are *a priori* rather than proven by experience, and philosophical rather than scientific, it is pertinent to point out that the basic assumptions of any alternative may have the same status.

A stronger consideration in favour of holism, though, is that while arguments for a non-holistic understanding of ecology have tended to emphasize how it can be assimilated to the model of physics, the model of physics in the twentieth-century has actually become more ecological. That is, the most basic criteria of scientificity – traditionally provided by physics – have been increasingly challenged from within. Ecology can thus be viewed as one of a number of disciplines at the cutting edge of scientific development which today are challenging some of the central assumptions of traditional, that is to say modern classical, science. On the traditional view, the objective of scientific knowledge was the discovery of necessary and universal laws of nature, and the criterion of scientificity was to be reductionist, on the assumption that the properties of a system can always be explained in terms of the simple properties of its parts. However, since the 1960s, as Marcello Cini points out, this paradigm has begun to undergo a significant transformation:

> Instead of seeking to unify various complex and irregular phenomena through the identification of simple properties and common regularities which represent their essential nature ... the new approach emphasizes, on the contrary, that even structurally identical systems may manifest behaviour which may be defined as 'wildly different'.[39]

Hence there has grown up a new transdisciplinary scientific community dedicated to the investigation of the phenomena of chaos, for instance;[40] an associated development, also originating in the abandonment of the epistemological priority of the categories of simplicity, order and regularity, is the birth of interest in complex systems.[41]

J. Baird Callicott argues that ecology and contemporary physics are converging towards a consolidated metaphysical consensus which may supplant that of modern classical science.[42] Modern classical science works with an atomic materialist ontology; this ontology is also reductive, implying that any composite body is ontologically reducible to its simple constituents; and mechanistic, in the assumption that 'All causal relations are reducible to the motion or translation from point to point of simple bodies or the composite bodies made up of them.'[43] This metaphysics has also informed the view of living nature as, in effect, an elaborate machine. By contrast, the ecological view of living nature, like the new physics, finds it inappropriate to view the world as an array of precisely demarcated things or substances.[44] In place of this object ontology is proposed an ontology of events or field patterns: from this point of view 'each living thing is a dissipative structure, that is, it does not endure in and of itself but only as a result of the continual flow of energy in the system.[45] An individual organism, like an elementary particle, is, as it were, a momentary configuration, a local perturbation, in an energy field. This is holistic rather than atomistic, organic rather than mechanistic:

> In both contemporary ecology and quantum theory at their respective levels of phenomena the oneness of nature is systemic and (internally) relational ... nature is a *structured*, *differentiated* whole. The multiplicity of particles and living organisms, at either level of organization, retain, ultimately, their peculiar, if ephemeral, characters and identities. But they are systemically integrated and mutually defining.[46]

Thus in contrast to the object ontology of classical physics and biology 'the conception of one thing in the New Physics and New Ecology necessarily involves the conception of others and so on, until the entire system is, in principle, implicated'.[47]

This has implications regarding basic ontological assumptions about the world. Holistic metaphysics brings with it the idea that all phenomena are ultimately interconnected (versus atomism) and exist in one sphere of being (versus dualism). These ideas have some far-reaching implications for thinking about the human relation to the rest of nature. They imply, for instance, that the human mind is not a kind of entity which is radically different from other kinds of natural, or material, phenomena; they also imply that human societies are a part of nature too and hence in principle amenable to naturalistic understanding. These are philosophically significant implications in themselves, but the implications are not exhausted in the spheres of epistemology and metaphysics: what makes of ecology a 'subversive subject', some claim, is that it implies a view of nature, and of human nature, individual and collective, which calls into question some of the cultural and economic premises widely accepted by Western societies.[48] This brings us to considerations about the broader penumbra of ecological ideas.

In ecological thought, humans are reintegrated with the rest of the natural world. I say *re*integrated since an ecological perspective is in some ways one which can be recovered from ways of life, closer to nature and to biological rhythms, that modern Western societies appear to have lost. Modern societies tend to be organized in thought and practice around dualistic oppositions which are challenged by ecological and holistic thought. These oppositions seem to be absent in less 'developed' societies. Anthropologists have recorded how tribal communities are often closer to nature and live by values from which there is much to learn.[49] A poignant illustration of this comes from the famous words of the nineteenth-century Amerindian Chief Seattle:

> Our dead never forget this beautiful earth, for it is the mother of the red man. We are part of the earth, and it is part of us. The perfumed flowers are our sisters; the deer, the horse, the great eagle; these are our brothers. The rocky crests, the juices of the meadow, the body heat of the pony, and man – all belong to the same family. The rivers are our brothers, they quench our thirst. The rivers carry our canoes, and feed our children. If we sell you our land, you must remember and teach your children that the rivers are our brothers, and yours, and you must henceforth give the rivers the kindness you would give any brother.[50]

These words point up how a different quality of the human relation to nature is possible: one not of domination or possession, or perhaps even of stewardship, but rather one of being with, belonging to a community, not only of humans but of animals and plants and even inanimate nature too. The world is seen as a dwelling place, home, *oikos*, rather than an array of resources there to be exploited, or subordinate beings to be managed or shepherded. Certainly there have been Western thinkers who have striven to regain this,[51] but to a large extent the concerns which ecology reawakens and emphasizes have tended to be either disregarded or underplayed in the value systems which have dominated Western culture.

In what follows I ask how these concerns translate into values – whether they can in fact be accommodated by existing value systems with a little modification, or whether it is a case of constructing radically new ones.

Ecology as a new value system

Although there are differences in detail between various accounts of ecologically grounded values, certain basic principles and assumptions are common to pretty well all of them. I shall briefly indicate what these are and then turn to the more problematic question of *how* the values are supposed to be grounded in ecology.

The core ecological values can be articulated in terms of three general imperatives.

Live in harmony with nature The most fundamental principle concerns the way the relationship between humans and nature is conceived. On a view which is prevalent and perhaps predominates in Western culture, the relationship is seen as one of opposition and struggle: 'Man' is set apart from the rest of nature and his destiny is to become its master and possessor. From an ecological standpoint, by contrast, it is emphasized that humans are themselves a part of nature: the general practical imperative which follows, therefore, is not to attempt to master and subdue, but rather to live in harmony with nature.

Overcome anthropocentric prejudice One ethical implication of an ecological worldview, then, is to challenge the valuing of the *specifically human* over and against the rest of nature. If humans are seen as a part of rather than apart from the rest of nature, this means relativizing the value of those peculiarly human traits which have traditionally been taken as the grounds for according humans a privileged moral status. For example, the powers of human *reason* were valued over and above any other powers of nature – either of 'external' nature or of the non-rational aspects of humans themselves such as passions and instincts – so as to impose a stark asymmetry on the human–nature relationship. Ecologists do not generally seek to deny the distinctiveness of specifically human faculties and capacities, but what they insist is that such specificity need not automatically be conceived in terms of superiority; it is this which they condemn as human chauvinism or speciesism.

Recognize intrinsic value in beings other than humans   Correlatively, if the value of the specifically human is relativized, the value of the non-human is taken more seriously. On a narrowly anthropocentric view, the only value any part of nature will have is the value humans happen to put on it. This means that, in practice, the reality of the natural world is reduced to that which conforms to a primarily economic or legal definition: land is merely property; elements, vital processes and even animals are merely resources. On this one-dimensional view, nature's values are simply those which can be reckoned with in cost–benefit analysis; the only response they call forth is the managerial manipulation required to maximize economic benefits. But if the perspective is shifted from economic to ecological imperatives, then nature is seen as having value in itself, independently of its usefulness to humans.

These, then, are the chief general principles according to which an ecological approach to values is claimed to be distinguished from an enlightenment approach. But one needs to be aware that in moving from these general principles to more specific values some difficult questions arise. Indeed, there are even certain tensions between the principles themselves which one might note. For instance, the injunction to live in harmony with nature depends for its plausibility and possibility on certain assumptions – such as, most obviously, that nature itself is harmonious. Yet if this is so, harmony is more likely to be found in the whole rather than necessarily in all its parts; for at 'lower', more local levels, one finds struggles for existence where nature appears 'red in tooth and claw' no less than cooperative and benign. This idea of harmony in the whole has been nicely captured in Lovelock's 'Gaia Hypothesis' whereby the world as a whole is regarded as a self-regulating organism.[52] The logic of this, however, could be argued to militate against intrinsic value theory, because, if nature will always find a balance, this does not tell us whether or how one balance will be better, more valuable, than another; indeed, it does not even tell us why a balance is necessarily a good thing – a question which is particularly pertinent in any situation where an overall balance can only be achieved at the price of individual suffering, for instance, of human or non-human beings. Thus whilst a holistic value theory may state that a whole is worth more than the sum of its parts, this leaves the question of what value if any the parts may have – a very important question, not least because any part is itself a whole.[53] Such tensions complicate the quest for identifying criteria of value; the basic problem, though, is that of accounting for values which are independent of human needs and interests, but are nevertheless to be the grounds of binding norms to guide human behaviour. The question of whether and how human norms can be derived from nature is a perennial philosophical question. I want now to consider what new answers ecologists have to offer.

Numerous writers on ecological values have claimed that guiding concepts in the science of ecology have an inseparable normative valency. Don E. Marietta, for instance, has noted that certain words used in ecological descriptions are also used in speaking of values: for example, stability, diversity, unity, balance (or homeostasis), complexity, integrity, order and health. Colwell has argued that not only are the words the same but 'human values are founded in objectively determinable ecological relations within Nature'.[54] Yet can such strong claims be substantiated? It would be quite uncontroversial to say that ecological science provides knowledge on the basis of which conceptions of ecological value can be developed. For example, if it is established that certain pollutants are doing harm, then it can be judged that to curb the pollution would be a good, a valuable, thing to do; or if it is established that our ecological life-support systems must either continually recycle or else perish, then, when considering human practices of production and consumption too, recycling must be deemed a good thing, a moral imperative even. What is more problematic, however, is the claim that values, or moral imperatives, can be *derived* from the findings of ecological science. It is one thing to accept that science can provide knowledge useful for informing moral choices; it is another to claim that values arise from the findings of science itself. The central problem here is that if one accepts the distinction between descriptive and prescriptive law then the attempt to treat statements of the one type as if they were statements of the other is to commit the 'naturalistic fallacy'.[55]

An environmental philosopher who believes that description and prescription can be related in ways that avoid the naturalistic fallacy is Holmes Rolston. It will be useful to examine some of his arguments as they promise to meet the challenge of grounding ecological values in ecological facts whilst also highlighting the pitfalls to avoid.

Rolston accepts, to begin with, that one needs to be wary of seeing moral imperatives as directly implied by ecological facts. Taking the question of recycling as an example, he notes that it might appear that from an ecological law, 'a life-supporting ecosystem recycles or per-ishes', a moral imperative can be derived, 'therefore you ought to recycle'. However the ecological law is actually non-moral, and although it circumscribes our options ('recycle or perish') it does not oblige us to choose the one rather than the other. To get an imperative which is moral and categorical it is necessary to introduce the *antecedent* moral ought, 'you ought to preserve human life'. Then it becomes possible to speak of recycling as a moral obligation; however, this obligation does *not* ulti-mately derive from any ecological law, but stems from a quite independent and traditional ethical injunction to value human life.

Rolston uses this mode of analysis to criticize the claims of Colwell. Colwell has taken what Rolston suggests is perhaps the paramount law in ecological theory – that of homeostasis – and attempted to translate this into moral prescription. Thus, according to Colwell:

> The balance of Nature provides an objective normative model which can be utilized as the ground of human value . . . The balance of Nature is, in other words, a kind of ultimate value . . . It is a *natural* norm, not a product of human convention or supernatural authority. It says in effect to man: 'This much at least you must do, this much you must be responsible for. You must at least develop and utilize energy systems which recycle their products back into Nature.' [56]

However, this is precisely the kind of claim which Rolston's mode of analysis shows to be confused in conflating the idea of a moral norm with that of a natural limit. Interestingly, though, the main lesson Rolston wants to draw from his account of Colwell's failure to set out the grounds of ecological value is not that it is insufficiently rigorous, but that it is insufficiently *radical*. This is because it is only secondarily ecological: it tells us that whatever values we do develop must be con-sistent with the balance of nature; but this need mean nothing more than pursuing a traditional ethic, ecologically tutored. 'To say that the balance of nature is a ground for human values', Rolston observes, 'is not to draw any ethics from ecology, as may first appear, but only to recognize the necessary medium of ethical activity.'[57] By contrast, Rolston sees the way forward to lie in the development of an ethic which is *primarily* ecological. The exemplary model of such an ethic, he believes, is Leopold's celebrated 'land ethic'. According to the land ethic:

> A thing is right when it tends to preserve the integrity, stability, and beauty of the biotic community. It is wrong when it tends otherwise.[58]

This is more radical, Rolston argues, because here morality is a derivative of the *holistic character* of the ecosystem.[59] Whereas in Colwell homeostatic connectedness did not really alter the moral focus, here, Rolston argues, there is a paradigm shift in that 'the values hitherto reserved for man are reallocated to man in the environment'.[60] Thus Rolston holds that the prescription 'you ought to preserve the integrity of the ecosystem' acts at a higher level, as itself an antecedent ought, and so parallels upper-level maxims in other ethical systems like that of preserving human life.

However, critical questions can be raised here. Rolston claims that a valuational element – 'the integral ecosystem has value' – is intrinsically related to the concepts utilized in ecological description.[61] But *how* exactly are they intrinsically related? He writes that the description and evaluation to some extent arise together, and that ecological description finds unity, harmony, interdependence, stability, and so on – things which are valuationally endorsed. As Rolston recognizes, though, in response to this it might be objected that stability and integrity, like beauty, may be qualities which exist primarily in the eye of the (human) beholder. He insists, however, that 'what counts as beauty and integrity is not just brought to and imposed on the ecosystem but is discovered there'. He argues that 'an "ought" is not so much *derived* from an "is" as discovered simultaneously with it'. He thus believes that the naturalistic fallacy is circumvented:

> As we progress from descriptions of fauna and flora, of cycles and pyramids, of stability and dynamism, on to intricacy, planetary opulence and interdependence, to unity and harmony with oppositions in counterpoint and synthesis, arriving at length at beauty and goodness, it is difficult to say where the natural facts leave off and where the natural values appear. For some observers at least, the sharp is/ought dichotomy is gone.[62]

Nevertheless, other, more sceptical, observers might reply it is difficult because *natural* values have *not* appeared, but have been imposed: and so, if the naturalistic fallacy has been avoided, it has only been by begging the question.

Rolston's strategy in reply to this objection is to seek to show how judgements of value are on a par with judgements of fact.[63] He begins by noting various reasons why it may seem hopeless to aim to establish objective natural values. In particular, because we have to reckon with how the relativistic conclusions of twentieth-century science – for example of Einstein, Heisenberg and quantum mechanics – have apparently demolished the possibility of claims to objective knowledge even in a 'hard' science like physics, let alone in the sphere of values. However, what Rolston emphasizes about this is that claims to objective knowledge of fact fall along with claims to objective knowledge of values: 'Subjectivity has eaten up everything, even the fact/value distinction.'[64] His next step is to show that the claims of relativity are only relatively valid. He asks us to consider, for example, the observation 'There is a hawk in the spruce beside that granite boulder.' This judgement, he grants, fades out on subatomic scales, but this does not alter the fact that we know something objectively, factually about hawks, spruce trees, and boulders: 'agnosticism and relativism about the ultimate structure of matter does not prevent objective knowing in a middle-level sense.'[65] I think Rolston is probably right about this: if we are concerned with the world at human scale and in terms of immediate human interests, everything is indeed as it appears to be. I think he may also be right when he continues:

> Just as we are getting incoming commands from 'out there' about length, color, hawks, and trees, so too we are getting some commands about value. We start with these as native range judgements, not as absolute ones.[66]

However, if this statement is true, it perhaps does not imply as much as Rolston wishes it to. For a sceptic might grant that a mid-range value judgement which is not absolute might come immediately to the unreflective mind of an observer, but still maintain that this tells us nothing about objective natural value: for, depending on the mindset of the observer, the hawk may be perceived as dangerous, good, evil, holy, beneficial to an ecosystem, or as bearing some other sort of value. At most, therefore, it could be that Rolston has referred us to the general point that people tend to associate values with facts – an anthropological and psychological generality which hardly suffices to make his case that value in general exists in nature, much less that nature yields specific values.

In order to bring this discussion to a constructive conclusion I think we need to separate out two distinct claims that Rolston makes. The first is that judgements of value may not be less secure than judgements of fact, a point he illustrates by saying that if the hawk may be perceived in different ways by different people, this applies to describing it as much as to valuing it: if an Iroquois Indian views the hawk as his totem, or the tree and boulder as the haunt of a spirit, the natural scientist who makes judgements about the natural kinds *Buteo*, *Picea* and granite is not doing anything radically different. This is because all judgements are theory laden. 'One has to decide whether this is a *Picea*, as one has to decide whether this is a *lovely Picea*.' Hence it follows that if facts are no more secure than values, values are no less secure than facts. The basic point here could probably be granted on any but the most positivistic conception of knowledge.

How secure judgements either of facts or of values are, though, is another question. Rolston claims that certain values come with the phenomena of life in such a way that scepticism in their regard appears less tenable than affirmation. An example he gives is that when a scientist says haemoglobin molecules are better than myoglobin molecules at oxygen transport, this 'purely descriptive' use of 'better' is inseparable from an expression of value: 'As soon as we have described hemoglobin evolution, we are ready to judge it a vital and valuable step upward in the advance of life. The phenomenon of things "being important" does not arise with our awareness; it is steadily there in quantized discoveries all along the way.'[67] The key idea here is that as nature has undergone processes of increased differentiation and complexity, accompanied by a growth in subjectivity and capacity for experience, specifically human values have emerged not as a radical departure but as part of a continuing development of the process. I think this is a potentially fruitful idea, connecting specifically human values in an evolutionary continuum with the rest of nature. It thereby promises to reconcile dualistic oppositions and provide a basis for a unified view of the human place in the world. This idea, however, also brings with it some further problems which need to be worked through properly.

Rolston's claim that judgements of ecological value emerge along with judgements of ecological fact implies that they are anchored in the nature of reality – that is, ontologically. However, a critic could argue that this is simply false: the judgements which Rolston claims to root in nature are actually constructs of human minds or cognitive practices; on the most plausible understanding of these constructions they are the products of social practices; and social practices cannot be explained naturalistically. On a strong formulation of this objection, naturalistic explanations of social practices would be held to be impossible in principle because all knowledge is socially constructed. However, the social constructionist thesis is no less questionable than the naturalism it opposes if pushed to the extreme of denying any basis of knowledge in reality. A milder formulation is more persuasive, though: given the present state of knowledge, it is at least contingently the case that the nature and behaviour of humans, especially as social beings, cannot fully be *explained* in wholly ecological terms. This does not prejudge the question of whether social phenomena may *ultimately* be understood in the same terms as phenomena of the rest of nature, but does emphasize that it *is* an important question. This means that even if societies may ultimately be understood naturalistically, or if the concept of the natural could itself be expanded, we nevertheless have to reckon in the here and now with social mediations.

My conclusion, then, is that the normative regulation of human affairs cannot necessarily be derived from ecological insights, at least to the extent that they follow a logic which ecology is insufficiently equipped to illuminate; so even if principles at a high level of generality could be established on an ecological basis, the application of these would require the understanding of human cultural and social beliefs and aspirations in their specificity. But this conclusion need not be seen as representing a detour away from properly ecological questions or an attenuation of their import. For precisely to the extent that ecology is claimed to have implications for social life and values, its aims are served by having the latter properly illuminated. Furthermore, it may help undercut the stand-off we have noted between Rolston's ecologism and an opponent's scepticism if it can be admitted that all knowledge is to some extent socially constructed:[68] for then it can be recognized both that the standards for judging reliable knowledge, the paradigms which are accepted for the time being, may represent only a provisional consensus, but also that they are not necessarily arbitrary *vis-à-vis* reality – if for no other reason than that society itself is part of reality. So paradigms can be contested, their rational standards questioned, to reveal any arbitrariness as inadequacy in the light of fuller – less arbitrary – understanding. We have noted that ecology is part of a current contestation which can perhaps be understood as the reality of ecology forcing itself against inadequate conceptions. Moreover, it is salutary to recall that science, even as narrowly understood, is itself a social practice, with all that entails,[69] given that there is often claimed to be a decisive difference between genuine ecological science on the one hand and ecologistic ideology on the other: as I have already suggested, it may be that the broader penumbra of ecological ideas cannot be so sharply demarcated off from the strict science as its critics might wish. It seems, indeed, that all is not light within – and it may yet prove to be not all dark without. The ideas of the penumbra may also have some claim to purchase on reality – perhaps even in ways that the science is so constructed as not to have access to. So, one cannot simply rule out claims for ecological thought which are of provenance other than the professional science. In pursuit of these claims, though, one cannot appeal directly to nature. It would be merely naïve to suppose that immediate access to nature in itself were possible. One may have the intuition that, at bottom, the whole world is natural, and that social/mental phenomena are complicated bits of it which generate an illusion of autonomy; but the illusion, if that it is, needs first to be investigated, understood and explained. One needs to direct one's attentions first to the constructions which assume the form of knowledge. Hence *critique of knowledge*, as social product, is indispensable to ecological thought.

1.3 Ecological Critique

What we have seen so far, in the attempt to arrive at a clear formulation of the ecological challenge to enlightenment values and rationality, is that there are tensions, ambiguities and even contradictions within ecology just as there are within enlightenment. This puts a serious question mark against the idea that ecology can be seen as straightforwardly opposed to enlightenment – and, indeed, it is significant to observe that there is a good deal of similarity between the two sets of tensions.[70] In this section, therefore, I put forward a different way of viewing the question, suggesting that the ecological challenge, precisely to the extent that it is a critical challenge, can be seen as a renewal of the enlightenment project itself.

If there are similar tensions in both ecological thought and enlightenment thought then this may quite likely be due to inherent difficulties in conceiving the relation of thought itself to reality. To address these we therefore need to reflect further on the nature of thought, reality and the relation between them: which means returning to questions of epistemology and ontology. Accordingly, I shall seek to show that more significant than the apparent opposition between ecology and enlightenment is an underlying set of problems that they could be trying to address together.

At root the common endeavour is to understand the nature of the world, the place of humans in it and the appropriate principles to guide human action. Ecology, as a natural science, contributes significantly to understanding the natural world; it also helps understand the human place in the natural world and to some extent informs principles to guide human action. Yet it is not in a position fully to determine appropriate action, or to explain the full range of human *social* behaviour: this requires the use of concepts and categories which simply cannot be worked up within ecology as a natural science. Understanding social behaviour and human action requires a theory with an adequate degree of reflexivity. I argue in the first part of this section that this is most appropriately sought along the lines developed within critical theory; I give reasons in support of the claim that if the enlightenment project is understood as one of critique rather than of domination it is not necessarily anti-ecological. We have already noted the distinction Kant draws between critical and positive knowledge.[71] The strength of critical knowledge is that it does not allow presuppositions to remain unchallenged, which means it is vigilant against error of the most insidious sort – that is, the sort that creeps in with the assumptions made before thinking even begins. A critical approach allows us to guard against a merely dogmatic and arbitrary conception of ecology. But if this rescues the enlightenment project from some of the more swingeing ecological objections, it does not suffice to establish it as an ecological ally since in the absence of substantive commitments it is not necessarily pro-ecology either. The weakness of critique, as such, is that it does not itself yield any substantive knowledge. If critique is to be turned to ecological ends, therefore, critical theory will also need to be informed by ecological understanding of a realist sort. In sum, if we can appreciate how thought in general can be both critical and realist we may get a better understanding of the real problems underlying the apparent opposition between ecology and enlightenment.

Enlightenment as critique

For thought to be critical it must raise to awareness and, as appropriate, problematize its own presuppositions. This applies to ecological thought too. My aim here is to outline a conception of critique which will be most useful to this clarificatory task.

Critique for Kant means the determining of the bounds and limits of knowledge: this is more than mere scepticism or doubt, for the critique of pure reason is an activity of self-knowledge. Nevertheless, Kant's critique of knowledge can itself be criticized for being insufficiently radical: it is limited by the fact that it does not criticize its own initial conception of what knowledge is. This point was made by Hegel who argued that Kant presupposes something is already known, for he *starts* with the idea of a knower (subject), a known (object) and the existence, if not the precise nature, of a relation between them (knowledge). This whole model is problematic, Hegel argues, for it sees knowledge as having the function either of an active *instrument* to 'seize hold of the truth', or of a passive *medium* 'through which the light of truth reaches us'. In fact, though, knowledge cannot fulfil either function:

> For if knowledge is the instrument for seizing hold of absolute essence, then it is immediately apparent that the use of an instrument or tool does not leave the thing as it is for itself, but entails some transformation and change in it. If, on the other hand, knowledge is not an instrument in our employ, but a passive medium through which the light of truth reaches us, then we are still unable to attain truth as it is in itself but only as it is through and in this medium.[72]

Hegel indicates that there is no secure point at which to anchor claims to knowledge, for knowledge cannot simply be the relation of the subject and object: rather this whole process of investigating is itself knowledge. Thus any critique has to be directed at a whole 'package' including knower, known, process, context and so on.[73] These packages of phenomenal knowledge include not only the strictly positive knowledge of the exact sciences, but also pre-scientific representations and cultural traditions. In other words, a society's common-sense beliefs and institutionalized values can also appropriately be subjected to critique. So, for Hegel, the attempt to do philosophy by purging presuppositions is simply untenable; what must rather be sought is to thematize, raise to consciousness, the presuppositions themselves. This will not yield absolute foundations for knowledge claims, but adopting this approach means that packages of knowledge can be subjected to *immanent* critique: that is, they can be criticized on their own terms, tested for their consistency, and if they fail to hold together then they refute themselves without the need to refer to any external criterion.

Immanent critique can be applied to all forms of knowledge, and Hegel's critique of philosophy is ultimately conceived as a critique of its cultural preconditions. As Marcuse commented:

> Hegel took the view that philosophy arises from the all-embracing contradictions into which human existence has been plunged. These have shaped the history of philosophy as the history of basic contradictions, those between 'mind and matter, soul and body, belief and understanding, freedom and necessity', contradictions that had more recently appeared as those between 'reason and sense' (*Sinnlichkeit*), 'intelligence and nature', and, in the most general form, 'subjectivity and objectivity'.[74]

For Hegel the presence of these dichotomies in philosophy is the expression of deeper rifts within cultural life. He sees the purpose of philosophy to be the overcoming of these rifts and the restoration of unity. Having in view how this restoration of unity would apply both between humans and between humans and nature, Hegel to some extent combines the enlightenment concern with emancipation with what we would now consider an ecological concern to overcome a way of life which is alienated from nature. His philosophy is holistic rather than atomistic and dualistic; it seeks to grasp what are first perceived as isolated entities in terms of an identity of opposites. This means trying not simply to connect and combine the opposites as they stand, but to transform them so that they cease to exist as opposites and become parts of a higher synthesis. This is to give full weight to the view that every part exists only in relation to the whole. Hegel's philosophical works can be seen to be grounded in the assumption 'that the laws of nature spring from the rational structure of being and lead in a continuum to the laws of the mind. The realm of mind achieves in freedom what the realm of nature achieves in blind necessity – the fulfillment of the potentialities inherent in reality. It is this state of reality which Hegel refers to as "the truth".'[75]

A problem which can now be discerned, however, is that Hegel's so-called 'pan-logism' treats every form of being as a form of reason. Indeed, in the *Phenomenology* Hegel speaks of external nature as a second, historicized, 'property of universal Spirit'.[76] Hegel's radicalizing of Kantian critique has in the end redoubled the view of humans as historical demiurge coming to the mastery of nature. In doing so, he may also have intimated a paradoxical question for ecology: that is, whether there is an ultimate 'whole' which does not imply 'absolute mind'.

At this point it is interesting to note how Marx radicalizes Hegelian critique so that in one way he improves the situation and in another exacerbates it. On the one hand, he transforms the Hegelian ontology so that history no longer appears as the process of absolute *Geist* (mind or spirit) coming to know itself, but is seen instead in terms of reality, nature, having primacy over thought. Attendant on this, emancipation of thought cannot proceed independently of social emancipation. Conflicts must be overcome not merely in thought, in philosophy, but in reality: 'It is not enough that thought should strive to realize itself; reality must itself strive towards thought.'[77] Marx thus effected a decisive move from philosophy and the criticism of knowledge, to social theory and the criticism of reality. This has the potential of offering a more realistic view of humans *vis-à-vis* the rest of nature. However his theory of human emancipation to some extent goes against this: his belief that by over-coming exploitative and oppressive social relations humans will be able to move from a 'realm of necessity' to a 'realm of freedom' rather installs historical humanity, if not exactly in the place of Hegel's *Geist*, at any rate in a privileged position *vis-à-vis* the rest of nature. So if Hegel can be said to have betrayed his own critical insights – including the insight that history can only be understood from within – by pursuing his ambition of gaining knowledge of history from some ultimate Archimedean point, it is arguable that Marx in a way makes this even worse by identifying as an Archimedean point of history the class of workers who were pro-ductively predominant at his time of writing. In giving this primacy to the productive workers, moreover, he systematically underplayed the importance of *nature*'s contribution to the process of production.

It is against this background that the development of critique by the Frankfurt School is particularly significant. Twentieth-century theorists like Adorno, Horkheimer and Marcuse departed from orthodox Marxism in ways which enabled them to be more genuinely critical and also potentially ecological. They were critical, for one thing, of the idea that human history can be portrayed as basically a success story. Particularly in view of the increasing implausibility of Marx's thesis concerning the emergence of a revolutionary proletariat in industrialized nations, and the rise of fascism in Europe, they considered it necessary to understand socio-historical reality in terms of determinations other than the eco-nomic. Hence one major area, neglected by Marx, which they developed along with other Western Marxists, was a critique not only of the eco-nomic sphere, but also of *culture*. In their examination of culture, they utilized categories drawn from thinkers less buoyant and more sceptical than Marx about the emancipatory possibilities of progress, to investigate the entwinement of myth and enlightenment, bringing into focus the 'subterranean history' of Europe, revealing the dark underside of the enlightenment heritage. They were thus also sensitive to respects in which Marx does not overcome the dominant ideology. For instance, he perpetuates a belief in economic growth and mastery of nature as pro-gress, allowing the emancipation of people at the expense of dominated nature. Hence, particularly important for our present concerns is how the Frankfurt School anticipated major ecological themes.[78] Aspects of Frankfurt School thought which are focused on in an ecological reading are their critique of instrumental reason and the attendant critique of enlightenment as domination, for in these respects they can be held to side with nature. There is a common concern to oppose the instrumental forms of reason and action which prevail in modern societies regarding both relations between humans and relations between humans and nature. The role of critical theory is to anchor moral criticism of prevailing human–human and human–nature relations in determinate criticism of the actual social relations and cultural forms which sustain them. The ecological potential of the Frankfurt School has been highlighted by Eckersley, for instance, who claims that their goal 'was to rescue reason in such a way as to bring instrumental reason under the control of what they referred to as "objective" or "critical" reason'.[79]

Nevertheless, although these things are rightly emphasized, there are also significant qualifications which have to be made, and which an overly simple ecologistic reading is liable to overlook. There is a greater degree of paradoxicality in the project described by Eckersley than she appears to allow.[80] If the critique of instrumental reason has remained a basic impetus for critical theory since the beginning, there have never-theless been significantly different views of where it leads. In the *Dialectic of Enlightenment* itself there is a significant tension which Seyla Benhabib alerts us to: the work in fact vacillates between two theses, she says, 'that of Adorno, which views reason to be inherently an instrument of domination, and that of Horkheimer, who acknowledges that reason had an emancipatory force which it has since lost under current conditions'.[81] The path taken by Adorno turns immanent critique into 'negative dialectics', and a denial 'that there is an immanent logic to the actual that is emancipatory'.[82] This leaves scope for irony and rhetor-ical condemnation, perhaps, but if it implies that an all-pervasive rationalization has eliminated crises and conflict tendencies within the social structure, then specific criticisms cannot find any anchorage. Viewing the genesis of civilization and its transformation into barbarism, the critique of enlightenment becomes a 'totalizing critique'.[83] One can draw comparisons between this and the claims of certain ecologists of an anti-enlightenment disposition who offer sweeping criticisms of Western civilization ancient and modern. But going to this opposite extreme from Enlightenment optimism totalizing critique can show too much: if soci-ety can no longer be shown to be a contradictory totality, then the utopian concept of reason can no longer be anchored in the present. It can therefore be argued that *if* critical theory is to be pursued at all, it must accept the hypothesis implicit in the second thesis – that associated with Horkheimer – that it is not Western reason as such which is defect-ive, but a specific instrumental form of it. This thesis, which does not wholly break from the enlightenment, has more recently undergone sig-nificant developments in the work of Jürgen Habermas.

Habermas has eschewed negative dialectics and returned to *immanent* critique of modern rationalization processes, locating instrumental reason within a larger and more comprehensive theory of rationality, so that although the logic of instrumental rationality governs human dealings with the non-human world, there is a logic of communicative rationality which governs interaction between human subjects.[84] His view is that in communication certain validity claims are necessarily invoked – claims about truth, rightness, sincerity, and so on. Even defective communication, such as lies and deceit, can only function because of these normative presuppositions. The basic idea, then, is that certain values people always already subscribe to can be identified through critical analysis of their own communicative practice.[85] It is the explicit thematizing of these values which constitutes Habermas's discourse ethics, whose fundamental principle is this:

> Only those norms can claim to be valid that meet (or could meet) with the approval of all affected in their capacity *as participants in a practical discourse*.[86]

This leaves the question, however, of those beings who may be affected by human decisions but do not have the requisite capacity to participate in practical discourse. Habermas's ethics is anthropocentric: only humans can participate in practical discourse because it involves both linguistic competence and a degree of reflection on communicative practices of which only rational beings would seem to be capable.

Thus a fundamental ecological objection to Habermas is that his communicative ethics is for humans only. As Dobson has observed, there is no guarantee that it 'will grant a more valued status to the non-human world than it has at present';[87] and Alford has put the point more strongly, noting that the very goal of Habermas's project is 'to prevent social relationships from becoming like our relations with the natural world'.[88] This summary has for many put the seal on the possibility of Habermas being seen as an ally of ecologists. Accordingly, when Eckersley notes how little impact critical thinking has had on green theory, she says this is due to the developments it has undergone with Habermas. The question this begs, however, is why contemporary ecologists have not simply availed themselves of the insights of earlier or greener members of the Frankfurt School.

My own view, as already intimated, is that this is not really an option because those insights are intrinsically bound up with the dialectic of enlightenment and cannot be sustained without taking account of those aspects of the dialectic which have been emphasized by Habermas –

whose thought is therefore not a deviation from or betrayal of those insights, but the extrapolation of something at the heart of the dialectic. The contemporary division of the legacy of critical theory between Habermasians and postmodernists is in fact the magnification of aporias at the core of critical theory – aporias which are already discernible in tensions between Adorno and Horkheimer and manifest in the *Dialectic of Enlightenment* itself. Unless one appreciates the good reasons for critical theory taking a Habermasian direction, and also for it diverging into postmodernism too, then not only will one fail to appreciate the highly ambiguous promise of critical theory as such, but one will be left at a naïve and unsatisfactory theory which is merely ecologistic.

Habermas is aware of the importance of ecological concerns, but he says little about them because he believes, on the one hand, that a radical rethinking of the human relationship to nature is not possible; but also, on the other, that it is not necessary. Radically rethinking this relation is not possible, he believes, because this would involve making knowledge claims which cannot be supported. The kinds of knowledge humans can gain of external nature are for Habermas quite precisely circumscribed: there exists, he says, 'only one *theoretically fruitful* attitude' in this sphere, that of the objective natural scientist.[89] He is sceptical about the 'possibility of giving a rational form to fraternal relations with a non-objectivated nature',[90] and doubts whether the way to treat problems of environmental crisis is by making a radical break with the differentiated structures of modern consciousness. Certainly, he says, the onus is on those who suggest such a break to show how they propose making knowledge claims in the areas he rules out: for example, those who envision an ultimate purposiveness to nature have to make clear how this idea avoids leading 'back to metaphysics, and thus behind the levels of learning reached in the modern age into a re-enchanted world'.[91]

Still, while Habermas is sceptical about non-instrumental attitudes towards nature having *theoretical* efficacy, he does not preclude the possibility of developing other attitudes and forms of knowledge with a purchase on nature. He does not deny that we can 'adopt a performative attitude to external nature, enter into communicative relations with it, [or] have aesthetic experience and feelings analogous to morality with respect to it'.[92] Thus, as Stephen White points out, Habermas's position at least allows one to address some of the *practical* concerns which animate efforts to rethink the human–nature relation. Ecological crisis can be 'a practical catalyst for reflection on how the ways in which we currently assault nature are leading to a more and more frustrating and self-destructive form of life'.[93] This need not involve a new philosophy of nature, but rather requires a new sense of what makes for human satisfaction: it would mean enhancing the moral-practical and aesthetic-expressive dimensions of everyday social life.

So Habermas does not think a radically new way of relating to nature is necessary since the outcomes desired by ecologists can be achieved through a frankly anthropocentric appeal to enlightened human self-interest. This is a suggestion whose pros and cons will be discussed more fully in the next chapter. At this stage, though, the point I'd wish to stress is that Habermas's position is properly understood not as representing a rejection of a more ecological mode of thought or ethic, but as a *challenge* to show how one might be possible. Although some of Habermas's most sympathetic critics suggest he is too rigid in drawing epistemological boundaries as he does,[94] he is trying to map them where they do appear to fall. The distinctions in theory and practice he marks have emerged historically in the West in the modern era. It is a specific *culture* which has generated those structures of rationality which have split reason into the three moments of modern science, ethics and aesthetics: 'philosophy', he says, 'had precious little to do with this disjunction'.[95] Philosophizing will therefore not suffice to overcome them, either; that will require a change in real conditions too. He does not preclude the possibility of those conditions being transformed; indeed, that is the *aim* of a critical theory of society with emancipatory intent.

For Habermas, critical theory is about identifying, and thereby seeking to promote, a progression of culturally embedded learning levels. It is arguable that the success of ecological thought and values will actually depend on this project since they essentially seek to extend their grip on human interventions in the world. It may therefore be that ecological thought already represents an advanced learning level. Thus Eckersley's own suggestion appears, at one point, to be not the abandonment but the extension of Habermas's ethics:

> We need to revise and extend Habermas's communication ethics to a full-blown ecocentric ethics that is informed not only by the internal relatedness embedded in human speech, but also by the internal relatedness and reciprocity embedded in ecological relations in general, which, in a very literal sense, sustain us all.[96]

I would endorse the spirit of this proposal but emphasize that its realization means overcoming that opposition between ecology and enlightenment which Eckersley takes as an organizing principle of her book. Thus one must beware of exaggerated claims for the newness of ecological thought: for a new learning level must build on rather than abandon previous ones. On the other hand, though, there is still some building to be done. Habermas's own position is not immune to a more considered critique. In particular, if he rightly emphasizes limits of knowledge, epistemic limits, one should not allow description of them to turn into defence of them. In this context Dryzek speaks of the 'subversion of ethics by epistemology' and advocates a greater openness to communication from non-human nature, arguing that practical reason places no restriction on the kinds of knowledge admissible.[97] A related point is made by Bhaskar who accuses Habermas of committing the 'epistemic fallacy' in failing explicitly to thematize ontology so that his system takes on a 'dualistic anti-naturalist' hue which is questionable in its own right and certainly hard to reconcile with ecology.[98] What is of value in Habermas, Bhaskar accordingly claims, needs to be set in a critical naturalist and transcendental realist perspective. I shall now briefly consider this proposal, as it may be that from this perspective some constructive suggestions may emerge as to how Habermas's challenge may actually be met.

Ecology as critical realism

If a renewal of critique is to aim at the realization of values grounded in ecology it presupposes that there is something ultimately non-contingent about those values. Yet if one is to avoid the fallacies of an unmediated ecologism – which is liable to suggest one can simply read off values from nature – one has to acknowledge the critical insight, elaborated above, that values always come socially mediated. This need not mean taking the view, however, that values are a purely social – and therefore contingent or conventional – construct. For society itself is a part of that non-contingent reality we call nature. So which values get constructed and how is unlikely to be arbitrary, even though the processes involved will be complex and not always easy to discover. Still, I believe we can make some assumptions of a general sort. In what remains of this chapter, accordingly, I want to make explicit the sort of ontological assumptions which are implied in the general view of nature, society and value relations being developed in this book.

The ontology implicit here is *realist* in the sense that predicates like 'ecological' and 'unecological' are taken to have determinate (even if not always determinable) purchase on real processes and states of affairs in the world. It is not naïvely realist, though, and recognizes that access to the real will not be direct or unproblematic. What I have in mind is the kind of 'critical realist' approach developed by writers such as Bhaskar and Sayer. Peter Dickens has summarized this in terms of a stratification of knowledge:

> At a general level relatively enduring generative structures are envisaged. These underlie the manifest phenomena of everyday life. Entities, such as humans, other organisms, and those of inorganic nature have latent powers or capacities . . . But . . . these structures and tendencies are not observable in an unmediated form. They emerge and combine in complex ways with contingent relations and tendencies. Indeed, the contingent factors may be such that the underlying mechanisms or ways of acting may not be experienced or observed. Explanation of manifest appearances critically relies, therefore, on *both* abstract laws and theories and on information of a less abstract kind.[99]

The world is conceived as structured, differentiated and changing. Social as well as natural phenomena are thereby seen as the product of a plurality of structures. Critical realism can be claimed to meet the major requirements of ecological holism whilst allowing sufficient differentiation and appreciation of dialectics to avoid the weaknesses of crude ecologistic versions. As Bhaskar notes: 'we have to see the natural and social dimensions of existence as in continuous dynamic causal interaction. Thus not only are many "natural" ills and disasters *socially* produced, but social production may have absolute *natural* limits and conditions.'[100] Critical realism recognizes that the social structure is embedded in, conditioned by, and in turn acts back upon the rest of nature; it thereby acknowledges the specificity of the social but without perpetuating the dichotomous opposition between society and nature such as finds expression in a Promethean view of the human relationship to nature.[101]

Nevertheless, while it may be that an ecological ontology is best thought of in terms of critical realism, this does not mean the latter is any automatic key to unlocking disputes or obviating debates in other quarters. There are liable to be significant differences *between* critical realists along lines which divide environmentalists and ecologists of other basic philosophical orientations.

One central question which ecology causes us to pose anew was already the fundamental problem of the philosophy of the social sciences: to what extent can society be studied in the same way as nature? Ecological thought would appear to require a form of naturalism, defined by Bhaskar as 'the thesis that there is (or can be) an essential unity of method between the natural and social sciences'.[102] If naturalism is to be defended in some form, though, it must be distinguished from two unacceptable forms which he describes as: '*reductionism*, which posits an actual identity of subject matter as well; and *scientism*, which denies that there are any important differences in the methods appropriate to studying societies and nature.'[103] There are thus also limits to naturalism, on Bhaskar's account, which derive from societies' distinctive emergent properties. In particular, he has noted three ways that social science differs from natural science:

1 Social structures, unlike natural structures, do not exist independently of the activities they govern. That is, they exist only in virtue of the activities they govern.
2 Social structures, unlike natural structures, do not exist independent of people's conceptions of what they are doing in their activity.
3 Social structures, unlike natural structures, are usually only 'relatively enduring'. The tendencies which are incorporated within them are not universal or unchanging over time and space.[104]

Interestingly, theorists who have sought to introduce critical realism into ecological thought have questioned Bhaskar here. Benton, for instance, puts the view, endorsed by Dickens, that these grounds for limiting the application of naturalism to social science look like a relapse into dualism.[105] Nevertheless, I believe Bhaskar is right to highlight certain problems with naturalism in the social sphere. Thus, for instance, although he does not seek to reinstate an absolute fact–value distinction, he does think there are reasons why factual judgements tend to be more secure in the natural sphere and value judgements in the social sphere: 'social phenomena only ever occur in open systems, whereas in the natural sphere it is sometimes possible to contrive, or observe phenomena in, locally closed (in physics and chemistry) or quasi-closed (in biology) systems.'[106] Knowledge becomes more difficult, less certain, as one moves from closed through semi-closed to open systems: thus, for instance, knowledge in maths may be more certain than physics; physics than biology; biology than ecology. Another difference is that objects of social scientific knowledge, although independently real, 'are causally interdependent with the knowledge of which they are the objects'.[107] In social science, therefore, the fact–value distinction breaks down more decisively: if one can demonstrate the sufficiency of a particular set of social conditions for a false, inadequate or partial belief, Bhaskar says, then, other things being equal, one can pass directly to a negative evaluation of them and to a positive evaluation of action rationally directed at

transforming them. This might mean that if a social structure systematically distorts communication between people, for instance, then it can
be described as bad; if it enables free intersubjective relations then it is
good.

There is a convergence here with the views of Habermas in that emancipatory norms can be anchored in critical social scientific knowledge.
There is also agreement that in the pursuit of emancipation 'the enlightenment which the depth human sciences may, but will not necessarily,
bring is a necessary but insufficient condition'.[108] Equally necessary, we
may add, is the enlightenment of ecology.

What I have sought to sketch here is the basic idea that the dialectic of
enlightenment is also the dialectic of ecology. This dialectic involves
tensions that we live in and have to address *from within* – which means
addressing them *as* humans, as social beings, with imperfect knowledge.
So if critique is not to become mere criticism which appeals to a utopian
vision that others may not share, which is not rooted in the norms and
values of the culture, and so is an abstract 'ought', one must seek out if
there are still norms and values with emancipatory content immanent in
modern culture. The question to pose today is whether critique can be
renewed with values grounded in ecology. That is one way of defining
the project of this book. Among the major questions that it has yet to
address concern what human emancipation means for the rest of nature,
and whether an instrumental relation to it is appropriate at least as a
means to human ends.

Conclusion

This chapter has sought to explain, in broad terms, the nature of ecological thought and values. Having acknowledged at the outset that
ecology itself can be understood in various different ways, the first
approach was to identify points of contrast with the prevailing rationality
and value systems of modern Western cultures which are particularly
associated with the enlightenment. This was to define ecological thought,
negatively, in terms of what it is not – at least to the extent that aspects
of the enlightenment worldview can be considered unecological. It was
also noted, though, that enlightenment concerns are not necessarily anti-
ecological and that its emancipatory and critical force might actually be
required by ecology when applied to the sphere of values. In the second
section, in the quest for an affirmative account of ecological thought, it
proved necessary to distinguish not only between ecology as a strict

science and as a broader concern of humans with their relation to nature, but also between competing views within each. Hence we surveyed different views of whether ecology participates in a new scientific paradigm, and if so with what implications. We noted that ecology does appear to imply a distinctive ethos, but also noted difficulties with trying to use it to ground determinate values and obligations. Indeed, here we came up against perennial philosophical questions concerning the relation of humans and values to nature; this was also to highlight the point that humans are not only natural beings, but also social beings. If recognizing this is not to lead to dualistic thinking, then it means taking a more dialectical view of the mediations between science and values, reason and nature. It thus becomes clear that the relation between ecology and enlightenment is not one of straightforward opposition; indeed, within each very similar tensions are at work. Moreover, I suggested, if ecology is to challenge conventional wisdom, then in doing so it partakes of the *critical* legacy of enlightenment thought itself. In this regard it is perhaps worth recalling a very simple point which is sometimes liable to be forgotten in the detail of a philosophical argument or the heat of a polemical debate: namely, that both ecological thought and enlightenment thought are concerned to get at the truth about *reality*, and to connect an understanding of this with an understanding of how humans might best live their lives. It is this I have tried to revive in the final section of this chapter. Certainly there are real disputes which can be introduced under the heading of ecology versus enlightenment, but these are disputes which will be better understood, and possibly resolved, by thinking beyond such dichotomies.

2
The Ethics of Ecological Humanism

In the previous chapter it was argued that enlightenment is not adequately understood as a dogmatic assertion of the claims of reason over
nature, nor should ecology be taken to mean the reverse; rather, they
converge on the project of critique. This alliance in principle, though, is
as yet only tentative, for there are still substantial differences to negotiate
regarding the standards and criteria for such a critique. However, before
looking at debates in specific spheres of value, it is necessary to say
something about valuing itself. For, as far as we know, only humans do
it. That is to say, whatever is *of* value in the world, only humans appre-
hend it in the *form* of value. The implications of this bit of human species
specificity need thinking through at the outset: hence the topic of this
chapter.

Humanism is perhaps one of the most distinctive characteristics of
enlightenment thought, and one of the most deeply rooted in modern
Western thought generally. It has also come under increasing criticism
from an ecological perspective. This is because there are some profound
ambiguities in the idea. The basic idea, which underlies the various,
sometimes contrasting, interpretations of humanism, is that the nature of
human beings is unique to humans, and is not to be adequately explained
by reference either to animal nature or to religion. From this basic idea
itself the reasons for the ambiguous character of humanism are already
discernible. On the one hand, bereft of divine guarantees for human
knowledge or destiny, without the assurance of having been made in
God's image, or as the centre or purpose of creation, humanity is decisively humbled in the cosmological scheme of things. Human self-
knowledge must proceed in a spirit of humility. On the other hand,

however, freed of an erstwhile humility before their Maker, humans themselves become the final arbiters of what is true or false, right or wrong: so an original faith in a higher authority may become a faith in the power of human reason and capacities. This faith itself has contrasting aspects, particularly in the sphere of ethics: on the one hand, it promotes an emphasis on the dignity, and equality, of all humans, thereby supporting benign and tolerant social attitudes; on the other hand, the emphasis on human autonomy can also lead to putting exclusive value on human interests, as opposed to the interests of the rest of nature, and to pursuing them through the attempted mastery and domination of nature. It is the latter aspect of humanism which is criticized by those concerned with ecological philosophy in general, and environmental ethics in particular.

In this chapter, accordingly, I am concerned to assess arguments for and against humanism in an ecological context. In the first section I consider how an affirmative attitude towards humanism can be justified, and how it may furnish the basis for an ethic which includes dimensions of environmental concern. The central argument is that a proper understanding of human interests entails recognizing how it is in the human interest to adopt principles of environmental concern. The second section examines ecological criticisms of a human-centred concern for the environment. It focuses particularly on the objection that in starting out from what sets humans *apart* from the rest of nature, it typically takes the specifically human to be the prime, and perhaps only, locus of intrinsic value in the world. I show that although the criticisms are well taken, there are nevertheless quite serious difficulties with the various attempts to provide a satisfactory alternative to human-centredness. Hence it remains open to argue, as I do in the third section, that the impoverished humanism and conception of human nature rightly criticized from an ecological perspective does not exhaust the enlightenment ideal, and that ecology, rather than undermining the latter, may help to revive it, and prove an ally in the continuing struggle to realize it.

2.1 Environmentalism and Enlightened Self-Interest

In this section I consider how an affirmative attitude towards humanism can be justified, and how it may furnish the basis for an ethic which includes dimensions of environmental concern. I begin by noting the reasons for 'transcendent' humanism – that is, the reasons why humans might justifiably be seen as set apart from the rest of nature – and the view that an accurate appreciation of human self-interest can form the basis of an ethic. I then consider how the humanistic conception of an enlightened self-interest can also apply to environmental ethics, drawing parallels between the idea that rational self-interest can be a basis of concern for other humans and the idea that enlightened self-interest can be a basis of concern for non-human beings.

Humanism in ethics

An account of human specificity as underlies humanistic ethics was quite well set out 50 years ago by Erich Fromm:

> The first element which differentiates human from animal existence is a negative one: the relative absence in man of instinctive regulation in the process of adaptation to the surrounding world . . . The emergence of man can be defined as occurring at the point in the process of evolution where instinctive adaptation has reached its minimum. But he emerges with new qualities which differentiate him from the animal: his awareness of himself as a separate entity, his ability to remember the past, to visualize the future, and to denote objects and acts by symbols; his reason to conceive and understand the world; and his imagination through which he reaches far beyond the range of his senses.[1]

Considered purely as an animal, the human is one of the weakest and most vulnerable. Yet this very biological weakness, Fromm believes, turns out to be the basis for humans' strength and the prime cause for the development of their specifically human qualities:

> Self-awareness, reason, and imagination have disrupted the 'harmony' which characterizes animal existence. Their emergence has made man into an anomaly, into the freak of the universe. He is part of nature, subject to her physical laws and unable to change them, yet he transcends the rest of nature.[2]

The human transcendence of nature which Fromm speaks of is therefore presented as something of a predicament: through the gift of reason the human is, without having chosen to be, a being condemned to make choices. There are echoes here of Kant, who saw the human as not merely a being of adaptation and survival, but a being of choice and purpose – free, rational and moral. To emphasize these characteristics is not so much arrogance as an appropriate response for this kind of being: for reason is a faculty, and a *problem*, bestowed on humans by nature. If humanistic ethics takes knowledge of humans to be the basis of establishing norms and values, with moral progress occurring through improved knowledge of human nature, and knowledge of human nature to be in important respects different from knowledge of the rest of nature, then this is to start not from a prejudice but from what appears to be a genuine dilemma.

Part of the existential predicament of beings of choice, Fromm emphasizes, is that they can choose badly. In our recent history, he believes, this is what has happened. Humankind appears to have given up the vision of living in harmony with nature and sought instead to conquer it; yet in attempting to transform it to human purposes, the conquest has become more and more equivalent to destruction.[3] Humanism therefore requires, above all, that humans go to work on themselves rather than on external nature. Human self-improvement would then appear potentially to be in the interests of both humans and the rest of nature. If humans are to lead better lives, it also appears to follow that their choices should be guided by a conception of human good which recognizes how that good is bound up with the good of nature.

Nevertheless, there is still the risk of seeing the good of nature to lie merely in serving the good of humans. For the consistent pursuit of human good can involve a conception of virtue which makes no necessary reference to the good of other beings. Humanists, generally, aim at the full development of human faculties and capacities, with the idea of virtue coinciding with the idea of humans' duties towards themselves. An evident problem with this is that it appears to make self-centredness the norm of human conduct, when the aim of ethics should arguably be to overcome it. This would seem to bear out ecological worries and constitute a powerful objection to humanism. To this objection, though, humanists have an answer – and the reply they can make in an ecological context, I shall shortly show, parallels the following point that Fromm develops within the human context.

When considering relations between humans, self-centredness can clearly be a problem. But when we then spell out what the problem is, it is appropriate to draw a distinction, as Fromm does, between self-love on the one hand and selfishness on the other. He argues that selfishness and self-love, far from being identical, are actually opposites: selfish people love themselves not too much but too little. He asks:

> is the selfishness of modern man really a *concern for himself* as an individual, with all his intellectual, emotional, and sensual potentialities? Has

'he' not become an appendage of his socioeconomic role? *Is his self-ishness identical with self-love or is it not caused by the very lack of it?*[4]

Fromm's reply, for which he claims psychoanalytic support, is that if people are incapable of loving others, it is because they are not capable of loving themselves either:[5] respect for one's own integrity, as well as love for and understanding of one's own self, cannot be separated from respect for and love and understanding of another individual. The confusion of self-love and selfishness, he claims, has also dogged the idea of self-interest. From a humanistic standpoint, human beings' true self-interest is the full development of their capacities and faculties. However, they can be deceived about what these really are, and Fromm believes this is particularly the case when people have a paramount concern with acquiring money and success. Although Fromm speaks of self-deception here, he recognizes this kind of deception has socio-cultural origins. 'Man, living in a market economy, feels himself to be a commodity. He is divorced from himself, as the seller of a commodity is divorced from what he wants to sell.'[6] In drawing attention to the idea of the commodification of human nature, Fromm is recapitulating a theme which is well established in the tradition of critical theory. As James O'Connor observes, human nature is instrumentalized in modern societies because the attempt to dominate nature requires 'a recasting of humans' instinctual organization in ways that allow the individual to be capable of exercising the kind of renunciations necessary for the transformation of external nature in systematic ways'.[7] This sets humanistic ethics in the broader context of social desiderata: for the overcoming of alienation and of the bifurcation of personality characteristic of modern societies cannot be achieved by individuals alone. Furthermore, the need for social change is also inseparable, on this view, from ecological considerations: 'just as the exploitative relationships which human beings have established against external nature have done great damage to other forms of species life, so have the alienated, exploitative relationships which humans have established against other humans done great physical, biological, and psychological damage to humans themselves.'[8]

To put the argument quite simply, then: just as love for others is not possible without love for self, so overcoming the commodification of nature is not possible without overcoming the commodification of *human* nature. According to this line of thought, environmental ethics would be seen as a part of the project of enlightening self-interest.

Environmental ethics

The positive ethical value of enlightened self-interest finds an analogy in environmental ethics. If in humanistic ethics the enlightened self-interest of an individual can be distinguished from mere egoism, in environmental ethics the enlightened self-interest of humans may be distinguished from 'speciesism' or 'human chauvinism'.[9] These latter terms describe the attitude of those who believe that only humans are bearers of intrinsic value, that only humans are worthy of moral consideration, and that the rest of nature is of merely instrumental value, as means, in the service of human ends. Environmental ethics in general is premised on the conviction that there is something wrong with such attitudes. There is a good deal of debate, however, as to how and to what extent they can be overcome. There are theorists, whose arguments will be considered in section 2.2, who hold that they are symptomatic of anthropocentrism – human-centredness – and this is something which has to be definitively purged from ethics. However, other theorists believe this aim to be problematic because, being humans, there are ways in which we cannot help being human-centred, and it is arguable that when anthropocentrism is entirely purged, so is anything recognizable as ethics. Hence, in the first instance, it may be more helpful to focus on what is *wrong* with anthropocentrism, to seek to identify those aspects of human-centredness which are most evidently remediable and in need of remedy.

What is wrong with anthropocentrism can be stated by drawing a parallel with egocentrism.[10] Just as egocentrism may be objected to because it allows a disregard for and possible detriment to others, so, similarly, anthropocentrism can be objected to because it licenses a cavalier treatment of other natural beings. In both egocentrism and anthropocentrism, then, there is the practical defect that one individual or species acts in ways which cause harm to other individuals or species. But there is also a cognitive defect: in seeing oneself or one's species as totally divorced from other people or species, one actually misconceives one's relation to the world and to others, failing to recognize how the self, or species, is constituted by others and by nature. Furthermore, just as egocentrism may also have a stunting effect on the self through failing to see how the self is actually constituted and fulfilled in association with others, so anthropocentrism can have a stunting effect on humanity in as much as it denies or loses sight of how humanity is a part of, constituted by, nature. Thus because the cognitive defect and the practical defect can be mutually reinforcing, there is as a consequence the rebound defect that in acting in ignorance one also does harm to oneself.

Now, particularly in view of the last point, a promising way out of this vicious circle would seem to be offered by enlightened self-interest, for by definition this includes a motivation to know one's own good and effectively pursue it: and if knowing this good means knowing how it depends on the good of others, then it also means pursuing their good. Certainly our knowledge is not exhaustive, but every gain in ecological understanding tends to strengthen the view of a necessary interdependence of all beings. So where doubt remains, the stronger and more prudent supposition is that even the apparently least significant microorganism may have some important role in our life-support system; and until or unless proven otherwise, enlightened self-interest cautions us to assume that it does. Enlightened self-interest, then, could be said to counsel a general principle of respect for nature.

This is the sort of view which can be identified in the positions of those environmental ethicists who may be described as moderately anthropocentric.[11] There is a spectrum of positions here, but they fall within the range of having neither a purely instrumental attitude to non-human nature nor an unqualified commitment to its intrinsic value. Thus, on the one hand, moderate anthropocentrists differ from 'strong' anthropocentrists, that is those who would deny that ethics should take account of non-human interests at all, and would therefore consider a purely exploitative attitude to nature morally acceptable. Moderate anthropocentrists significantly qualify this view. They do recognize that humans are the distinctive addressees of ethical imperatives; and since only humans (as far as we can know) confer values, only humans can be considered moral agents.[12] However they also see a necessity to extend the sphere of reference of moral consideration, so that whilst non-human beings may not be considered moral *agents*, they nevertheless can and should be recipients of moral concern – moral *patients*, as they are sometimes called.[13] A purely instrumental approach to nature is therefore not appropriate. On the other hand, however, they remain anthropocentric because of the kinds of reason they are prepared to recognize as grounds for moral concern about other natural beings. These may not be crudely instrumental reasons, but they do make reference to human interests:

We preserve wilderness and the maximally diverse ecosystem for reasons scientific and aesthetic. Natural museums serve as laboratories. Useless species may later be found useful. Diversity ensures stability, especially if

we err and our monocultures trigger environmental upset. Wild Beauty
adds a spiritual quality to life.[14]

The underlying assumption is that if humans become sufficiently enlightened about their own best interests, then they will also pursue the best
interests of non-humans: 'An enlightened anthropocentrism acknowledges that, in the long run, the world's good always coincides with
man's own most meaningful good.'[15]

What moderate anthropocentrists have a problem with is the idea that
we can talk of non-human beings having their own, independent, intrinsic value. This is not so much to *deny* them intrinsic value, though, as
to point up the paradoxicality of attempting to ascribe it. One aspect of
the paradoxicality, as indicated by Norton, is that enlightened self-
interest may also be operative in certain worldviews that others might
consider as attributing intrinsic value to non-human nature: 'The Hindus
and Jains, in proscribing the killing of insects, etc., show concern for
their own spiritual development rather than for the actual lives of those
insects.'[16] This is not necessarily to challenge the sincerity of others'
beliefs in the intrinsic value of non-human nature. Rather, it is to emphasize that we are talking, precisely, about beliefs; and these beliefs are not
amenable to any test which could confirm or deny their veracity.[17] Thus
moderate anthropocentrists argue that beings other than humans may be
of value in and for themselves, but if they are, this value is not the
possible object of human knowledge. The kinds of things which can be
of intrinsic value, as Attfield points out, 'are not objects, people or other
creatures, but experiences, activities and the development of capacities',
so that talk about the intrinsic value of living creatures 'should be taken
as talk about the intrinsic value of their well-being or flourishing'.[18]
What anthropocentrists question is whether moral agents will generally
have sufficient access to the experiences of non-human beings to pro-
nounce on their value. Talk about development of capacities presupposes
some notion of purpose or ends at which development aims: but whereas
in the human case we can know our ends because we formulate or discover them ourselves, in non-human cases we can have no such
subjective, or intersubjective, knowledge. The only ends we can attribute
to non-human beings are those apprehended from without, hence objectively: but the crucial point is that without intersubjective knowledge of
these ends we can have no assurance of the reliability of such attribution.
So if moderate anthropocentrists hold that we must remain agnostic on
this question, this does not mean actually *denying* intrinsic value to non-
humans: the claim is that we can actually neither affirm nor deny it.

Sometimes a further claim is made: namely, that there is no *need* to attribute intrinsic value to non-humans in order to achieve the ends that such attribution is intended to serve. It is argued that enlightened self-interest can lead to behaving *as if* non-human nature had intrinsic value – or, more accurately, it can lead to granting as much consideration to non-human nature as non-anthropocentrists can consistently claim. Norton, for instance, argues it allows the development of arguments against current, largely consumptive attitudes towards nature because they do not fit into a rationally defensible worldview; it can also emphasize the value of nature in *forming* rather than simply in satisfying human preferences.[19] This approach has evident strategic and political value. For one thing, it has the advantage over more ambitious attempts to talk about intrinsic value in nature that there is a discernible motivational path to actualizing it which does not require a leap of ecological faith. Real progress in the protection of the natural world will be more likely if it is perceived by humans to be in their own interest. Moreover, there are principled as well as pragmatic considerations: given that it is humans who are responsible for abuses of nature, it is appropriate not to deny the specificity of humanity in this respect.

However, critics of this general approach believe it places overly restrictive limits on the moral considerability of non-human beings. The whole line of reasoning which would base environmental ethics on the principle of enlightened self-interest is at least viewed with suspicion, and often rejected outright, by those who take a more radical, anti-anthropocentric, approach to environmental ethics. An evident ground for suspicion is that whilst enlightened self-interest may lead a human to identify harm to other beings and its causes, it may not provide a motivation to do anything about them unless they also harm the self; and this does not necessarily offer very secure guarantees for the welfare of other species. In practice the connection between the pursuit of particular human goods and the welfare of the rest of nature may be too loose and contingent to offer adequate protection of the latter.

Such considerations lead to a crucial divergence between what are sometimes called 'shallow' and 'deep' positions on the question of whether a concern for non-human nature will be better promoted by further *enlightenment* of human self-interest or by a more radical purging of anthropocentrism. On the question of the intrinsic value of nature, moderate anthropocentrists adopt shallow positions which can be characterized as benign agnosticism. They are not committed to a recognition of the intrinsic value of non-human beings, but nor do they seek actively to *deny* intrinsic value to the rest of nature. Because they simply remain sceptical as to the possibility of attributing it, they can argue that there is no necessary connection between anthropocentrism and an actual *devaluation* of the rest of nature. Moderately anthropocentric environmentalism would issue in a gradualist, or reformist, strategy whose aim is to heighten awareness that it serves no one's interest to (over-)exploit natural resources or treat other beings cruelly or inhumanely. However, what leaves critics of anthropocentrism unsatisfied is the way this all ultimately depends on the interests or preferences of humans. The deeper or more radical theorists would argue that its shallowness lies in the idea that what is truly human is sufficient to grasp the value and integrity of non-human nature. Anthropocentrism, even in its moderate forms, can be criticized both on the strategic grounds that it offers insecure guarantees given that self-interest for the most part is not yet, and may never be, sufficiently enlightened, and on the principled grounds that non-human nature has intrinsic value which anthropocentric ethics do not recognize.

2.2   Ecological Anti-Humanism

Humanism can be found objectionable from an ecological point of view because it focuses on what sets humans *apart* from the rest of nature, and, in doing so, typically takes the specifically human to be the prime, and perhaps only, locus of intrinsic value in the world. In this section, alternative, ecologically grounded, moral views are to be examined. Two basic kinds of alternative will be considered. One seeks to extend intrinsic value to non-humans, but in such a way that it is not appropriately referred to as an anti-humanism; indeed, for reasons we will shortly see, it might better be described as humane moralism or an expanded humanism. However, exactly for those reasons, this approach is not radical enough for proponents of the second form of ecologically grounded ethics, whose best known adherents are deep ecologists.

Before considering these two kinds of ethics, however, it is worth briefly clarifying what exactly we are going to look for in them. It has already been argued that anthropocentrism in general need not, and moderate anthropocentrism in particular does not, entail a *denial* of intrinsic value to non-human beings: what it does is point to the difficulties in ascribing value to them. There is, then, a significant difference, which any critic of anthropocentrism has to be aware of, between denying our ability accurately to attribute intrinsic value to non-humans, and denying the existence of such value. Moderate anthropocentrists would tend to play safe when the question of comparing the values of different beings arises, believing our possible knowledge of these values to be quite strictly circumscribed, and therefore being sceptical of how reliable any claimed ethical judgement might be. Anthropocentric reasoning *vis-à-vis* talk of intrinsic value in non-human nature is thus only superficially objected to as callous; it is more accurately reckoned with as a specific form of scepticism. Criticism of anthropocentric ethics, therefore, as well as the proposal of an alternative, means meeting this sceptical challenge.

The main sceptical challenge, then, concerns the *possibility* of ascribing intrinsic value to non-humans. However, moderate anthropocentrists, particularly when talking about strategy, also voice scepticism about even the *necessity* of doing so. Before looking at attempts to meet the former, more difficult, challenge, I shall briefly indicate the reasons which can be given to show that there is a need to try.

Moderate anthropocentrists, as we have seen, are essentially agnostic about values in nature, but reasons can be given why this agnosticism will not do. A major assumption made by moderate anthropocentrists is that if humans get clear enough about their own best interests, then they will realize that these coincide with the interests of the rest of nature. This amounts to an assumption of an underlying rational harmony between the interests of human and non-human beings. In making this assumption, moderate anthropocentrists are able to avoid stating any grounds for discriminating in favour of humans against nature and so give the appearance of ecological benignity. But they avoid siding with humans against the rest of nature only by assuming that there need ultimately be no conflict between them. Now, for one thing, I am not sure whether we can know if this assumption is true, since to know this, the requisite enlightenment would have to have occurred. Meanwhile, what we do know is that in the present, unenlightened, state of things there are serious conflicts between human interests, as they are currently perceived and pursued, and the interests of other natural beings. On the one hand, then, we cannot be certain whether further enlightening human self-interest will in fact promote the good of the rest of the planet; and, on the other, we can be certain that at present we are seriously harming life on the planet; it therefore seems we have good reason for remaining agnostic about the assumption of an ultimate harmony of interest and in the mean time addressing the problems which we do know about now.

Given, then, that there might be good reasons for *wanting* to attribute intrinsic value to non-humans, we turn now to the question of whether, and if so how, it is *possible* to do so.

Intrinsic value theory

The first type of approach to this question starts from the position that humans are loci of intrinsic value and seeks to extend recognition of intrinsic value to other beings. Particularly interesting exemplars tend to be biocentric, or life-centred. As Paul Taylor, an advocate of this type of theory, explains:

> From the perspective of a life-centred theory, we have prima facie moral obligations that are owed to wild plants and animals themselves as members of the Earth's biotic community. We are morally bound (other things being equal) to protect or promote their good for *their* sake.[20]

Adopting this moral stance involves two main ideas: that each living thing has a good (well-being, welfare) of its own, so that one can say quite simply, without reference to any other entity, that it can be benefited or harmed; and that it is necessary to regard these living beings as possessing value such that moral agents can think of themselves as having binding obligations towards them.

Now as regards the idea that each living thing has a good of its own in as much as it can be benefited or harmed, I see no good reason to withhold assent. Certainly, philosophical objections can and have been levelled against the idea that criteria of harm, welfare etc. can get an adequate purchase in the case of non-human beings: for example, because it is claimed that a being must have conscious feelings, desires or purposes in order to have a good of its own.[21] However, it seems to me that there are no more compelling reasons for accepting such particular definitions of 'having a good of one's own', than for granting the basic moral intuition of the biocentric outlook concerning living beings, even if they are non-sentient. As Attfield, taking trees as an example, puts it: 'not only can trees grow, blossom and decay: they can thrive and wither, be endangered by fire and be protected from commercial pillage. Now what can thrive, reach maturity, be endangered and be protected itself, I contend, has a good.'[22] For Attfield, as for Taylor, the good of an individual non-human organism consists in the full development of its biological powers.

However, once it is granted that non-human living beings may *have* their own good, the sceptic remains to be satisfied on two points. One sceptical challenge is to specify *what* that good consists in, since it is arguable that in a significant number, if not a majority, of cases, we will not necessarily know exactly what that good consists in. The other challenge is to explain why it may also be a good 'for us', by which I mean something that can provide the basis for an obligation on the part of moral agents. Now biocentrists do not generally appear to think that the first challenge presents much of a problem – or, at least, that too much of a problem can be made by speciesists who wish to resist giving any moral consideration to non-humans when some basic criteria of harm and advantage can quite straightforwardly be applied.[23] I shall have occasion to return to this after considering what they say regarding the second point, to which they devote more attention, as to how the good of a non-human can be the ground of an obligation for moral agents.

The answer turns on its good having *intrinsic value*. It is worth distinguishing between approaches which are qualified and unqualified in their commitment to the intrinsic value of the good of non-rational beings. A representative of the qualified view is Robin Attfield. For Attfield, whatever has a good of its own has moral standing – that is, merits moral consideration. His position is that if we grant consideration to humans then we cannot consistently deny it to other living beings, and the onus is on a would-be opponent of this view to name some morally relevant difference between humans and other living beings which would justify considering humans as moral patients and non-humans not. He believes this will prove hard to do. However I call Attfield's a qualified view for the outcome of consideration may be rather meagre: he writes that 'there might well be a preponderant need most of the time to treat plants, and, perhaps, some other creatures, as resources, valuable though their lives are in themselves'.[24] For Attfield, the moral standing of a being is established separately and prior to any judgements as to its moral *significance*. All beings which have standing have intrinsic value, but some of them will have very little of it – indeed, too little to be a determinant of any obligation of a moral agent. It therefore appears that a qualified approach may not necessarily lay the ground for claiming anything more than a frankly anthropocentric one.[25]

An unqualified approach, by contrast, is more determinedly antianthropocentric: on such an approach, all beings are supposed to be of *equal* worth. This can be illustrated by reference to Paul Taylor's idea of 'inherent worth' which ties considerability more tightly to strong value commitments: for Taylor, to say that a being possesses inherent worth is to say *both* that its good is deserving of the consideration of all moral agents, *and* 'that the realisation of its good has intrinsic value, to be pursued as an end in itself and for the sake of the entity whose good it is'.[26] In this way, granting standing is not a prelude to deliberating about moral significance, it is already to take up a specific moral attitude which has definite normative implications: 'Living things are now viewed as *the appropriate objects of the attitude of respect*';[27] and respect is not a formal preliminary but is itself a moral commitment. Yet if this commitment applies equally to all living beings it raises awkward questions about how it can lead to any determinate judgements about values;[28] there may also be a further problem of arbitrariness and indeterminacy regarding the kinds of beings to consider.[29] A major question, therefore, is why the attitude should be assumed in the first place. Taylor accepts that this does not automatically follow from granting that non-human beings can have their own good. Rather, he says, it depends on a *belief system* – the biocentric outlook. For Taylor, biocentrism means, in particular, seeing individual organisms as teleological centres of life. Along with the beliefs, according to Taylor, comes an ability: '*Conceiving of it as a centre of life, one is able to look at the world from its perspective.*'[30] In looking at the world from that perspective, Taylor says, we recognize objects and events occurring in its life as being beneficent, maleficent, or indifferent. We can take their point of view just because we can recognize what does them harm and what benefits them. But can we? Some strong knowledge claims are implicit here.

We are brought directly back to the other element of scepticism mentioned above – namely, the question concerning the limits of our possible knowledge regarding the good of beings radically different from ourselves.

An unqualified commitment to the intrinsic value of non-humans, and the attendant claim to have radically purged anthropocentrism from ethics, can be met with sceptical considerations. Two in particular are worth mentioning as they both alert us to a risk of causing unwitting harm in the very attempt to combat it. The first problem arises from limits of possible knowledge: Taylor's factual judgement that individual organisms are teleological centres of life need not be controversial even for an anthropocentrist;[31] anthropocentrists are sceptical, however, about the idea that humans can see the world from the point of view of other species. There is an evident risk that anthropocentrism is merely supplanted by a practice of anthropomorphizing – that is, projecting human characteristics, needs and interests on to other beings which may in fact be radically different from anything humans can imagine. If one's knowledge of other entities' needs and interests is less secure than one imagines, then one may believe one is pursuing an entity's good when one is in fact doing it harm. I think it is quite possible this will be the case more often than people like Taylor seem to assume. The other problem is that it is not usually possible to maximize an aggregate of goods without passing an optimum point beyond which some entities' goods are pursued at the expense of others', which means it will be necessary to prioritize the good of some over the good of others. This, of course, is part of the very stuff of ethics, and is where the worth of an ethical theory is really tested. Although Taylor is more ambitious and arguably more consistent in his biocentrism than Attfield, he does less well on this test. Taylor's view is that all living things possess the *same* inherent worth.[32] Yet either we are to make distinctions or we are not. In making them, we have noted, Attfield grasps the nettle: in squaring up to the fact that as soon as we prioritize one good we thereby sanction an attendant harm, he allows determinate criteria which leave him open to charges from purer biocentrists of conceding too much to anthropocentrism. Taylor's more determined attempt to preserve biocentrism from any anthropocentric contamination, however, raises a number of serious questions. One is this: when expanding the sphere of moral consideration, why stop at living beings? Biocentrists do not want to draw the boundary of moral considerability at sentience, but they do draw it at living beings. Yet, as Thompson asks, 'why should we regard rocks, rivers, volcanoes, molecules as being of less value simply because they happen to lack the properties associated with life?'[33] If Taylor's use of analogy from humans to non-rational and non-sentient living beings works, Thompson suggests, there is nothing to stop it being more vigorously extended: for example, once we appreciate how crystals form we can see they have enough relevant similarities to living beings to fulfil Taylor's criteria for 'having a good of their own'. The same can be said, she suggests, of any natural entity, whether a rock, a molecule, an atom, or a solar system. Moreover, once this line of argument is embarked on, even machines can plausibly be held to have a good of their own. This points towards the conclusion that the argument Taylor uses to overthrow human chauvinism has such loose criteria as to undermine the very possibility of an ethic. Seen in this way, it appears that biocentrism is only preserved at the price of ethical vacuity. But even if this conclusion could be resisted, Thompson also points out, there is in any case the problem of how to determine what *counts* as a living being.

It is perhaps natural to think that particular plants and animals are the individuals that we need to be concerned with. But why shouldn't we count the parts of an animal or plant as individuals, their cells, organs, or molecules? Why not the complex consisting of an animal or a plant and its various parasites and bacteria? Why not the plant and the soil that nourishes it? Why not an interrelated system of animals and plants?[34]

Thompson claims there are no clear criteria for picking out the relevant individuals.[35]

To sum up the problems, then. The challenge for intrinsic value theories was to meet anthropocentric scepticism regarding the possibility and necessity of locating intrinsic value outside the specifically human, or rational, sphere. Its particular motivation was to counter the perceived arbitrariness of anthropocentric criteria of value and the insecurity of its guarantees for the welfare or flourishing of non-human beings. It now transpires that, on the one hand, guarantees are not necessarily more secure: biocentric approaches to environmental ethics, like Attfield's, which ultimately depend on humanist ethics, may well in practice be able to grant no more than moderate anthropocentrism can. On the other hand, as we have seen in the case of Taylor, biocentrism appears to be able to avoid anthropocentrism only at the price of arbitrariness.

Interestingly, though, when it comes to revealing the arbitrariness of biocentrism, anthropocentric sceptics find themselves in the company of deep ecologists. Both, essentially, pose the critical question, 'Why stop here?' For deep ecologists, though, the question is posed not as a prelude to a *reductio ad absurdum*, in the manner of Thompson, but as an invitation to go further. Biocentrism, as the name itself implies, takes the moral universe not to be centred on or exhausted by members of the human species. Intrinsic value is to be found in all living beings. Deep ecology, however, believes this is not to go far enough: it refuses to limit intrinsic value to living beings, and argues for intrinsic value of rivers, rocks and ecosystems and so on.

From this point on, therefore, if one is not convinced by biocentric arguments, one has a choice between granting that the extending of human values to non-humans does not necessarily mark an advance on avowedly moderate anthropocentric positions, or attempting a more radical approach to intrinsic value which breaks the continuity with humanist thought altogether.

More radical approaches

A more radical approach must begin by rejecting what Richard Sylvan has referred to as the 'greater value assumption': the assumption that even if humans are not the *sole* item of moral value, the irreducible value of non-humans never normally exceeds that of humans, and can be less.[36] Rejecting this assumption allows 'that natural things other than humans have value in themselves, value sometimes perhaps exceeding that of or had by humans'.[37] This tends to support the principle of 'biospheric egalitarianism' – that is, a 'belief in the equal right of all life to live and blossom' – which the founder of deep ecology, Arne Naess, considers to be 'an intuitively clear and obvious value axiom'.[38]

However, more recent developments of deep ecology have had to take account of certain fairly evident problems with biospheric egalitarianism: for instance, it is not wholly clear in what sense it would be meaningful to say of prey and predator that they have an equal right to flourish; and if one does attempt to use it to support determinate judgements, these can be strongly counterintuitive, as Attfield points out: 'if the death of a human would result in a greater number of flourishing lives (e.g. maggots) than the number of lives which the same human being sustains when alive (e.g. intestinal flora), then it would be better for the human being to die.'[39] Now Naess cautions that the term 'equality' should not be understood in a sense which implies quantitative comparisons: 'Equal right to unfold potentials as a principle is not a practical norm about equal conduct towards all life forms. It suggests a guideline limiting killing, and more generally limiting obstruction of the unfolding of potentialities in others.'[40] But if this saves the principle from literal-minded absurdity, it leaves it open to the objection that it fails to generate the criteria needed to serve as a guideline.

In response to such objections, some deep ecologists have chosen not to offer a defence but rather to become increasingly explicit that they are not primarily concerned with making ethical claims at all: they choose to emphasize instead a concern with questions of metaphysics and ontology. Thus Warwick Fox, for instance, has sought to demonstrate that the main emphasis of deep ecology is neither ethical nor axiological, but metaphysical.[41]

Nevertheless, given that the question we are here concerned with is whether there is a well-founded alternative to humanism in ethics, what needs to be asked is whether a 'deep' ontology can provide it. One might expect this could be the case since, most fundamentally, the objection to anthropocentrism is that it is based on a view of the relation of humans to nature which is fundamentally flawed, or shallow.

The underlying problem here may perhaps be cast in a helpful light by a significant line of criticism opened up by Kenneth Goodpaster when he writes:

the mere enlargement of the class of morally considerable beings is an inadequate substitute for a genuine environmental ethic. Once the class of morally considerable beings is enlarged, no hint of a method for assessing or commensurating the newly recognized claims is provided.[42]

In emphasizing this indeterminacy in the idea of extending moral consideration to other beings, part of the problem to which Goodpaster draws attention is the inadequacy of attempting to extend essentially *individualistic* ethics. A *genuine* environmental ethic would therefore require working out radically alternative accounts of bearers of moral value. Once this is granted, then it appears that a wholly different approach needs to be adopted – a more decisive alternative to the method of proceeding by analogy. Goodpaster, like Callicott and Rolston whom we looked at in the previous chapter, believes a paradigm example of a genuinely environmental or ecological ethic to be Leopold's land ethic. The principal precept of this, it will be recalled, is:

A thing is right when it tends to preserve the integrity, stability, and beauty of the biotic community. It is wrong when it tends otherwise.[43]

What, for Callicott, is especially noteworthy about this formulation 'is the idea that the good of the biotic *community* is the ultimate measure of the rightness or wrongness of actions'.[44] For him this means that the land ethic is holistic, its implicit ontological basis being the idea of a field ontology, which, as we saw in the previous chapter, is an ontology not of (discrete) objects but of (interconnected) events: this applies to individual organisms which are conceived as configurations in an energy flux, and so also to human organisms. Thus from the idea of a field ontology emerges the idea of a 'relational self'. This idea has been illustrated by Paul Shepard:

In one aspect the self is an arrangement of organs, feelings, and thoughts – a 'me' surrounded by a hard body boundary: skin, clothes, and insular habits . . . The alternative [aspect] is a self as a center of organization, constantly drawing on and influencing the surroundings . . . The epidermis of the skin is ecologically like a pond surface or a forest soil, not a shell so much as a delicate interpenetration. It reveals the self ennobled and extended . . . as part of the landscape and the ecosystem.[45]

Callicott similarly suggests it is impossible to find a clear demarcation between oneself and one's environment: gases and fluids flow continuously in and out; organisms are continually, if selectively, transubstantiated into and through oneself.[46] Rolston, too, takes this view, and has summed it up in the striking observation that the human vascular system includes arteries, veins, rivers, oceans, and air currents: in short, 'The world is my body.'

Rolston, like Callicott, believes the idea of a relational self is central to a non-anthropocentric ethic – involving a shift of ethical perspective centred in the dissolution of any firm boundary between humans and the world. If, traditionally, the intrinsic value of oneself is taken as a given, with the principal problem then being that of accounting for the value of 'others', be they human or non-human, this problem is now out-flanked:

> If the world is one's body and one's consciousness not only images in its specific content the world around, but the very structure of one's psyche and rational faculties are formed through adaptive interaction with the ecological organization of nature, then one's self, both physically and psychologically, gradually merges from its central core outwardly to the environment. One cannot, thus, draw hard and fast boundaries between oneself, either physically or spiritually, and the environment.[47]

For Rolston, this expansion of the self to coincide with the entire eco-system is presented as an advance on an anthropocentric perspective, and he claims this shift of perspectives ultimately invalidates the effort to understand ecological ethics as disguised human self-interest.

Nevertheless, the bottom line is that I have a duty and interest to protect and preserve nature because I am one with it. Hence nearer the mark may be Callicott's conclusion:

> Ecology, thus, gives a new meaning as well as new substance to the phrase 'enlightened self-interest'.[48]

With these words, though, we have just about come full circle. The search for an alternative to the anthropocentric principle of enlightened self-interest appears to lead right back to that very principle. The argument which would outflank anthropocentric sceptics appears to undermine itself.

Radical ecologists would wish to resist this conclusion. Rolston himself claims that a relational self involves something nobler, broader and more far-sighted than enlightened self-interest. This is an idea which has been further promoted in terms of 'the ecological self'.[49] Something similar has also been argued by Warwick Fox, for whom 'transpersonal ecology' aims at a cultivation of a 'wider sense of self', one which 'extends *beyond* one's egoistic, biographical, or personal sense of self to include all beings'. As Eckersley explains:

> The movement from an atomistic *ego*centric sense of self toward an expansive, *eco*centric or transpersonal sense of self is seen as representing a process of psychological maturing. In other words, transpersonal ecology is concerned to expand the circle of human compassion and respect for others beyond one's particular family and friends and beyond the human community to include the entire ecological community.[50]

Put this way, though, the claim for transpersonal ecology scarcely lives up to its billing as part 'of the vanguard of the cultivation of a new worldview, a new culture and character'.[51] The most ecological thing about this may turn out to be that old established ideas – for example Stoic, Christian and quotidian – are being reused or recycled with green labels! But this does not move us beyond the starting point of any moral inquiry into questions as to which particular obligations one has to whom and why.

The social dimension

Overcoming the arbitrary favouring of humans over other sorts of beings requires a non-arbitrary conception of the human relation to them. This relation may be as intimate as radical ecologists argue, but it is still a relation rather than an immediate identity. So while there is undeniably an ontological continuity between self and environment, just as there is between human beings, there are also discontinuities which have to be properly accounted for. Real continuities are in fact constituted as ensembles of mediations, and among these are mediations at a social level. Hence if holism is to have a connection with values at all it needs to recognize human, and social, specificity.

So if Goodpaster has identified a real problem, I am not convinced that the solutions just considered are very promising. Accordingly, I would like to develop his criticism in a rather different way. Stressing the need for a transindividual standpoint, he writes:

> The oft-repeated plea by some ecologists and environmentalists that our thinking needs to be less atomistic and more 'holistic' translates in the present context into a plea for a more embracing object of moral consideration. In a sense, it represents a plea to return to the richer Greek conception of a man by nature social and not intelligibly removable from his social and political context – though it goes beyond the Greek con-

ception in emphasizing that societies too need to be understood in a context, an ecological context, and that it is this larger whole which is the
'bearer of value'.[52]

Having got to this point, however, Goodpaster quite frankly admits to
being unsure how to proceed further. This should perhaps not be surprising. It is not that a return to ancient Greece is simply not an available
option, but that the immediacy of ethical life which it apparently symbol-
izes for him is anyway not recoverable without relinquishing the
principle of subjective freedom – something which is arguably neither
possible nor desirable. At any rate, there is little reason to suppose that
the differentiation and fragmentation of contemporary social life will be
overcome by wishful pleas for holistic thinking alone.

In this context, it is well worth emphasizing that Leopold's own conception of an expanding ethical realm explicitly depends on historical
processes of ever more general emancipation (for example, of slaves,
women and other categories of human moving from being considered
property to being considered persons). Such processes of emancipation
themselves have precisely arisen through the break-up of traditional
social bonds of the ancient Greek type.

So if Goodpaster is certainly right that social life needs to be understood in its ecological context, what should be emphasized is that it
precisely needs to be *understood*. Goodpaster himself appears to think in
terms of a leap from the atomistic standpoint of the rights or intrinsic
value of individual beings to the moral value of all-embracing ecosystems: he alludes to the social dimension only to jump straight to the
ecological dimension. Yet a pause here would be of some avail. Humans
are of course part of nature as individual organisms, and they can be
considered at all ontological levels of biology. But the holistic perspective itself would also bid us recognize the significance of the irreducibly
social dimension of the interface of humans and nature. In the first
instance, I would therefore suggest, societies *as they are* must somehow
be seen as bearers of value – and to the extent that they embody dis-
values they need to be revalued. Part of this revaluation may follow
ecological criteria – but these alone will not suffice.

2.3   The Meaning of Ecological Humanism

Human specificity remains to be reckoned with. If transcendent humanism underestimates the fact that humans are natural beings, ecologism
neglects the implications of the fact that they are also social and cultural

beings. There are important features of human life, behaviour and society which, it seems, cannot be accounted for in the same terms used to describe the rest of nature. In particular, there is the question of human autonomy and, associated with this, the meaning of human emancipation in an ecological era.[53]

Ecological considerations raise new questions about the meaning of human emancipation. It is rendered particularly problematic if conceived, as traditionally it often has been, in terms of a move from a sphere of necessity to one of freedom. For the sphere of necessity is taken to comprehend both the order of nature-imposed necessity and the order of coercive and exploitative human relations; and while emancipation in the latter sphere would seem, prima facie, to remain a justified and necessary aim, what the ecological perspective casts doubt on is the possibility, and perhaps even the desirability, of emancipation from nature-imposed necessity.

However, to appreciate the force of these doubts, and their implications for any project of human emancipation, it is necessary to distinguish three different meanings of the idea 'emancipation from nature-imposed necessity'. For, I shall argue, they are not all equally objectionable from an ecological standpoint.

Firstly, if overcoming natural necessity means engaging in nature-transformative activities to meet human needs for food, shelter, good health and so on, the aim need not be ecologically objectionable so long as the transformation of natural ecosystems involved is sustainable: that is, it is not such as to undermine their capacity to reproduce themselves without an application of non-renewable external energy other than human labour.[54] In this way, then, it may be possible, through the application of human ingenuity to nature's enabling conditions, to push back the natural limits to human productivity. We may call this the aim of *subsistence*, recognizing that levels and qualities of subsistence may be socially and historically variable.

A second and altogether different aim, however, is that of *transcending* natural limits. Even if few people would be so foolhardy as to suppose humans can alter the laws of nature, many nevertheless think and act *as if* they believed those laws were not wholly binding: that is, they cherish the idea that *any* obstacle nature throws in the way of the expansion of human productive capabilities can and probably will be surmounted by technological ingenuity.[55] When this is taken as axiomatic, it amounts to a belief in the possibility of transcending natural limits. This may be called the *Promethean* aim.

In principle, then, we can distinguish between the aim of pushing back natural limits – which really means working more efficiently within them – and the aim of transcending natural limits: the former may be possible, the latter is not.[56] Yet a problem with specifically modern discourses of emancipation is that they do not always draw a clear distinction between what I am calling the subsistence aim and the Promethean aim. The meeting of subsistence needs is seen as just a part of a process of continuous *expansion* of human needs through which human fulfilment comes to be realized. This is true for supporters of capitalist enterprise; it is also true of capitalism's critics to the extent that they share Marx's view that 'man produces even when he is free from physical need and truly produces only in freedom from such need'.[57] This effectively premises human emancipation on an indefinite expansion of productive forces.

There is, though, a third conception of emancipation from nature-imposed necessity which is quite distinct from either the subsistence aim or the Promethean aim: this is the emancipation of human creativity, the realization of freedom in a humanistic sense, by developing human potentials in all spheres – affective, creative, aesthetic, spiritual, cognitive and so on. This is what I would call a distinctively *humanist* aim. Certainly, this humanist aim, like the Promethean aim, may be understood in terms of a transcendence of nature-given determinants. Yet 'transcendence' here has a different sense, seeing truly human potentialities not as pitted *against* nature, but as *autonomous* of the order of natural causality: this means the possibility that human flourishing need not depend on the ability to force nature to conform to human ends. Human emancipation can thus be seen not in terms of an extension of humans' power over external nature, but rather in terms of an attempt to develop human capacities of internal development and adaptation. It may therefore be argued that if human emancipation is conceived in terms of learning to live within natural limits, rather than seeking to overcome or continually push them back, this will mean the development of self-mastery, discipline, and a responsible exercise of freedom such that *distinctively humanist* ends are pursued in ways which do not depend on the Promethean aim. On this view, then, the humanist aim is anti-ecological not *per se*, but only to the extent that it is conceived in Promethean terms; the pursuit of human goods is not intrinsically hostile to the goods of the rest of nature, but only when human goods are conceived in an ecologically ignorant or hostile manner.

Nevertheless, it may be too easy to slip from humanism into Prometheanism: the very idea that humans are in some measure autonomous of the natural order leads very easily to the making of normative claims, if not directly for humans' superiority, at least for a right of self-determination, and from here to a right to determine the destiny of non-humans too.

The question, therefore, is how to comprehend the specificity of human autonomy, and value it, while keeping an ecological perspective on the human place in the world. In what follows I shall examine two contrasting answers to this question – one from Richard Lichtman and one from Ted Benton – which between them highlight the difficulty of how to acknowledge the specificity of human autonomy while also taking account of the naturalness of human beings.

Two approaches to human nature

Richard Lichtman has put forward the view that human nature cannot be fully described in terms borrowed from the study of the rest of nature. He argues that although non-human nature is ontologically prior to and independent of human existence, human nature as such is something *acquired* through acculturation. This is the case ontogenetically, since children only develop to maturity under the influence of culture: 'Human nature is self-constituting because we are born incomplete.'[58] It is also the case phylogenetically, for the human species was partly constituted *as* a species through cultural mediations:

> The final stages of biological development occurred simultaneously (for a million years) with the origins and initial stages of cultural history. Society is not a fortuitous addition to individual psychology, but a necessary constituent of its very possibility.[59]

Culture, then, is an intrinsic component of human nature as such; and it is not possible to specify *human* nature in purely biological terms even in principle, for the human biological organism itself did not reach its final evolutionary form before the introduction of culture. The self-transformations made possible for humans in society, therefore, cannot be treated as derivations of underlying biological or psychological determinants, of an innate human nature:

> were the veil of culture removed, we would confront neither a noble nor a brutal savage but a proto-being without definable shape or function, unformed matter to the active potentiality of social definition . . . whatever in our being is not permeated by culture, simple reflexes and primitive responses, is not distinctively human.[60]

Now Lichtman is aware that this might look like leaving human *nature* as something of a blank slate, but he pre-empts potential criticism on this score by pointing out that even a blank slate 'must have such properties as will permit the acceptance of the chalk, as the wax accepts the stylus, the inscribing tool'.[61] So what is at issue, he argues, is not *whether* there is a common human nature – for there is necessarily a structure of capacities, tendencies and sensibilities that humans bring, incompletely formed, to their life world – but rather what kinds of thing can be said about it. Lichtman asks what our common human nature must be like for specific manifestations of it to be possible; and he deduces two general characteristics. The first given of our human nature is the power to complete what is *not* given in our nature: this works through various natural and social interactions, including 'engagement in a transcendent normative structure to order what would be an otherwise formless and consequently impossible life'.[62] From this is deduced the second attribute of human nature: 'since humans never create or appropriate social existence in general but always some particular, concrete social existence, we must come to understand our species' capacities as abstract, meta-propensities to enact and transform the presented materials of which we make our life.'[63] These are our self-reflexive capacities: we not only conceptualize our experience, we also reflect on our conceptualization; we have self-consciousness and an awareness of others' self-consciousness and their awareness of our own. These second-order powers, though, do not determine the specific character of our first-order powers: that is, there is always a specific socio-cultural form to the *appearance* of human nature.

Lichtman cites anthropological evidence which indicates how the view of human nature prevalent in contemporary Western societies – as possessive, individualist, and egoistic – reflects only *one* way that human capacities and propensities may actually develop, and certainly not the best. His principal theoretical contention, though, is that one cannot draw general conclusions about human nature directly from a study of the many *particular* ways of being human. An important corollary of this is that there can be no list of fundamental – that is, first-order or empirically identifiable – human needs:

> All needs are socially mediated and therefore socially constituted, not in the sense that they have no origin in the disposition of individuals, but that what they are dispositions for can only be granted through culture ... In structuring needs society also prioritizes them, so that the basic principles determining human activity cannot be derived from 'needs' but only from

the structure of values that confer form and meaning on the needs themselves.[64]

This is a crucial point of Lichtman's argument, and one at issue in the controversy which ensues. For Lichtman it implies that the knowledge most necessary to emancipation 'grasps the openness of our future and our responsibility for its determination'.[65] Yet the critical import of this affirmation can be misread, partly owing to the hyperbole that Lichtman allows himself in stating his case against the view that our nature is formed innately – as, for example, when he states 'that we collectively elicit, form and educate the possibility of our human existence, creating in the process something that has never before existed',[66] or that we 'remain what we make ourselves, except as we are made against our own enlightened self-determination'.[67] In such passages the reader gets a sense that enlightenment values are pitted *against* nature, reproducing the Promethean ideology expressed with greatest hubris by the idea that 'Man produces himself.'

So while it is clearly not Lichtman's intention to perpetuate the modernist devaluation of nature, his emphasis on what is distinctive about humans in contrast to other beings leads him to underplay what humans and other beings have in common. Indeed, it may also be that it cuts him off from a fuller understanding of humans themselves.

So argues Ted Benton, who criticizes Lichtman for giving little or no elaboration of what our common human nature consists in, and leaving human nature too malleable: 'if there are no "given" or "innate" dispositions of a positive kind,' he argues, 'then there would seem to be no grounds for regarding one social or cultural framework for the formation of a specific *kind* of human nature as more appropriate to human well-being than any other.'[68] The only limit to cultural relativism Lichtman appears to admit, says Benton, is the order of external nature, for he appears to assume that human development can take place in an *indefinite* range of socio-natural contexts.[69] Lichtman's emphasis on culture, in Benton's view, gives short shrift to the biological component of human nature and perpetuates a dualistic perspective which goes against what we should be learning from ecology, that humans are a part of and not apart from nature.

So where Lichtman concentrates on what *distinguishes* humans from other natural beings, Benton wants to highlight their commonality. He notes, for example, how certain supposedly human-specific characteristics are also to be found in the animal world: in particular, the capacity for and disposition to social coordination of their activities. Moreover, he also notes, there are many significant differences *between* animal species. Recognizing such points should encourage us to look at humans as one species among many others, not as an ontologically distinct and privileged entity. It is characteristic of the dualistic tradition, Benton remarks, to accept that the human *is* an animal, but an animal with a special something extra (soul, will or reason, for example). Among the consequences of this is that some human needs are then seen as truly human and others as merely animal. Benton believes that the supposed differences between humans and other animals need to be seriously qualified – and here a naturalistic perspective commends itself:

> a naturalistic approach begins with the common predicament of natural beings and moves from that basis to render intelligible their specific differences in constitution, structure and modes of life.[70]

A naturalistic specification of human nature must start from a recognition of the natural beinghood which humans share with other living creatures; it would then proceed by differentiating out and elaborating what is specific to humans. If this differentiation is not to slide into the dualistic mode, though, it will not present the powers, potentials, or requirements of humans as something they possess over and above those they share with animals. Thus without denying that there are certain things which only humans do (e.g. composing symphonies or constructing weapons of mass destruction), nevertheless, Benton argues,

> those things which only humans can do are generally to be understood as rooted in the specifically human *ways* of doing things which other animals also do.[71]

Here we have the key idea which perhaps most clearly distinguishes Benton's approach from Lichtman's.

So what kinds of thing does this approach allow to be specified about human nature? Benton suggests that, as natural beings, there are three interconnected features which humans share with other natural beings: they have natural needs whose objects lie outside themselves, independent of them; they have natural powers which *enable* them to satisfy these needs; and need-satisfying activity in relation to external objects 'is essential to the "confirmation" or "manifestation" of the essential powers of the species'.[72] Once it is granted that any species has its own distinctive 'species-life', then it is possible – and possible for *any* living species (plants as well as animals), not only for humans – to distinguish between conditions necessary for mere organic survival and conditions for *flourishing*. An important implication of this is that a critique of alienating and exploitative social conditions could then be carried out on behalf of living species other than humans:

> Under regimes of private property, conditions which enable the survival of workers are provided but the conditions for them to confirm their powers and potentials in the living of their characteristic 'species-life' are denied to them . . . precisely the same framework of analysis can be applied in the critique of the mode of life imposed upon many of the other living species caught up in this distorted mode of human life.[73]

Benton thus claims to carry the aim of social emancipation across the species divide. Linking ecological critique with other radical critiques of the pervasive dualisms of modern Western thought, Benton thus appears to offer a way of reconciling the aims of human, and not only human, emancipation with the demands of ecology.

Limits of naturalism

Despite its promise, I believe there are some difficulties with Benton's proposed naturalistic approach to human nature. One is that while it may, as he suggests, allow illuminating comparisons between humans and other animals, it is another matter whether it will be adequate to the treatment of aesthetic, cognitive, normative – in other words cultural – dimensions of human needs. In fact, if his interpretation were taken to involve the strong claim that all natural beings have similar fundamental needs and all that distinguishes them is the specific *way* in which they are satisfied, then it would look decidedly vulnerable to a charge of reductionism. Benton recognizes this:

> Surely not *all* of human cognitive and aesthetic activity is displayed in the practices through which physical needs are met, nor yet even in those practices through which we meet the whole range of needs which we share with (some) other animal species? What of those needs – self-realisation needs – which appear to be peculiar to self-conscious and historical beings?[74]

The response he offers to this important question, though, while making clear that he is not committed to a strong, reductionist, claim, seems to weaken quite considerably the potential of his position as a distinct alternative to Lichtman's. Not wishing to deny the self-realization needs, he says, 'the commitment is to viewing them as *in some sense* consequential upon those needs which are common to natural beings, or upon the species-specific ways in which those common needs are met.'[75] However, it seems to me that nobody but the most extreme idealist would attempt to deny that peculiarly human needs are *in some sense* consequential upon their more generally animal needs; and I am not sure that a dualist would need to. At any rate, the point would be, precisely, to spell out that sense.[76]

If 'in some sense consequential' is to mean something more than the uncontroversial point that certain basic biological needs (e.g. eating) have to be satisfied before other (cultural) needs (e.g. composing symphonies) can be satisfied, or can even arise, then it might be interpreted in one or other of the following ways. On the one hand, the fulfilment of a higher or supervenient need is *eo ipso* the fulfilment of a more fundamental need, for example a kind of sublimation. If so, then presumably the biological need could also be directly fulfilled without such a mediation; in which case, though, there would be nothing left of the higher need which really has the impelling quality of a need at all. If, on the other hand, it is consequent on the fulfilment of biological needs that *qualitatively* new needs arise, then it would not appear to be possible to explain these in terms of the former, since they would no longer be specific ways of meeting some more general need, but would be entirely irreducible, autonomous needs. Now presumably Benton would not wish to draw either of these conclusions, since the former would be reductionist (and he distances himself from it in the passage cited above) while the latter is dualist (severing the connection he wishes to maintain between peculiarly human and more general animal needs). Apparently, then, he has in mind a third way, perhaps thinking in terms of complex needs which retain elements of more basic simple needs, but also incorporate a further element such that the whole need is something more and other than the sum of its parts – an emergent need which is neither reducible to the simple basic need nor entirely autonomous of it. So 'higher' needs might be thought of as, or on analogy with, emergent properties.

However, promising as this line of reasoning might at first sight appear, I do not think it will resolve the problem. One reason is that on Benton's own account it would appear to be the species *powers* which are emergent properties, not the needs. Thus, for example, whilst it makes sense to say that the human species has developed the power to compose symphonies or construct weapons of mass destruction, it cannot be said that the species, or even many (if any) individuals or groups, have a *need* to do so. So even if one allows, with Benton, that species' powers develop as a response to need, nevertheless, at least in the human case, once these powers are developed they are not necessarily directed to need fulfilment. This, in fact, is precisely the reason why Benton wants to develop a theory of needs in the first place – in order to distinguish, in the critical evaluation of human practices, between those directed to need fulfilment on the one hand, and the pathological or at least in some way infelicitous exercise of human powers on the other. But it seems to me that Benton expects more from his theory of needs than it will be able to yield, and that he is seeking to hold together an unsustainable set of claims: firstly, that the development of human species powers gives rise to new needs; but then also that only some of these needs are 'real'; and finally that a naturalistic account of how powers develop new needs will tell us which of these new needs are *really* needs. The question this leaves us with is how any (normative) distinction between real and apparent needs can be generated from an account which would show that *all* new needs are produced by the development of species powers.

So whilst one might accept that species powers are emergent properties which may be accounted for naturalistically, this does not tell us what uses they might or ought to be put to. This leads us to question what Benton advances as a major advantage of his approach over Lichtman's: namely, the possibility of drawing normative distinctions between needs delineated on a naturalistic basis. He says Lichtman's insufficiently determinate characterization of human nature would leave us without a normative standpoint from which to criticize late capitalist civilization and envisage a preferable future;[77] yet the claim that his naturalistic approach promises clearer guidance needs to be critically examined.

Now although Benton believes that biological sciences will yield knowledge which will give unequivocal guidance for arriving at appropriate preferences in the cultural sphere, he does not want to make the reductive suggestion that one can simply read off what is preferable in a normative sense from biological data. Indeed, within biology, the term 'preferable' might reasonably be taken to mean something like 'more apt for survival'; and, as we have already seen, in order to avoid reductionism in his account of the full range of human needs and to accommodate their normative dimension, Benton wants to distinguish between survival and flourishing – so that judgements as to what is preferable would refer not to mere survival but to conditions for *flourishing*. To maintain the naturalistic character of his account, though, he argues that this distinction holds for non-human beings too. His position, then, hinges on the possibility of offering a naturalistic account of flourishing.

However, there is room for scepticism about the prospective reliability of such an account and its guidance to political values. For one thing there is the question of whether we can learn much about human flourishing from comparisons with other species: it could in fact be that in so far as we can talk about flourishing in other species at all, it is only on analogy with what flourishing means in the human case. Thus, for example, it may be plausible enough to speak of non-human flourishing in cases where particular animals are so directly caught up in the purposivity of industrial production as to evoke clear parallels with humans, such as the animal victims of factory farming or laboratory experimentation; but outside such relatively clear and narrow bounds, wherein human sympathies are quite easily transferable, it becomes increasingly doubtful whether the criterion of flourishing, as something distinct from survival, will have any clear purchase. Saying this is not to *deny* that non-human beings can flourish, but to point to the limits of possible human knowledge regarding what flourishing can mean for them. Flourishing, in any sense adequate to the purpose Benton assigns it, has an irreducibly subjective dimension; knowledge related to flourishing, therefore, can only be had in cases of beings with whom some kind of intersubjective relation is possible. It is not necessary in the present context, however, to enter into controversy concerning the range of beings with whom intersubjective relations are possible because even such relations are not a sufficient condition for knowledge of what others' flourishing means. Even beings who relate intersubjectively do not always agree what flourishing means for them, and humans in particular have conceptions of it which vary quite considerably according to time, place, social location and so on. The aim of Benton's naturalistic project, of course, is to restrict the range of possible conceptions of flourishing whose fulfilment would be acceptable in a future which was preferable. In doing so, however, he is vulnerable to Lichtman's counterargument that he risks imposing one culturally specific conception in the guise of a naturalistic specification. This is perhaps the core of Lichtman's disagreement with Benton: 'Benton seems to believe that if we could specify human nature and its needs, we could then determine "what it needs", that is, what is good for it.'[78] Benton puts much weight on the role of the kind of positive knowledge sought by sciences such as ethology and ecology. Lichtman does not seek to deny the necessity of this kind of knowledge; but what he does deny is that it would be sufficient for thinking through future possibilities, for this involves other necessary conditions: in particular, distinctively human values like justice. Thus, he observes:

Societies can exist without justice, for example; large numbers of them have. For justice is not a want that must be satisfied if humans are to survive, but a transcendent value that determines what in the social order is worth surviving.[79]

A broader implication of this is that ecological sustainability is not necessarily incompatible with social injustice. For this reason ecological and ethological knowledge cannot inform us directly as to which future possibilities will be preferable.[80]

If Benton is right that a distinction between survival and flourishing is important for a political project of human emancipation, then I think he is mistaken in supposing that a humanist discourse should be ousted in favour of a naturalistic discourse. In humanistic traditions, the distinction between survival and flourishing has been presented in terms of subsistence and dignity – the two non-Promethean aims of emancipation from nature-imposed necessity which, I argued in the opening to this section, give content to the overall objective of social emancipation. What I called the distinctively humanist aim is the realization of autonomy.[81] Humans of course pursue this for their own good, but there is no reason why this should be at the expense of non-humans. In fact, it is the precondition for respecting the good of any other beings: autonomy is a precondition of any ethic at all, since ethical prescriptions can only apply to autonomous agents. Hence there is also a very good reason why we should be very cautious about blurring the distinction between human, or more precisely rational, autonomy and the capacities in non-humans for independent self-direction that we will want to respect: if autonomy is understood as *moral* and *responsible* freedom, then those beings who enjoy it will also have *obligations*. Rather than embark on the implaussible and unjustifiable enterprise of attributing obligations to non-humans, a humanist approach to the ethics of environmental concern, in placing the emphasis on human agency, allows us to focus on the problems that humans cause – for themselves and for non-human beings too.

Conclusion

The main question for this chapter has been whether it is possible to acknowledge the specificity of humans as *valuing* beings without assuming they are the only beings *of value* in the world. In the first section we looked at the arguments of those who think that humans in some ways cannot help being anthropocentric, but that this need not mean being speciesist; in fact, we saw some argue, environmental ethics can be developed on the basis of the enlightened self-interest of human beings. We also noted as a general problem with this approach, though, that it may not make a secure enough connection in practice between human and non-human values, especially when human interests conflict with interests of other beings; and this leads to the question of principle of whether what is required is really a further enlightening of human self-interest, or, by contrast, a more radical attempt to purge anthropocentrism from ethics. In the second section, therefore, we examined two ways of attempting to conceptualize the irreducible and intrinsic value of beings other than humans. What we found, though, is that one does not radically break with humanism, whilst the other arguably undermines its own claims to break with anthropocentrism. For this reason it was proposed, in the third section, rather than to look at which beings are bearers of moral value, to adopt a different approach. Part of this involved recognizing that perhaps the chief problem with anthropocentrism is not that it licenses a cavalier treatment of the rest of nature – since we have seen reason to think it need not do so – but that *anthropos* itself is an abstraction: focusing on 'humanity in general', it abstracts from the vast differences, such as those of sex, race, class and geographical distribution, which divide humanity. As long as such differences assume invidious forms, ecological morality will remain a mere ought (*Sollen*), relatively impotent to effect the transformation of those human social relationships without which the relation of humans to nature is unlikely to be transformed. Hence it was sought to reintegrate ecological concerns in a social perspective, recognizing that whilst there are some basic needs which are universal, other needs will be more culturally variable.

We can therefore acknowledge that values are socially constructed at some levels but without thereby being committed to a thoroughgoing relativism. In line with the critical realist approach sketched in the previous chapter, we can accept that the relation in which we stand to things and states of affairs *is* amenable to a realist account, and at a *deep* level values may be non-arbitrary. That is to say, we are so constituted as to be disposed to find values in similar states of affairs – not always, and with latitude and malleability. Hence, as I tried to show in the discussion of Lichtman and Benton, we cannot necessarily be certain about specific potential value agreements (on pain of imputing them without warrant) but this does not leave us open to just any possible conclusion. Ultimately, then, Lichtman and Benton illuminate, from different perspectives, one problem and the requirements for solving it.

Thus if we disagree about values, these disagreements may ultimately prove to be resolvable. I see three types of requirement, which can be related to the three sections of this chapter: certainly it means looking harder at 'the world out there' (with environmental scientists), and empathizing more determinedly with it (with deeper ecologists), but it also means investigating the presuppositions of our own human values and knowledge (with critical social theorists). Hence a recurring theme of this book is that sound critical social theory is as important as natural knowledge and ecological goodwill.

This chapter amounts to a provisional defence of talking about specifically human values or goods, since their pursuit need not be detrimental to the rest of nature, and, perhaps, if properly understood, could be to its good. It has also suggested that there may be more convergence between proponents of enlightened self-interest and those who advocate heeding deeper ecological intuitions than is often apparent in the literature, which overstates an opposition between anthropocentrism and anti-anthropocentrism. Nevertheless, real disagreements of other sorts remain. For instance, just as *anthropos* is an abstraction which does not refer to any single real entity, so it is that real humans are often not united in interests or beliefs. So, having defended our entitlement to *pose* the question as to which human values to promote, we shall now need to answer it. In the next chapter we will consider different views of the good life, asking after the objective grounds of needs and motivations and how these relate to practices with harmful ecological consequences. Following that, chapter 4 will ask how needs can be the basis for justice – especially when they compete with one another and with other principles. Then chapter 5 turns to questions of politics, in awareness not only of ecological realities, but also of how people sometimes think differently from theorists, philosophers or politicians about what their needs or interests are, or what is right.

3

Environmental Economics, Sustainable Development and Political Ecology

In the previous chapter it was affirmed that human development can in principle be considered an intrinsic good which is not inherently hostile to nature. Indeed, it was suggested that an enlightened conception of human development – development of both potentialities and welfare, individual and collective – would necessarily heed natural limits and promote the ideal of working in harmony with nature.

Yet it has to be acknowledged that such an enlightened conception of human development is not the one most usually pursued in the modern world. A different conception of development prevails – one which is defined, above all, *economically*. The goal of economic development is, of course, to maximize human welfare; but on the prevailing view of it, welfare is measured first and foremost by the quantity of goods consumed, and human potentialities are measured largely in terms of their productive employment. This conception of development, so closely tied to the idea – and ideal – of economic growth, is in many respects the antithesis of ecological ends. For it is precisely the drive to maximize the production of material goods which is provoking the overuse of resources, destruction of habitats, disturbance of ecosystems, and so on.

Now the economic conception of human development is widespread and deeply rooted, and there are powerful reasons why it should be. Economic activity in its most general sense – the production, circulation and consumption of material necessities of life – is a *sine qua non* of human existence. Moreover, productive activity can be seen not only as the key to human survival, but also as a precondition of human flourishing in non-economic senses, to the extent that the arts, culture, science, benevolence, and the pursuit of humanistic ideals in general are made possible by the existence of a strong and secure economic basis. Thus although the traditional ideals of humanism may not be reducible to economic goals, they do seem to depend on them. Hence, enlightenment humanism must face a further challenge from an ecological perspective: namely, that even if humanist *values per se* are not anti-ecological, their realization depends on economic development which is.

To sum up the problem, then: enlightenment ideals appear to pre-suppose and support the objective of economic development; but economic development cannot occur in practice, so ecological critics argue, without riding roughshod over the environment and other species; it therefore runs wholly counter to the ecological ideal of living in harmony with nature.

However, if this is so, then the question is how to develop a conception of the good life which is consistent with ecological constraints *and* with effective motivations. For, as was just noted, there do appear to be good reasons for pursuing economic development. If ecological ends are to be more than unrealizably utopian aspirations, it means reckoning with people's motivations as they *are* as well as saying how they *need* to be – and finding a way from the one to the other.

This, then, is the underlying question of the present chapter. There are three distinct lines of approach to it which will be set out in its three sections. The first approach is one which would see just how far existing economic practices might be pushed in an ecological direction: in other words, it investigates the scope for a *reform* of conventional economic theory and practice. A strength of this approach is that, in stressing how ecological harm is also human harm, it builds on existing motivations and practices; a weakness, however, according to its critics, is that it does not seek to challenge them radically enough. A second approach, by contrast, is suggested by writers who, sceptical as to whether there is any commensurability at all between the different imperatives of the eco-nomy and of ecology, advocate a radical rejection of economic imper-atives and call for a purely ecological alternative. This approach allows a fuller view of the scope of changes which need to be made to the existing economic system; but a potential weakness is that it is able to offer insufficient advice on how to institute the desired changes. Because there is something to be said for each of these broad approaches, I seek in the third section to indicate how one might develop an approach which would combine the strengths and valid insights of the other two but without their respective shortcomings. Thus I affirm, with representatives of the first, that we have to reckon with the reasons why economic growth is currently a priority, whilst agreeing, too, with the radical critics that those reasons can no longer be reckoned entirely good ones. What is required is an ecological redefinition of the economy which may provide the theoretical framework of an ecological reconstruction of the economy.

It should therefore be stressed that the arguments of this chapter move at quite a high level of generality. It is presupposed that too much of current economic activity is unecological in its effects, and this is something the three approaches broadly agree on. Moreover, there need be little serious disagreement about *identifying* what are the problems. Economic activities, for example, which pollute, use up scarce resources, disturb ecosystems or destroy habitats can be considered unecological in a fairly straightforward sense.[1] The disagreement focused on here, though, concerns what the *causes* of the problems are, and, therefore, what the best sorts of *solution* would be. Differences here depend, most fundamentally, on the *conception* of economy which underpins the conflicting perspectives. For what is claimed to make a practice unecological depends on the *interpretation* of that practice. It is primarily differences at this level of interpretation which will occupy us in this chapter.

3.1   Environmental Economics

Environmental economists start from the assumption that a good deal of economic activity today is unecological, but they do not take this to mean that there is something wrong with economic activity *per se*; rather, there are, contingently, some defects in the way it is presently conducted. In other words, economic activity needs serious reform, but it is reformable. In this section, therefore, I shall look first at the basis for reform, and then at the methods by means of which they believe it may be carried out.

The rational basis of reformist approaches

Environmental economists consider it to be neither necessary nor desirable to criticize economic activity *as such*; nor would they consider it necessary radically to redefine the scope of economics, the discipline, for in both its practice and its theory economics is already the science of managing scarcity, its prime concern being the study of the allocation of scarce resources to alternative ends. Hence they can argue it has always been concerned with how to negotiate limits like those now highlighted as environmental issues. What is needed, therefore, is better execution of this task, refinement of its tools and methods, and in particular the paying of due attention to the environmental inputs and outputs of economic systems. What environmental economics aims to do, therefore, is bring economic conceptions of value more into line with ecological values. Conventional modern economics places positive importance and value on some kinds of phenomena which from an ecological perspective would have a negative value, while on the other hand placing little or no value on other kinds of phenomena which have considerable ecological significance. However, for reformist economists, these two modes of valuation may not be irreconcilable. For instance, many sorts of economic policy which yield high economic benefits in the short term may be criticized because they provoke high ecological costs; but it may also be that they provoke high *economic* costs in the longer term too. Hence, in such cases, the problem may, for instance, be one of adjusting the rate of discount. In general, it is possible to take the view that if economic theory and practice pay insufficient heed to ecological factors, then the solution is to make economics take fuller account of them. In this way, environmental considerations lead to the *reform* of the bases for costing and accounting within economics, not their abandonment.

So the general line of argument of reformist environmental economists is that there is the sound basis for a descriptively and normatively adequate theory in modern economic theory, but that this is unrealized to some extent because it has taken too narrow a view of what the economy is. It abstracts from its connection both with ecology and with a more enlightened conception of the good life for humans. Thus, on the one hand, it has disregarded how economic activity takes place in the same world as ecological processes, and is ultimately part of a single set of systems; on the other hand, in treating the economy as a self-subsistent process, it has also tended to lose sight of how at root it is composed of human activities and should ultimately be understood as aiming at the good life for humans, but is not to be *equated* with the good life. In other words, the economy has both a natural and a social existence which are actually excluded from its own theory. But just as this abstractness did not always prevail in economic theory, so it need not continue to do so. On the contrary, if the most fundamental abstraction concerns the very conception of the economy, economics could already be reformed by recalling it to a previous conception of the economy which did not occlude crucial ecological and enlightened considerations. The concept of economy has itself undergone marked shifts in the course of Western history, along with changes in economic practices. Going back to the original meaning of the Greek *oikonomia*, its sphere of reference was the 'management of the household', with the criterion of good management being the increase of its use value to all members of the household (*oikos*) in the long run.[2] If one generalizes from this core description to conceive of the economy, more globally and broadly, as including the production of all use values in any site, ultimately in the entire eco-sphere, and to conceive members of the 'household' as including all beings who could possibly stand to benefit, then it can be seen that economy is not *intrinsically* anti-ecological – for, indeed, such a broad description of economy would correspond, in important ways, to a definition of ecology itself. As was noted in the opening chapter, the very name of 'ecology' was coined with the same etymological root as 'eco-nomy'. So 'ecology', etymologically, would be 'science of the house-hold' – which would be a curious choice of name for a biological discipline were it not that some clear analogies were perceived between ecologic and economic phenomena. Thus the name of the science stuck, perhaps, because it preserved the sense of, while improving on, the name hitherto available to its practitioners as a general designation of their object field – namely, 'nature's economy'.[3] So if 'ecology' at root means the study or science of the *oikos* and 'economy' means its management, then there would seem to be good reason to see ecology and economy as mutually dependent allies.

But if economy, considered under this general description, is not intrinsically anti-ecological, some specific forms of economy neverthe-less are. The contemporary problem is precisely the prevalence of such forms of economy: these depart significantly from the general description just given and come much closer to what the Greeks termed 'chremat-istics', in stark contrast to *oikonomia*. Chrematistics refers to 'the manipulation of property and wealth so as to maximize short-term mon-etary exchange value to the owner'.[4] Unlike *oikonomia* which had a connection with the good life, chrematistics had merely to do with mak-ing money, and was thus to be condemned.

Interestingly, chrematistics was to be condemned for reasons that can be advanced on essentially humanistic grounds; similarly, contemporary chrematistic forms of economy can be criticized in terms which need make no direct reference to ecological concerns as such, but which can in fact be derived from an enlightened conception of human interests. Before turning to specifically ecological considerations, therefore, it is worth noting how the distinction between *oikonomia* and chrematistics alone suffices to point up some of the most glaring inadequacies of contemporary economics. Three chief respects in which *oikonomia* dif-fers from chrematistics have been summed up by Daly and Cobb:

First, it takes the long-run rather than the short-run view. Second, it considers costs and benefits to the whole community, not just to the parties to the transaction. Third, it focuses on concrete use value and the limited accumulation thereof, rather than on abstract exchange value and its impetus toward unlimited accumulation.[5]

A major problem with modern economics, then, is that it has departed from the classical conception of *oikonomia* to operate almost exclusively in terms of chrematistics.

Corresponding to this shift is a change in the conception of what constitutes a good life for human beings. The human values assumed by modern economics are predominantly those of an individualistic and materialistic hedonism which is morally and spiritually quite unambitious. The good life amounts to little more than the fulfilment of the immediate interests of those with something to buy or sell on the market. These values sustain the quantitative assumptions of economics that more is straightforwardly better, whilst banishing as extraneous any considerations as to the quality or possible limits of human satisfactions. It is worth highlighting the specificity of modern economics in this respect, for such values are neither universal nor eternal. It is certainly not essential for economic activity that individuals' immediate self-interests be taken as intrinsically worthy of promotion regardless of long-term consequences or consequences for third parties; or that economic activity be pursued only for exchange value, as opposed to the production of useful objects. Indeed more was not, and is not, always automatically better: humans can also form concepts, for example, of 'too much' and 'wrong sort' – questions which make reference to the *purpose* of economic activity, which, when it goes beyond meeting survival needs, necessarily makes reference to improving the *quality* of life. Qualitative questions have been obscured – indeed, rendered obsolete – in modern economics. But they can and must be recovered. If this is necessary from an ecological point of view, it is no less necessary from a purely human point of view.

If the goals of the economy are to be oriented to a more enlightened conception of the good life, this will clearly require some quite decisive changes in economic theory and practice. In particular, what needs to be questioned is the way the market and market behaviour are taken as exhaustive of the activities making up the economy; standards applicable to the market are taken as given rather than contingent and possibly problematic; in general, human beings, their activities and their welfare are reduced to quantifiable categories. On this basis deductions and calculations can be made with the appearance of scientificity, but it means that other factors – which on a different view might be as, or more, central to the economy – are all but dismissed under the category 'externalities': negatively there are social and ecological costs which do not figure in balance sheets; positively there are all contributions to human well-being for which no money is paid. The very concept of economic success is growth in GNP, which, essentially, measures the volume of monetary transactions, regardless of what is traded. The equation of growth with success is *assumed* in neo-classical economics: questions as to the rightness or wrongness of growth or its effects are simply not considered. A telling commentary on the status of growth in economic thinking has been provided by Keynes, nurturing the hope that somehow growth will gradually slow down as people gain the wealth and leisure necessary to pursue less materialistic satisfactions: 'The love of money as a possession – as distinguished from the love of money as a means to the enjoyments and realities of life – will be recognised for what it is, a somewhat disgusting morbidity.'[6] Yet before this can come about, he says, it has to be endured for some time still:

> For at least another 100 years we must pretend to ourselves and to every-
> one that fair is foul and foul is fair; for foul is useful and fair is not.
> Avarice and usury and precaution must be our gods for a little longer still.
> For only they can lead us out of the tunnel of economic necessity into
> daylight.[7]

The tone of regret scarcely alleviates the cynicism of this, however, which appears only the greater when one wonders whether the right time will ever come, and if it does, whether it will not already be too late. In truth, the idea that economic necessity can be overcome is a piece of hubris which does not stand up to examination in human, ecological or even economic terms; the idea that the pursuit of goodness and virtue, justice and spiritual truth can be postponed until universal prosperity is attained is, as Schumacher says, an unrealistic, unscientific and irrational hope. For Schumacher, Keynes's assertion that 'foul is useful and fair is not' is the antithesis of wisdom: from an economic point of view, the central concept of wisdom is permanence, he says. 'Nothing makes economic sense unless its continuance for a long time can be projected without running into absurdities. There can be "growth" towards a limited objective, but there cannot be unlimited, generalised growth.'[8] Yet the value of unlimited growth has become axiomatic in modern economics: it is seen as good not only as a means to the end of wealth production, but as an end in itself. The overriding economic goal is thereby distanced from an enlightened conception of the good life by a second remove.

A critique of economic growth is also a central theme of enviromental economics, and I shall shortly be examining how this critique is developed. Firstly, though, I should like to sum up how the concept of economy has passed through three stages to become, in modern economics, pure chrematistics.

In the classical Aristotelian tradition, wealth was valued only as a means in the pursuit of a truly human conception of the good life. In classical political economy, wealth begins to assume the status of an end in itself; and now that *growth* is perceived as a means, wealth can be seen as the *end* at which it aims. This view of wealth as an intermediate end is a significant step along the road to losing sight of the ultimate end of wealth and seeing it as an end in itself. This is the process which modern economic theory has completed. In modern economic theory, reference to human ends becomes so attenuated that growth comes to be seen as an end in itself. Criteria for defining wealth are now abstracted from human ends, and a cynicism is institutionalized where everything has a price but the value of nothing is appreciated. So the historical expansion of the economic sphere has been accompanied, both in thought and in practice, by a process of increasing abstraction of the economy from the broader contexts in which it actually exists. The principal stages of this process of abstraction can be summarized as follows:

1 Wealth is seen as a means to the end of the good life (Aristotelian tradition).
2 Growth is seen as a means to the end of wealth (classical political economy).
3 Growth is seen as an end in itself (modern economic theory).

This summary is obviously highly schematic, but I think it is helpful in providing a set of analytic distinctions which in turn will provide the basis from which the project of a reform of economic theory and practice can be described. That is to say, we can see in general terms what would be involved in the recovery of a broader perspective on the economy. It would mean, first, disposing of the view that growth is an end in itself; then, disposing of the view that wealth is an end in itself, the possibility of re-engaging economic activity with an enlightened conception of the good life is opened up. Describing the project at this level of generality, one is able to conceive it in ways which do not involve turning the clock back or abstract utopianism; moreover, it can also be seen to be consonant with the aims of environmental economics.

Economics and sustainability

Environmental economics differs from conventional economics in that it does not uncritically accept the assumption that growth is an end in itself. However, it does not necessarily reject the idea that growth may be desirable as a means to other ends: in this respect it also differs from the more swingeing critiques of economics made by radical ecologists.

Addressing the question of the desirability of growth as a *means*, one has to reckon with reasons why economic growth is currently a priority. One answer is that, at present, many economic institutions can only function in the expectation of growth: practically all activities based on credit and investment, for instance, depend on this.[9] Nevertheless, this begs the question of whether and why the institutions themselves are desirable and worth saving. A potentially compelling reason why they may be is that they in turn promote aggregate social wealth. An important question for environmental economics, therefore, is whether economic growth serves as a means to the end of wealth (I set aside for the moment the more radical question of whether wealth itself should be pursued as an end in the first place). Now a straightforward answer in the affirmative would be that it does by definition: growth represents an increasing GNP, and GNP measures wealth. But when one considers some of the things GNP measures one is brought to question the concept of wealth involved; it certainly appears to be a poor indicator of economic welfare or well-being. As Michael Jacobs points out, it includes things we would rather have less of (pollution control, road accident surgery, etc.), and excludes both the value produced by unpaid work (housework, childcare, etc.) and the free services of the environment.[10] Hence today there is increasingly widespread acknowledgement that growth in GNP does not in itself mean aggregate well-being is actually increased.

The answer, therefore, to the question of whether growth is desirable as a means to an end must, on any meaningful definition of ends in terms of real wealth, be 'not necessarily': one can have growth without an increase in real prosperity if this is understood as having to do with meeting real needs, providing satisfying work, interacting with nature and expanding intellectual, spiritual and practical horizons.[11] Yet although this is a sceptical answer, it is a less decisively negative verdict on growth than that often made by ecological critics. The key point is that if growth in GNP does not necessarily do any good, then by the same token it does not necessarily do any harm. As Jacobs has pointed out, growth of itself does not automatically lead to resources running out, or add to pollution, or make ecosystems unstable. It is a fallacy, he says, quite prevalent in green thinking about economics, to suppose that it does. Yet it is precisely because GNP does not distinguish between 'good' or 'bad' economic activities – between, say, a pound spent polluting and a pound spent controlling pollution – that it is not necessarily better as an indicator of things getting worse than of them getting better: it 'can go up with less degradation and down with more'. Accordingly, Jacobs argues, 'it is not so much *growth* that is the problem, but simply the *amount* of consumption, whether this is increasing or not'.[12] If this is so, then growth, in itself, is not the issue at all. Once the rationale and criticisms of growth have been taken stock of, then the task, on this view, becomes that of working out a constructive alternative. This is the task that reformist environmental economics has taken on.

We are now in a position to appreciate why there has been, as Pearce has noted, a shift of emphasis in recent years, away from the limits-to-growth approach:

> In the 1970s it was familiar for the debate about environmental policy to be couched in terms of economic growth versus the environment. The basic idea was that one could have economic growth – measured by real per capita incomes – or one could have improved environmental quality. Any mix of the two involved a *trade-off* – more environmental quality meant less economic growth, and vice versa. Perhaps the most forceful, if least scientific, expression of that view came with the publication of the Club of Rome's *Limits to Growth* in 1972.[13]

This analysis led to a polarization of views which was not entirely helpful, according to Pearce, for whilst environmental 'doomsters' overstated the negative relationship between economic growth and environmental quality, their opponents, who claimed a potential complementarity between growth and the environment, tended to understate the potential for economic change to damage the environment.

This stalemate has been overcome, economists like Pearce claim, by shifting the focus of debate on to *sustainable development*. This allows a more constructive and nuanced approach to the problems already broadly identified.

Advocates of sustainable development accept the substance of the point that critics of growth have long been making, namely, that what has been called economic growth in the past has been measured by some very misleading indicators. Accordingly, a broader range of indicators of economic well-being – not simply incomes as in GNP – has to be employed to take into account the quality of life.[14] Hence it is also recognized that at a deeper level the nominally value-free assumptions of conventional economics have to be replaced by some explicit value commitments. As Pearce points out, 'development' is a value word; it embodies ideals and aspirations and concepts of what constitutes the good society. Development is thus a richer and broader conception than growth. It implies change leading to *improvement* or *progress*, says Pearce, and an economy 'which raises its per capita level of real income over time but does so without making any transformations in its social and economic structure is unlikely to be said to be "developing"'.[15] A society undergoing development is likely to be experiencing an advance in material well-being – which means increased income, at least for the poor, and includes environmental quality, the preservation of existing freedoms and advances in freedoms where existing ones are inadequate, and a growing sense of independence and self-respect.[16] Development, then, is constituted by a set of social goals which are broader than those related to material wealth production alone, even if, for Pearce, those remain centrally important.[17]

Turning to the question of what makes development sustainable, it is to be noted that there are various particular definitions of sustainable development, and it is likely to remain an essentially contested concept.[18] Nevertheless it is usually characterized with reference to the three desiderata identified in the Brundtland Report which go under the headings of environment, equity and futurity. Thus, firstly, concern for the environment means combating pollution, for instance, and avoiding depletion of non-renewable resources. Threats to the sustainable use of resources, though, come as much from inequalities in people's access to resources as from the ways in which they use them, according to Brundtland, so that it is futile to attempt to deal with environmental problems without a broader perspective that encompasses the factors underlying world poverty and international inequality. Both environment and equity need to be perceived in the context of futurity: the unifying thread of sustainable development is a concern with the intergenerational allocation of resources, as is clear from the key definition of sustainable development as 'development that meets the needs of the present without compromising the ability of future generations to meet their own needs'.

The aim of sustainable development involves considerations both aggregative and distributive. That is, on the one hand, there are questions as to what the good life or good society is; on the other, there are questions as to who is entitled to share in it, how, and how much. In practice, the two kinds of consideration may not be adequately treatable in isolation from one another, but it may be helpful in analysis to separate them out when considering what sort of practices make up the development to be sustained. In the next chapter, equity and futurity, as questions of distributive justice, will be discussed more fully; here I shall focus on the question of *what* is to be distributed, and also how it is to be measured.

Pearce, following Brundtland, says we should leave the next generation a 'stock of wealth' no less than the stock we have inherited.[19] He notes two contrasting understandings of this, though: on the one hand, it can be taken to apply to 'natural capital' only; on the other, it can include both natural *and* man-made capital. The latter interpretation normally allows the substitutability of man-made for natural capital, and this may be undesirable for ecological reasons: for example, many environmental assets are not substitutable and hence need straightforward preservation; moreover, depletion of environmental assets is often likely to be *irreversible*, and hence substitution itself would reduce future generations' substitutable capital.[20] Hence there are good reasons for advocating that the stock of *natural* capital be kept constant.

There are then two different ways that natural capital can be understood. On one, the requirement would be that *physical stock* should not decline; but this may be an unpromising objective for three reasons, which Alan Holland summarizes:

> One is that working out a criterion for non-declining physical stock turns out to be a less simple matter than might first appear, particularly where living things are involved, because of the constantly changing relations between them. A second is that, whatever criterion is used, it would seem prima facie virtually to rule out the use of non-renewable resources . . . A third is that . . . not all physical capital is equally useful to humans, and some perhaps is of no use at all. So the reason for attempting to maintain the level of physical stocks, in an undiscriminating sense, remains somewhat obscure.[21]

The other variation requires that not the physical *stock* but its economic *value* be kept constant: in other words, 'that there should be no reduction in the flow of services yielded by the stock of natural capital'. This is the approach adopted by Pearce and his colleagues. It allows more flexibility than would be possible on the constant stock variation, for it would allow some use of non-renewables, provided technology was opening up new possibilities for exploitation. Holland points out that it also restores the rationale for preserving natural capital, understood as those aspects of nature which are usable in human social and economic systems.

Once natural capital is defined in terms of the economic value it yields, it becomes of crucial importance to know what money values to place on environmental services, and to be clear how these are arrived at. Indeed, the need to place proper values on the services provided by environments, states Pearce, is one of the central themes of environmental economics.

The central problem, and the reason why this is necessary, is that many of these services appear to be provided free because of an implicit bias in the way economies work. Unlike goods and services which have prices that can be observed in the marketplace, the general functions which environments serve (e.g. as a waste sink) are not invariably bought and sold in the marketplace. Because of this, they have 'zero price'; and if something is provided at a zero price, more of it will be demanded than if there was a positive price. The most likely outcome, therefore, is that when their allocation is left to the unfettered market, the services of natural environments will be *overused*. Accordingly, Pearce believes, to try and correct this bias and ensure a better allocation of resources, it is important to have some idea of what the environment is 'worth'. While acknowledging that this project will offend conservationists and radical ecological critics, he emphasizes that seeking to put money values on certain aspects of environmental quality is to underline the fact that environmental services are *not* free.

The absence of markets makes economic valuation more difficult, but by no means impossible. Concern for the environment can be thought of in terms of positive preferences for cleaner air and water, less noise, protection of wildlife, and so on. Hence environmental values can be determined by reference, not to actual market prices, but to the virtual market, so to speak, of preferences. The existence of such preferences makes possible the evaluation of different courses of action in terms of cost–benefit analysis.[22]

Preserving the environment is never a free option, and costs of some sort will always bite somewhere. While cost–benefit analysis is not the only way to arrive at environmental policies, it is, Pearce says, the only one which explicitly makes the effort to compare like with like using a single measure of benefits and costs. There are, he argues, several reasons why it is important to place monetary values on environmental gains and losses: firstly, placing money values on preferences enables the *degree* of concern to be measured; secondly, he believes, supporting any particular environmentalist case with a monetary expression of that concern makes the case more strongly than if any one argument is used alone; thirdly, it may permit comparison with other monetary benefits arising from alternative use of funds.

To sum up, Pearce's view is that, suitably reformed, 'economics provides a potentially powerful defence of conservation and a novel array of weapons for correcting environmental degradation'.[23] On this view, environmental economics is presented quite straightforwardly as enlightened self-interest: 'an improvement in environmental quality is also an economic improvement if it increases social satisfaction or welfare.'[24] The bottom line of all this is that economics will take care of the environment because, being dependent on the environment, it is in its own interest to do this:

> Very simply, if the 'true' value of the environment were known, we would not degrade it as much.[25]

Problems with environmental economics

There are various practical problems with environmental economics which its proponents are quite ready to acknowledge. These have to do with the technicalities of environmental accounting and audits, for instance, or the various ways of identifying and measuring preferences, and so on. More centrally for our present concerns, however, there are some questions of *principle* that need to be addressed.

The first and most general is whether environmental goods can or should be given a price at all. Some critics object that valuing the environment is neither desirable nor possible because there are some things in life which simply cannot be valued in money terms, things which are beyond exchange value altogether.[26] Pearce's response to this is that often we do value things – such as human life for instance – in money terms: 'We quite explicitly draw boundaries round the kinds of expenditures that we are prepared to make to save life.'[27] The reality is, he says, that in contexts of scarce resources we are condemned to make choices: so if we cannot avoid doing so, we can at least try to make them as fully informed as possible.

A second objection addresses not the principle of valuing as such, but the possibility of measuring different sorts of value with one measuring rod, be it money or whatever. This is the problem of commensurability.[28] Now all that commensurability of values requires, according to the authors of the Ramsey Centre Report Attfield and Dell, is that one be able to make judgements such as 'This is more valuable than that.'[29]

They grant that making such judgements may often be difficult and complicated, but believe it will generally be possible. In order to illustrate their point they consider the case of comparing enjoyment of art or natural beauty with saving lives:

> It may look as if one could not say that a certain amount of aesthetic enjoyment was more or less valuable than one life: that such a comparison did not even make sense. But governments do make such comparisons, and it is hard to deny they make sense. For instance, the government of the United Kingdom has decided that it is justified in subsidising the Covent Garden Opera, even though it knows perfectly well that the money it spends could save a certain number of lives if it were transferred to the NHS. cancer-screening programme.[30]

So the bottom line of the reply to each of the objections is that if hard choices will always have to be made, then it is no use offering as a criticism what is essentially only a complaint about that fact.

That, at least, is how matters appear from the standpoint of those committed to valuing the environment. Other perspectives may nevertheless be possible. For the hard choices which confront people at different times and places do not always do so with the force of brute facts. Both what the options are and how they are now evaluated will often depend on the prior choices humans have already made. Thus, for one thing, as John O'Neill points out, environmental objects and states, like any others, are necessarily evaluated under different descriptions:

> A location is not evaluated as good or bad as such, beautiful or ugly as such, but, rather, as good, bad, beautiful or ugly under different descriptions. It can be at one and the same time a 'good A' and a 'bad B', a 'beautiful C' and an 'ugly D'. A location may have considerable worth as a place – it may embody in a particularly powerful way the work of a community – but little worth as a habitat, an ecological system or as a landscape.[31]

Such different descriptions are likely to depend on the different practices and perspectives from which evaluation is made. Perhaps even more telling is the point that present options will often have been created by past actions. Choices typically do not arrive out of the blue and simply have to be dealt with by harassed humans, but rather emerge in the context of humans' ongoing and continuing practices. So although choices may be inevitable within any given practice, the continuance of the practice itself may not be. What this sort of perspective suggests is that reformist positions like Pearce's exhibit an inbuilt bias of non-criticality *vis-à-vis* existing practices.

From a more radical perspective, an environmental economics assessment of costs and benefits begs a number of questions. For one thing, if environmental goods are evaluated with reference to the ends the valuer has in mind when expressing a value judgement, then *whose* preferences are to count? For proponents of cost–benefit analysis this question is not seen as representing a serious problem: their assumption is that with enough goodwill, enough information, and the freedom to discuss it, reasonable people will generally be able to arrive at consensual decisions. One specific objection to this follows from sociological observations of how different people are presently placed in very different positions *vis-à-vis* environmental problems, on the one hand, and decision-making processes on the other. From this it follows that before preferences can be freely and rationally discussed, it is necessary to establish the prerequisite conditions of social equality; until all preferences have an equitable chance of being heard and being effective, decision-making will continue to promote the interests of those who have power. That the interests of other people might not be represented is a question I take up again in the next chapter; at this stage, with the interests of non-humans and the environment more particularly in mind, we have the question of why human preferences only, if at all, should matter.

This is to open a line of criticism which strikes at the underlying argument of environmental economics as such: namely, that taking care of the environment is in humans' interest. To question this is to question whether environmental economics adequately grasps its own *raison d'être*. For if it makes and needs make no reference to sources of value other than actually or potentially verifiable human preferences, this leaves no independent concern for the good of any beings other than humans: all we need now, and all we want to leave as a bequest to our heirs, are adequate resources for human use. A point that Alan Holland notes about this is that it also leaves no reason to care whether the resources to be used, now or in the future, are natural or man-made. On *what grounds*, Holland therefore asks, can Pearce consistently speak of natural capital which must not be depleted? If humans are getting the services they need, then it should not matter to the theory whence they come.   .

Another source of value appears to be implicitly at work. Yet it is arguable that environmental economics cannot recognize it even in principle. Holland focuses this point by reference to the central idea of natural capital. He points out that on Pearce's definition of natural capital in terms of the flows of services it yields, one is actually talking about services which human activities can *get* it to yield – and this varies considerably according to the state of knowledge, productive forces and social arrangements. This means 'the economic value of natural capital is only as secure as the technology, social conditions and cultural needs which enable that value to be realized, and these can be quite fragile.'[32] A static physical stock of natural assets can, through the application of technology, yield a dramatic rise in natural capital; alternatively, constant levels of natural capital could be maintained with dwindling stocks of natural assets. The distinction between man-made and natural capital thus, to some extent at least, breaks down, which means that the imperative of maintaining natural capital constant becomes difficult to understand and to operationalize. It also becomes unclear why it should be desirable: given that some *man-made* capital is non-substitutable and some natural capital is substitutable, it is not all and only natural capital that is indispensable. So there does not ultimately appear to be, on Pearce's account, any reason why natural capital specifically should be held constant. Applied consistently, therefore, the criterion of constant economic value need do little to protect natural assets.

Although economists like Pearce evidently *care* about natural assets, this must be for reasons extraneous to their official theory. Perhaps there is an appreciation of values to be sought beyond economic categories altogether, discovered, as Grove-White and O'Donovan put it, with the importance of a 'reality that exists, prior to us and independently of our interests as we have conceived them, [and that] "dawns" on us, forcing us to reappraise what we had thought important hitherto.'[33] But there is a radicality in this suggestion which seems to escape environmental economics. In environmental economics such intuitions are admitted in the form of 'existence values': 'existence value is a value placed on an environmental good and which is *unrelated to any actual or potential use of the good.*'[34] These show up, for instance, in campaigns for remote environments or species which it is not realistic to expect the campaigner ever to use, notes Pearce, yet they can be treated like any other form of preference as far as economists are concerned: they can be reduced to some or other form of altruism – bequest motives, gift motives, or sympathy – which makes economic analysis more complex, but they can nevertheless be subsumed in the conventional model of rational economic behaviour. 'Essentially, it says that the well-being of one individual depends on the well-being of another individual.'[35] In other words, environmental economists can by definition recognize no sources of value in nature other than those which assume the form of human preferences. If this is a strength of environmental economics in relation to its own goals, it nevertheless leaves those goals themselves open to a more radical line of questioning.

3.2 'Ecology into Economics Won't Go'

We have seen that reformist environmental economics like Pearce's can be criticized for retaining too many assumptions of conventional economics: in particular, for retaining a strong connection between development and economic growth, and an instrumental attitude towards natural resources. In this section we will be considering arguments from more radical positions which provide a critique of the very project of environmental economics, asserting an incommensurability between ecology and modern economics such that there is not simply a contingent difficulty in putting a price on nature or natural services, but an irreconcilability of fundamental assumptions. The section begins by examining some key factors in a radical critique and redefinition of 'development'; it then explores the arguments of those who would take this critique to imply the rejection of economics, or its subsumption under ecology.

Towards an ecological critique of development

There are a number of factors involved in a more radical critique of development. These and their interconnections have been particularly well set out by Vandana Shiva, whose work is drawn on in the following.

Firstly, the conventional approach in economic theory and practice takes an instrumental view of nature. The dominant development paradigm disregards the complexity of the processes of life on earth, and sees the planet merely in terms of resources, 'raw materials', to be exploited, 'developed', thereby 'adding value', and exchanged for money on the world market. This approach aims at the maximization of production, and disregards the destruction and degradation which attend it. Shiva observes that the 'act of living and of celebrating and conserving life in all its diversity – in people and in nature – seems to have been sacrificed to progress'.[36] In this destruction of natural and cultural wealth and diversity, she argues, reductionist categories in science are dialectically linked to reductionist categories in economics which reduce all value to market value, and register only those activities and processes that are monetized and involve cash transactions. Moreover, Shiva also points out the paradox that while devastating the planet and being able to destroy the real economies of entire countries, the global economy is increasingly dealing with mythical constructs on computers: 'During the post-war period, capitalist "growth" came from industrial expansion; today wealth comes from *unproductive* and fictitious economic exchange ... Only about five per cent of commodity transactions on futures markets relate to actual delivery of goods.'[37]

Secondly, the domination of nature is connected with the domination of women. Numerous writers have argued that men's domination and mastery over nature have also been associated with new patterns of domination and mastery over women. For Shiva they are two aspects of 'the same process of devaluation and destruction that has been characterised in masculinist history as the "enlightenment"'.[38] Nature and women do not acquire value through domination by modern Western man; they lose both through this process of subjugation. 'Activity, productivity, and creativity ... are expropriated as qualities of nature and women, and transformed into the exclusive qualities of man.'[39] According to the dominant view of the productivity of labour as defined for processes of capital accumulation,

> 'productive' man, producing commodities, using some of nature's wealth and women's work as raw material and dispensing with the rest as waste, becomes the only legitimate category of work, wealth and production. Nature and women working to produce and reproduce life are declared 'unproductive'.[40]

Shiva argues that just as the devaluation and derecognition of nature's productivity have led to the ecological crises, so the devaluation and derecognition of women's work have created sexism and inequality between men and women. Furthermore, she argues, the devaluation of subsistence economies[41] based on harmony between nature's work, women's work and man's work has created the various forms of ethnic and cultural crises that afflict the contemporary world. Which brings us to a third factor.

Thirdly, the domination of nature and women is also the domination of values of specifically Western culture. The connections between the exploitation of natural resources and the exploitation of the poor South by the affluent North are well documented.[42] It needs also to be recognized that economic exploitation goes hand in hand with cultural domination. Shiva notes that contemporary development activity in the Third World 'superimposes the scientific and economic paradigms created by western, gender-based ideology on communities in other cultures'.[43] The dominant development paradigm, which environmental economics seeks to reform, but not radically to transform, embodies a system of values which represent 'the arrogance of the west'. This arrogance, argues Shiva,

> is grounded in a blindness towards the quiet work and the invisible wealth created by nature and women and those who produce sustenance. Such work and wealth are 'invisible' because they are decentred, local and in harmony with local ecosystems and needs. The more effectively the cycles of life, as essential ecological processes, are maintained, the more invisible they become.[44]

So the diverse traditions of the world, with their distinctive technological, ecological, economic, political and cultural structures, are forced to conform to a conception of development derived from the particular evolution of the West.

These three factors taken together amount to a powerful indictment of modern Western conceptions of development; and Shiva herself believes the conventional concept of 'development' would more appropriately be called 'maldevelopment'. A truer definition of development would take account of the perspectives of the poor South, women and ecology. Shiva sums up her view:

> Women producing survival are showing us that nature is the very basis and matrix of economic life through its function in life-support and livelihood, and the elements of nature that the dominant view has treated as 'waste' are the basis of sustainability and the wealth of the poor and the marginal. They are challenging concepts of waste, rubbish and dispensability as the modern west has defined them. They are showing that production of sustenance is basic to survival itself and cannot be deleted from economic calculations; if production of life cannot be reckoned with in money terms, then it is economic models, and not women's work in producing sustenance and life, that must be sacrificed.[45]

Existing economic models are inadequate to ecological realities – something which is highlighted by observing that subsistence economies and activities traditionally associated more with women than men are less so. The question raised here, then, is whether a conception of development, more appropriate to the complexity of reality as indicated by these considerations, may be constructed on a wholly new basis. This is the question of a radical alternative to environmental economics.

The economy in radical ecology

By contrast to reformist approaches which press environmental considerations into the service of economic models, a radical approach would subsume economy under ecology. It would attempt to redefine human development in primarily ecological, as opposed to economic, terms.

The inbuilt non-criticality of environmental economics has already been noted: its politics is inherently reformist; it is, in the words of Dobson, 'the green politics of carbon dioxide scrubbers on industrial chimneys, CFC-free aerosols and car exhausts fitted with catalytic convertors'.[46] Green radicalism, by contrast, would call into question the very use of aerosols, cars and other industrially produced commodities. Indeed, it would seek, in the words of Porritt and Winner, 'nothing less than a non-violent revolution to overthrow our whole polluting, plundering and materialistic industrial society and, in its place, to create a new economic and social order which will allow human beings to live in harmony with the planet.'[47]

At its most radical, the green vision is one of human goods being subsumed entirely under broader and deeper ecological conceptions. In deep ecology, there is the idea of dwelling in mixed communities, for example, whereby the other inhabitants of the bioregion, including animals and plants, would be considered no longer simply as economic resources, but also – perhaps instead – as neighbours. This would be to effect a radical displacement of what has become our conventional view of the world, and to bring it more in line with Leopold's land ethic, an ethic which 'enlarges the boundaries of the community to include soils, waters, plants, and animals' and thereby 'changes the role of *Homo sapiens* from conqueror of the land-community to plain member and citizen of it'. This would be to transform our relation to the land, which at present is still 'strictly economic, entailing privileges but not obligations'.[48] The idea of 'economy' as actually or potentially a neutral description of humans' material basis gives way to a view of humans as one species among a number – whose specific needs or interests will not always and necessarily be a sufficient reason for encroaching on other species.

The transformation of economic imperatives into this sort of ethical imperative is something Leopold sees not only as desirable, but as an ecological *necessity*. Considered ecologically, he writes, an ethic is a limitation on freedom of action in the struggle for existence: 'The thing has its origin in the tendency of interdependent individuals or groups to evolve modes of cooperation. The ecologist calls these symbioses. Politics and economics are advanced symbioses in which the original free-for-all competition has been replaced, in part, by cooperative mechanisms with an ethical content.'[49] In this passage is made explicit the crucial deep assumption that economy can be subsumed under ecology. There is also an indication of what the explanation for this would be:

> That man is, in fact, only a member of a biotic team is shown by an ecological interpretation of history. Many historical events, hitherto explained solely in terms of human enterprise, were actually biotic interactions between people and land. The characteristics of the land determined the facts quite as potently as the characteristics of the men who lived on it.[50]

A key concept in this kind of explanation is that of ecological succession, which refers to what some see as a youth-to-maturity development analogous to that of an individual organism. Edward Goldsmith has argued that the idea of ecological succession can be used as a general framework for talking about the process of building mixed communities, and one which provides a perspective quite different from the economic. The ideal corresponds to nature's own tendency to develop towards a climax situation, whereas conventional economic development tends to cause a reversion to a pioneer situation.

> A pioneer ecosystem, that is to say an ecosystem in the earliest stages of development, or one that has been ravaged by some discontinuity such as a volcanic eruption or an industrial development scheme . . . is the least 'living' of ecosystems . . . Such an ecosystem is among other things highly productive, which of course endears it to our modern production-oriented society which can cream off the apparently surplus biomass.[51]

A reason why a pioneer ecosystem is productive, Goldsmith states, is that as soon as it comes into being, the 'healing processes' of nature are activated so that the ecosystem might rapidly go through the different stages of succession to arrive as closely as possible to the original climax. Thus the climax ecosystem, by contrast, is very unproductive:

> This must be so both because the climax is the most stable state possible in the local biotic, abiotic and climactic circumstances, and because the achievement of such a stable state appears to be the basic goal of living things. Once achieved, change is kept to a minimum.[52]

Looking at matters in this way, the human economy appears as a kind of irritant in an otherwise harmoniously self-regulating natural world. This kind of perspective has been put forward particularly eloquently and persuasively by James Lovelock as the Gaia Hypothesis. Lovelock stresses the interrelatedness of all things within an overall self-regulating whole: 'the entire range of living matter on Earth, from whales to viruses, and from oaks to algae, could be regarded as a single living entity, capable of manipulating the Earth's atmosphere to suit its overall needs.'[53] The dominant development paradigm, however, disregards the complexity and interrelatedness of processes on earth.

We can now elaborate on Shiva's observation that 'development' is something of a misnomer. Its aim is to cream off the best of available resources to yield exchange value on the world market. As de la Court observes, 'capital accumulation in the world market aims at a world which is constantly in a pioneer situation (in contrast to the climax situation). It is very productive, but with very little diversity and little internal self-control.'[54] Given that the changes being brought about by modern societies are in fact reversing ecological succession, it is appropriate to consider industrial development or progress as an anti-evolutionary process. Basic facts of ecological reality are systematically disregarded in economic theory, whose categories are simply not equipped to grasp them: even such fundamental concepts as production and consumption appear quite differently when viewed ecologically.

It is worth stressing, then, that ethical criticisms of the dominant development paradigm are supported by considerations of a more strictly scientific nature. Focusing solely on 'what we can get out of it' is to take a view of an ecosystem which is not only objectionable, but also mistaken. For one thing, humans do not in fact take out resources from nature or put back waste, for the whole process – and they themselves – are within nature. This is something becoming increasingly well theorized by bioeconomics – which reminds us of many facts abstracted from conventional economics:

> Every economic phenomenon, every activity which produces goods or generates services, can be described as a flow of material and energy which begins in the environment, passes through the factory, house, city, humanised territory – that is, through ecosystems modified by humans or through artificial ecosystems – and returns, sooner or later, to the environment.[55]

A merit of this approach is to remind us that the human economy is ultimately grounded in physical processes.

One important point that becomes evident from this approach is that no good is ever in fact consumed; it may only be transformed into another thing. If one burns coal, for instance, one sets in train various chemical and physical processes which, for example, combine carbon with oxygen and dissipate energy – but nothing is lost in the process, something is merely displaced. Conversely, it can also be misleading to talk of producing. Humans tend to give themselves more credit than they deserve in this regard. For instance, to cite an example Martinez-Alier takes: 'it is geologically incorrect to say that production of oil in Mexico was about 2.7 million barrels per day in 1983.'[56] In 1983 that much oil was *extracted*, and thereafter transformed into some useful energy and some polluting gases; the *production* of that oil, however, was something that took place over a geological timescale.

These points about the physical truth underlying economic concepts like production and consumption lead us to consider the true origins of material wealth. An interesting perspective has been offered by Soddy, arguing that real wealth comes solely from the sun:

> Without the sun the world would be lifeless, not only because there would be no plants and animals, but also because even inanimate nature would stand still.[57]

On this view, wealth is essentially a *flow*; the sun's energy becomes useful by being harnessed, in the first place, through the process of photosynthesis. Hence, as Soddy has put it, 'the first capitalist was a plant.' Plants accumulate solar energy, whereas humans expend it. The energy stored in fossil fuels has been concentrated by millennia of plant activity. 'Coal burned was burnt forever. It cannot be burned and kept in the cellar at the same time, and still less can interest continue to be accumulated on the value of burnt coal.'[58] The notion that consuming such resources yields economic growth looks absurd from this perspective. Soddy's main point is thus that economists mistake real capital for financial capital: many investments do not increase productive capacity in the physical sense, rather they increase the destruction of non-renewable resources.

Such, then, are the facts abstracted from in conventional economics; acknowledging them means taking a different starting point. If wealth is always essentially some form of useful energy embodied in an object, it is subject to the laws of thermodynamics. The first law of thermodynamics says that energy can be neither created nor destroyed: this means it can only be embodied in more or less useful forms. The second law of thermodynamics then tells us that although the total amount of energy in a closed system will remain constant, the energy will tend to dissipate into less useful forms – or, in other terms, that entropy will increase. These two laws of thermodynamics, it is argued by ecological economists like Georgescu-Roegen, must be the starting point for economics. The economic process itself is entropic. Thus while the raw materials from nature are equal in quantity to the waste materials ultimately returned to nature, there is a qualitative difference between the equal quantities of raw and waste material. Entropy is the physical measure of that qualitative difference:

> It is the quality of low entropy that makes matter–energy receptive to the imprint of human knowledge and purpose ... We cannot with any currently imaginable technology power a steamship with the heat contained in the ocean, immense though that amount of heat is. Nor can windmills be made of sand or ashes.[59]

On this view, then, all resources, and indeed all items of value, are characterized by low entropy.

But where does low entropy itself come from? Is there some other law which overrides the second law of thermodynamics? The answer, in fact, is that the consequences of the second law are not wholly negative. In particular, it is precisely by transforming energy from high- to low-utility states that organisms and ecosystems maintain their own highly organized, low-entropy (low-disorder) state. Odum illustrates the process with an oak leaf: if this receives 100 units of dilute energy from the sun, then in the course of transforming this, 98 units are dissipated as even higher-entropy energy; the remaining 2 units, however, are less entropic, more concentrated, in the form of sugars.[60]

Hence there are two basic sources of usable energy: the solar, the energy currently coming from the sun; and the terrestrial, the stored energy on the earth. The difference between them is also significant for economics:

> these two ultimate sources of life sustenance differ in their patterns of scarcity. Radiant energy from the sun is practically infinite in total amount (stock), but it is strictly limited in its flow rate – that is, the amount that arrives on earth during any period. Energy stored in fossil fuels and minerals is strictly limited in its total amount (stock), but relatively unlimited in its flow rate – that is, we can use it up at a rate largely of our own choosing. We cannot use tomorrow's sunlight today, but in a sense we can use tomorrow's petroleum, coal, iron, and helium today.[61]

Daly and Cobb note that since the industrial revolution began its intensified exploitation of fossil fuels and mineral materials, it has shifted dependence from the relatively abundant to the relatively scarce source of the ultimate resource: low-entropy matter–energy.

As Keekok Lee points out, it is the second law of thermodynamics which shows *why* there are limits to economic expansion which are not surmountable even in principle: work may be performed, but only by diminishing the amount of available energy for further work in the future. As resources of low entropy are dissipated, the attempt to substitute them involves a greater expenditure of energy and increase of energy. There is no technical solution to this. The second law of thermodynamics, says Lee, assures us that scarcity is absolute, not merely relative.[62]

This reappraisal of the real basis of wealth yields a more decisively ecological account of value than appears in reformist environmental ethics. Hence with regard to doubts raised earlier about the idea of natural capital, for instance, it now appears there are good ecological reasons for thinking that there are definite *limits* to the extent that man-made capital can be substituted for natural capital; for whatever apparent success there may be in the short term, substitutability involves increasing costs, and ultimately insuperable barriers.[63] Productive activities have developed to such an extent that those costs and barriers can no longer be ignored; the idea that development of knowledge and technology might overcome them is beginning to appear, in the words of Keekok Lee, as 'fantastic'. The bottom line is that it is concentrations of low-entropy energy that make production possible – and sustain life itself. Indeed, if production is seen as a means to the end of life, then energy for sustaining life *directly* should be given priority over uses of energy in production which has at most an indirect connection with the sustenance of life. We should therefore note the crucial distinction Soddy draws between 'vital' and 'laboral' uses of energy:

> Vital use refers to photosynthesis in plants and to carbon oxidation in the nutrition of animals and human beings . . . The laboral use of energy refers to the use of humankind of instruments which are moved by the wind, by waterfalls, by steam or internal combustion engines, etc.[64]

This distinction expresses, in such a way that the economic implications are quite clear, that established in energetics between endosomatic and exosomatic uses of energy.

There are connections here with questions concerning the good life too. The good life would be based on the development of internal as opposed to external goods – that is, those which depend on and promote human faculties and capacities rather than on material consumption. A lifestyle frugal in material possession and consumption, but rich in spirit, would involve less squandering of low-entropy resources in exosomatic uses.

The ecological critique, then, completes the project sketched out in the previous section: it carries us from a critique of growth as an end in itself to a critique of wealth as an end in itself – or at least to a radical reappraisal of the real nature of wealth.

Limits to the radical ecological critique of economics

The ecological critique recalls economics to the physical realities it abstracts from. It would nevertheless be a mistake to think it possible to go beyond economics on the basis of a theory focused first and foremost on physical realities. For one thing, there are some goods which Hirsch calls 'positional goods', the existence of which give rise to 'social limits to growth' with scarcities being created by particular patterns of consumption and distribution rather than anything intrinsic to the nature of the product or its production.[65] For another thing, although industrial processes are the product, in physical terms, of technological developments, the question of technology can never wholly be separated from questions of the *ownership* of the means of production. This can be illustrated by reference to Ivan Illich's concept of 'radical monopoly', that is, 'when one industrial production process exercises an exclusive control over the satisfaction of a pressing need, and excludes nonindustrial activities from competition.'[66] The kinds of activity that get squeezed out are 'healing, consoling, moving, learning, building their houses, burying their dead ... These activities have use value without having been given exchange value.'[67] The establishment of radical monopoly happens, he says, when people give up their native ability to do what they can do for themselves and for each other, in exchange for something 'better' that can be done for them only through big technology. One can in fact go further than Illich does in connecting questions of technology with questions of ownership, since it is arguable that people often do not so much 'give up' older ways of life as have taken away the possibility of pursuing them. It tends to be the case that the industrial processes which succeed in driving out more traditional ones are undertaken by particular vested interests. So one needs to be cautious about generalized criticisms of industrialism which pay no heed to the property relations which sustain it.

In the final analysis, economic arrangements involve forms of organization which cannot be fully understood ecologically. It is therefore necessary to recognize that ecology and economy are interconnected but not reducible one to the other. Hence, if there is a problem with more radical ecological positions, it may be summed up as the fallacy of 'ecologism': that is, in this context, the attempt to discuss economic phenomena as if they could be wholly grasped in ecological terms – for they cannot.[68] Ecology cannot simply take the place of economics; it cannot explain the human allocation of energy and natural resources to different uses. Ecologists, as Juan Martinez-Alier writes, 'are quite good at explaining the movements of birds and fish, but today they are unable to explain the geographical distribution of the human population'.[69] They are certainly not in a position to explain the drastic differences in resource use:

> Some use perhaps one ton of petroleum yearly (in the form of fuel for tractors, fertilizers, herbicides, transport, fridges, electric kitchens, etc.) in order to feed themselves while other members of humanity do not use a single drop of petroleum.[70]

Any attempt to account for such things in terms of ecological categories like 'carrying capacity' is bound to appear arbitrary and ideological. To illustrate this point Martinez-Alier refers to how human ecologists have commended the very low level of energy use by highland shepherds in the Andes as an adaptive device. He observes:

> One could as well say that the shepherds not only 'adapt' to ecological conditions, but to the land tenure system ... Peruvian peasants have attempted time and again, at least from the Spanish conquest onwards, *not* to adapt to the destiny that the colonial power, the authorities from Lima, the local landowners, and the world economic and political system, reserved for them.[71]

Thus in Martinez-Alier's view, the dynamics of human history are better understood 'as the result of a struggle between rich and poor, the forms of which vary according to the changes in relations of production, than as a history of social organisms which "adapt" to ecological conditions.'[72]

If the explanatory role of ecology has to be importantly qualified in this way, then some of the more sweeping claims for the distinctiveness of an ecological worldview need to be qualified. In particular, it cannot be a case of simply supplanting an economic worldview by an ecological worldview. The problem, then, is one of trying to get economic rationality genuinely and constructively informed by ecology. For if management of ecosystems is in some ways unavoidable, then the imperative is that it be conducted according to sound principles. Martinez-Alier concludes that the economy and the ecology of humans are embedded in politics. This conclusion is one I would endorse and shall explore in the next section.

3.3 From Political Economy to Political Ecology

We have arrived at the central problem that while mere reform of economics does not appear adequate to ecological ends, radical ecological alternatives do not appear adequate to the range of concerns which economics deals with. Although the criticisms which can be levelled at reformist environmental economics from deep ecological, feminist, and South perspectives all appear to be well taken, they also present some incompatible demands. For instance, the reasons for a critique of conventional economic and development theory from the South's perspective are significantly different from those of deep ecology. The situation regarding feminism is even more complex: although some, like Shiva, emphasize the potential for alliance between women's struggles against oppression and struggles for nature, others resist too close an identification of the two since just that connection has so often been used ideologically to oppress women; nor would they want necessarily to assimilate feminist struggle to that of oppressed male workers. In short, despite their powerful criticisms, the critical perspectives do not offer, singly or collectively, a complete and adequate alternative to the economic perspective.[73]

In view of these considerations, the difficulties with environmental economics may come to appear in a less harsh light: not only has no fully coherent alternative so far suggested itself, it may also be that some of the reasons for maintaining a reformist approach have not been obviated by the criticisms. Hence the dilemma appears to be that the pursuit of ecological values can proceed neither with nor without economics.

In this section I cannot hope to offer a complete solution to this dilemma, but I shall attempt to sketch the form a possible solution is perhaps most likely to take. This is to find a conceptual orientation, at least, where constructive and critical dialogue is possible. If simply *abandoning* economics is not an option, in theory any more than in practice, then the aim must be to seek a transformation, perhaps more radical than that implied by environmental reformists, but nevertheless without effecting the kind of radical break dimly envisaged by ecologism. What will ultimately be needed is a theory which can account for how the economy can be both a part of ecology but also relatively autonomous of ecological determinants. In what follows I shall simply be sketching what seem to me to be the most likely, promising, parameters of this kind of theory. I shall refer to it as 'political ecology' to indicate how it must take over but deepen the insights of political economy.

The human metabolism with nature

If a unified theory of economics and ecology is to be possible, it will neither hypostatize an opposition between economy and ecology nor posit a straightforward identity of the two. It must be capable of comprehending the relation of ecological processes and human practices without simply subsuming the one under the other. In order to do so, it must be able to grasp the real relations between them: which means focusing on their mediations. The locus of these mediations, and hence the object field, can perhaps best be described as the 'human metabolism with nature'.[74] This idea captures fundamental aspects of humans' existence as both natural and political beings: these include the energetic and material exchanges which occur between human beings and their natural environment both at an individual level (reproduction of the human organism), and, more importantly in the present context, at a social level (through the activities of extraction of materials, agriculture, construction, manufacture etc.). This metabolism is regulated from the side of nature by natural laws governing the various physical processes involved, and from the side of society by institutionalized norms governing the division of labour and distribution of wealth etc.

Now the idea of a human metabolism with nature, in much this sense, originated with Marx: it served to characterize the materialist basis for his critique of political economy.[75] However, there are respects in which Marx's radicalization of classical political economy does not go far enough. In particular, both classical political economy and the Marxian critique effectively consider the human metabolism with nature almost exclusively in the dimension of human intention – labour – while all but disregarding unintentional effects, and the input of nature itself. What is also necessary, therefore, as contemporary attempts at an ecological reconstruction of Marxism are tending to show, is a radicalizing of Marx's critique of political economy on the basis of a fuller and more differentiated elaboration of his own materialist premises. This will also need to be informed by aspects of a feminist critique of Marxism. For the human metabolism with nature involves not only the day-to-day repro-duction of individuals and social relations, but also procreative reproduction – something which Marx, as much as the political eco-nomists, effectively consigns to the sphere of unmediated nature, with the consequence that the parturitive labour of women, in particular, but also nurturative and domestic labours more generally, are drastically undertheorized and depoliticized. In other words, the entire human metabolism with nature – including all aspects of human reproduction, and not just those activities which happen to be defined, in some ways arbitrarily, as productive – need to be comprehended.

If the materialist conception of history remains a touchstone in this, it is because the relation of economy and ecology needs to be theorized in its concrete mediations as these have actually permeated social and polit-ical processes. In very broad terms this means considering how relations of dependence and control between people develop out of and into rela-tions of dependence and control between people and their natural environment. This means viewing history not with the ready-made cat-egories of 'economic' or 'ecological', but with the aim of seeing how these categories themselves have emerged and developed. It is certainly noteworthy that at other times and places there has not always been a radical separation of economy and ecology. In tribal or subsistence com-munities, for example, there appears to be an absence of differentiation between economic and ecological ideas as we would conceive them, with ecological systems being preserved and their constituents respected for reasons which do not reflect any distinction between instrumental and intrinsic values. Even in feudal economies, human wealth remains suffi-ciently tied to the land for there to be little reason to conceive a radical distinction between economy and ecology, which is not to say that feudal practices have caused no ecological harm, but only that the economic and the ecological would be perceived as together constituting an undiffer-entiated sphere of necessity. By contrast, in modern economies there develops a notion of economic freedom as quite distinct from natural necessity. This notion arises from the fact that the sphere of economic activity does indeed gain some autonomy from the natural world, and in two major respects. On the one hand, there is the freedom generated through the growth in human powers of technological manipulation real-ized through the achievements of science and industry. The productivity of human labour is increasingly distinguished from natural fecundity, and the modern period sees the rise to prominence of labour theories of value - from Smith to Marx – which effectively attribute all wealth- and value-creating power to human labour. On the other hand, there is the development of the market system which entails the general alienability of land, labour and capital. These factors of production had hitherto been seen not merely as social phenomena, but as aspects of the natural world. With the generalization of the market system, however, this naturalness can be increasingly abstracted from: the *specificity* of nature becomes an indifferent generality. The social reality of land, labour and capital is now merely quantitative: its sensuous reality becomes a matter of indifference. In this way has developed what is the antithesis of an ecological perspective on production, involving the kinds of abstractions that, as we have already noted, are uncritically theorized by modern economists in general.

However while Marx's critique of political economy shows how this abstraction takes place in the process of converting labour into capital, it nevertheless pays little heed to the role played by nature in meeting economic objectives, or indeed to the effects on nature of pursuing them. For Marx, what is wrong with the capitalist mode of production is that it perpetuates an exploitative relation between capitalist and worker, but he says virtually nothing about the exploitation of the rest of nature.[76] Indeed, he retains the belief that human emancipation must be premised on the continuing growth of productive forces. He attributes a positive value to capitalist accumulation in so far as this means the material concentration of productive forces, for he sees this as a *sine qua non* of human emancipation, providing the material basis for the worker's effective claim for true, communist, freedom. Thus his objective appears to be a transition from an unequal to an equal partnership in the domination of nature. It implies the Promethean view of the human relation to nature which ecologists object to.

The Marxian critique of political economy is therefore not a sufficient basis for an ecological critique of political economy. It is a different question, though, whether Marx's theory is, while not sufficient, nevertheless a *necessary* factor in such a critique. There are ecologists who argue it is not, seeing as quite separate phenomena the subjection to the market of human labour on the one hand, and of land – or nature more generally – on the other. Focusing on the exploitation and subjugation of nature, they see the root of ecological problems as lying in the processes of *industrialization*. The Marxian emphasis on *capitalism* as the root problem they believe to be misleading since capitalism is not the only system of social relations capable of supporting anti-ecological productive forces, and socialist states have often proved to be worse on this score. It therefore does not suffice to present capitalism as the root of all ecological evil, or to suppose that the traditional tools of Marxism, applied to capitalism, would solve ecological crises *en passant* as it were.

However, the validity of the Marxist analysis of capitalism cannot be denied or declared irrelevant just by claiming that ecological crises are caused by the industrial system of production as such. For one thing, if industrialization is the problem, it is because of the *scale* it has reached, since it is obviously possible for small-scale industry to be less harmful than the widespread application of more 'primitive' practices. There has always been ecological devastation: but in the past it was normally confined within a locality. The history of modern manufacture itself was from the outset one of ecological disruption; but whereas at the beginning local manufacture had local ecological effects, the global industrial system now has global effects. Thus ecological devastation has become systematic in the same sense that commodity production is: that is, not as the result of a prior plan, but according to the inherent logic of a process which tends towards an infinite exploitation of finite natural resources. Now capitalism has this tendency as its very essence, being a commodity-producing system which needs continuously to grow to survive; whereas it is arguable that if socialist systems have also embodied a similar logic, they have done so *contingently*, but do not need in principle to continue growing indefinitely. Be that as it may, though, there is another reason for not accepting that industrialization as such is the cause of ecological problems: this is simply that the impetus to excessive growth comes not from the industrial means of production themselves, for they could sit quite idly without humans to press them into service, but from the way human affairs are motivated and arranged. Questions of social organization, power, ownership and the division of labour are inseparable aspects of any mode of production: to the extent that Marxism insists on examining them it is a mode of analysis which remains necessary.

This is what is missing from ecologistic positions which fail to consider the social in its specificity; environmentalists, for their part, are just as inclined to see ecological crises as the unmediated effect of industrial production or overpopulation. Yet if no connection between such phenomena and the social division of labour is theorized then the regulation of the human metabolism with nature from the social side is inadequately grasped. What is needed, then, is to examine both sides of the human metabolism with nature, the social and the natural: the opposition between two radical positions – Marxism and ecologism – has thereby to be overcome. With this in mind it becomes appropriate to engage in a constructive critique, rather than rejection, of Marx's theory.

The problem, then, is that whilst natural limits to the growth of productive forces cannot adequately be theorized without reference to social relations, they do need to be theorized. This is the central problem picked up as a challenge by those theorists who are now seeking to develop an ecologically reconstructed Marxism.[77] This project would involve an ecological elaboration of the basic categories used by Marx in his theorization of society in terms of the human metabolism with nature. At a high level of generality Marx characterized society in terms of two fundamental categories:

1 The material and energetic exchanges which take place between humans and nature in production are wrought by what Marx calls *forces* of production.
2 The relations between humans which regulate the human metabolism with nature, for example the division of labour and property rights, are called *relations* of production.

Ecological Marxism, however, raises to prominence a third factor. If society first appears as arising in opposition to nature, this opposition is, in some ways, only apparent: for both the material infrastructure, and the human constituents, of society are in fact themselves part of nature. Thus nature enters the social world, conditioning and limiting it, in both these ways. Hence a third category, which is present but in a subordinate position in Marx's theory, needs to be accorded no less importance:

3 The natural limits of both human and non-human nature which regulate the metabolism from the side of nature are examples of the *conditions* of production.

Now using these three basic categories – the forces, relations and conditions of production – it may be possible to offer a constructive perspective on the essential theoretical dispute between Marxism and some of its ecological critics. In his critique of the capitalist mode of production, and his projection of a communist alternative, Marx focused on contradictions between forces and relations of production: in particular, he criticized capitalist relations as fetters on a fuller development of forces of production. Now the ecologists argue that since it is precisely the development of the forces of production which is wreaking ecological havoc, what we need, if anything, are more effective fetters.

Hence, instead of criticizing capitalist relations, they insist on criticizing industrial *forces* of production. However, Marxists would point out that it is not possible to transform the forces of production without engaging with the social relations which maintain them in being. So where the ecologists would reduce Marx's two-dimensional dynamic (between forces and relations of production) to the one dimension of forces of production, ecological Marxists seek to extend the framework of analysis to incorporate the third dimension – that of *conditions* of production. Thus O'Connor, for example, suggests it may be possible to theorize a 'second contradiction of capitalism':

> An ecological Marxist account of capitalism as a crisis-ridden system focuses on the way that the combined power of capitalist relations and productive forces self-destruct by impairing or destroying rather than reproducing their own conditions.[78]

This approach can be claimed to offer the advantage – over environmentalism and ecologism – of an integrated account of social, economic and ecological crises.[79]

Nevertheless, what needs to be emphasized in the present context is that in expanding the framework of analysis to incorporate an account of production conditions, an ecological reconstruction of historical materialism will entail a more radical critique of political economy – and its presuppositions – than is to be found in Marx. Marx's critique of political economy was intended to elucidate the dynamics of the *capitalist* mode of production, but this critique will offer too restricted a view of the problem: for capitalism is not the sole cause of ecological crisis; and the effects of ecological crisis cannot be fully grasped in terms of a crisis for capital. An insufficiently reconstructed Marxism could persist in the error of believing it can. Orthodox Marxism has always recognized the existence of 'natural barriers', but has seen them, like the barriers represented by social relations, as obstacles to be overcome. If an ecological Marxism merely adds to this a view of how what is specific to capitalism is the way natural barriers assume the form of crisis, then the implicit hope may be fostered that if the specific crisis form is removed, what is left will be the nature-given barriers which productive forces have always encountered, and will continue to push back: the aim would thus remain that of further developing productive forces. An ecological Marxism would have to incorporate a different political aim. This point is reinforced by the observation that there can be increasing ecological destruction for a long time, without this having a reflection in capitalist crisis. Now, recognizing this, O'Connor suggests it may be precisely the role of new social movements to accelerate the process – to translate ecological crises into crises for capital.[80] Nevertheless, there remains the question of whether ecological crisis, which appears on O'Connor's account in the form of a crisis of reproduction of production conditions, is not actually something more and other than this. This question gives form to the ecological intuition that nature, internal and external, is something more and other than a condition of production. I think the answer is likely to be – one which is gaining ground in debate – that ecological concerns cannot be fully accounted in discussion of production conditions, unless these are so broadly defined as to problematize the Marxian conception of production itself.

Viewed ecologically – indeed, viewed properly *materialistically* – production is not simply a unified or homogeneous set of activities which can either advance or experience setbacks. It may appear this way from the standpoint of capital and its theorists who see production merely as the precondition for the process of valorization, but they abstract from the specific material and ecological existence of productive conditions and, indeed, of productive forces which are themselves also a part of nature. Worth noting, moreover is that the idea of natural capital, which we have already seen to be important to environmental economics but ecologically problematic, will warrant analysis in no less detail than Marx's original analysis of economic capital. It might then be shown that there is no clear fault line of contradictions between forces and conditions of production; indeed, that the distinction between productive forces and conditions becomes increasingly arbitrary as the material character of production is analysed. In revealing this arbitrariness, political ecology might follow recent feminist critiques of the primacy of production in Marx.

Beyond the paradigm of production

Production is the most fundamental category in Marx's theories of society and history. It is by reference to its mode of production that Marx believes the specific character of any society may be explained. When he writes that human history begins when people begin *producing* their means of subsistence he is quite clearly making a claim about the primacy of production in general. Now a problem which has been pointed to, and with growing insistence in recent years, is that there is something of a hiatus between the kind of claim Marx makes for the primacy of production in general and the conceptualization of specific forms of production – such as in commodity production. Thus Linda Nicholson,[81] for example, points out a variety of meanings of 'production' in Marx: sometimes he appears to mean any activity which has consequences; at other times he refers, more narrowly, to activities which result in objects; and then again, more narrowly still, he refers to those activities which result in objects which can be bought and sold, that is commodities. This variety of usages yields a problematic ambiguity: for as Benhabib and Cornell also argue, the concept of production based on the model of an active subject transforming, making and shaping an object given to it, is inadequate for comprehending activities like child bearing and rearing, and care of the sick and the elderly.[82] But if these activities do not conform to the object-producing model of production, they are nevertheless crucially important to the basic material practices of reproduction of society which Marx intends under production in general. Hence it may be argued that, under capitalist conditions, production in general assumes at least two distinct forms: the production of commodities and the reproduction of people. Although the distinctiveness of the latter is recognized by Marx, and especially by Engels, it is nevertheless undertheorized. As Mary O'Brien writes:

> Marx talks continuously of the need for men to 'reproduce' themselves, and by this he almost always means reproduction of the self on a daily basis by the continual and necessary restoking of the organism with fuel for its biological needs. Man makes himself materially, and this is of course true. Man, however, is also 'made' reproductively by the parturitive labour of women, but Marx ultimately combines these two processes. This has the effect of negating biological continuity which is mediated by women's reproductive labour, and replacing this with productive continuity in which men, in making themselves, also make history.[83]

There is thus a tendency for Marx to negate the sociality and historicity of reproductive activities, to view them either as natural and historical or else as historical effects of changes in productive relations, and so to accord them a subordinate or marginal role.

Accordingly there are feminist arguments for a 'displacement of the paradigm of production', and these are directly relevant to the project of political ecology. Broadening the concept of the economic to include not only productive but also reproductive activities allows the development of a more ecological perspective. For while from an economic perspective production appears as a self-contained and self-generating sphere, from an ecological standpoint it may be seen as one facet of the broader set of natural phenomena – of which human activities are just a part – which can be described as reproduction. Conversely, whereas from an economic standpoint reproduction, if significant at all, is only a moment of production, from the standpoint of ecology production appears as a moment of reproduction, as a mediation of nature's own activity. However much humans believe they are working against nature, they are in fact always working *with* nature; indeed, nature is working *for* them, as the labourer works for the capitalist. Thus where political economy reveals the source of value to be labour, political ecology reveals the source of labour, and hence ultimately of value itself, to be nature.

That said, however, it has to be remembered that nature is not *immediately* the source of value, as value is a *form* arising from human practices. In the previous chapter we discussed problems with deriving values more directly from nature, and in this chapter too it has been emphasized how neglecting social mediations encourages the fallacy of ecologism. This problem is paralleled within certain streams of feminism by the problem of essentialism; it is heightened in their combination in some forms of ecofeminism.

There has been considerable debate within feminism in recent years concerning the relation of production to reproduction. Some versions of ecofeminist theory advocate the *primacy* of reproduction: as Valerie Bryson notes, these have grown out of a strand of feminism which takes motherhood and associated experiences to be celebrated as giving rise to 'womanly values' to do with nurturing, cooperation and peace, to be contrasted with male attributes of self-interest, competition and aggression;[84] they equate men's treatment of women with their treatment of nature, and insist that only women's values can save the planet from ecological disaster.[85] However, as Bryson points out, this sort of view can be criticized for a biological determinism which contradicts current scientific thinking and flies in the face of much historical evidence. Moreover, it 'would seem to confirm traditional roles and divisions, allowing men to continue to destroy the planet while celebrating alternative virtues at home'.[86] This essentialist equation of nature's and women's values is therefore suspect both scientifically and politically.

Nevertheless, reproduction and nature do need to be accounted for, and not merely as social constructs. So it may in fact be appropriate, as Kate Soper says, to be essentialist at a certain level: that is to say, one must recognize a distinction between deep and surface concepts of nature.[87] The idea here is consistent with the realist view I discussed in chapter 1 that the nature which enters social mediations has certain 'essential' qualities of its own. This is *not* the essentialism of ecofeminism however; for as, Soper observes, men are just as clearly situated within 'nature' and governed by biology as women are, and both men and women are clearly involved in reproduction ... [Therefore] to approach reproduction as if it were inherently a more 'natural' and 'female' domain obscures the politically important discriminations which need to be made with respect to *all* human practice (both 'productive' and 'reproductive') between those aspects which are biologically/naturally constrained (and thus far 'essentially' given), and those which are socio-economically conditioned, and whose specific 'material' constraints are in principle removable.[88]

The view here, then, is not that the production/reproduction dichotomy should be inverted, as essentialist ecofeminists would have it, but that it should be *overcome*. At the level of theory, the aim is not to supplant the primacy of production by the primacy of reproduction, but rather to theorize the human metabolism with nature in all its facets. If what makes ecology political is how processes of production and reproduction enter social relations of power and property, then, taking a cue from feminist theory, this will mean including those social relations of power and property, such as the domestic and the familial, which have been excluded from political economy. This appears to give support to the suggestion that a politics which is ecological, feminist and socially just will find its theoretical ground in the theory I am describing as political ecology.

This theory does not deny the relative or partial truth grounding political economy that productive activity is fundamental to human social being; nor does it deny the force of Marx's critique of exploitation of labour in capitalist productive processes. But it does revalue and reconceptualize productive activity itself, and extend that critique to the exploitation of non-waged labour and the 'labour' of nature itself. This means revaluing reproductive activities; it also means identifying reproductive aspects of productive activities, and making distinctions *within* production. Perhaps production and reproduction would then be seen no longer as two entirely separate spheres, but rather as one sphere within which some activities are sustainable and others are not. This would significantly expand the parameters of political economy to those appropriately described as political ecology.

Conclusion

This chapter opened with the general question of whether a conception of development corresponding to true human needs is necessarily bound up with the sort of economic development which tends to have ecologically deleterious consequences. The first response to this question considered was that of environmental economists like Pearce who would seek to reform conventional economics so as to allow 'proper valuation' of the environment. We noted that this was an improvement on an unreformed economics which sometimes treats environmental goods as having *no* value at all, but we nevertheless also found it reductive in its methods and its assumptions. In the second section, therefore, we considered more radical alternatives, the strength of which is to accord the ecological basis of economic activity theoretical and practical primacy; the problem they are not fully able to grapple with, though, is that economic practices, being social as well as natural phenomena, cannot be comprehended in ecological terms alone, and to think they can is the fallacy of ecologism. In the third section, therefore, we were concerned with the question of how to overcome the limitations of reformist environmentalism on the one hand and ecologism on the other. It was argued that this would require developing a theoretical perspective which is able to take account of the human metabolism with nature in both ecological and social terms; it was suggested that such a perspective could usefully develop Marxist and feminist insights. Taking this perspective on the economy holds out the promise of overcoming the antithesis of reformist versus radical perspectives, because, on the one hand, it supports the general line of argument that women and nature and subsistence workers should be made to *count* in economic thinking and that this means making their values *visible* in economics,[89] which is what reformism aims at; but if they are to become visible, they must nevertheless become visible *in their own terms*, which means taking, on the other hand, a radical line on the irreducibility of values not currently reckoned with in economics. Taken together, this implies a two-pronged, long-term project which will certainly involve significant difficulties and tensions, but which nevertheless has an underlying coherence.[90]

Other aspects of this project are to be taken up in the remaining chapters. This chapter has investigated whether a conception of the good life could move from an economic to an ecological definition. It is clearly necessary, though, not only to redefine what constitutes economic activity and how it relates to the good life; there is also the question of how benefits and burdens are distributed within and across societies. Moreover, an economy which is *ecologically* sustainable may nevertheless coexist with a social and political order which does not respect the other two ideals of enlightened development – equity and futurity. Hence the critical elucidation of sustainability, which has proved necessary in the context of ecological economics, will need to be applied to these other two ideals as well. These are distributive questions, questions of social justice, to which we turn in the next chapter.

4

Rights and Justice in Ecological Perspective

This chapter is to inquire into the implications of ecology and natural limits for human rights and social justice. Human rights and social justice are key planks of most green platforms and manifestos. The Brundtland Report builds them into the very definition of sustainable development: of its three desiderata, the goals of securing equity for people living today, and rights for future generations, are quite obviously questions of justice and rights; the third, concern for the environment, there is also reason to believe, can be assimilated to the existing discourse of human rights, which is worth doing since that discourse is established, respected, and to some extent implemented. In short, there are reasons to think that the implications of ecology may be to increase the scope and importance of human rights, and thus inform a constructive development of what is arguably one of the most important legacies of the enlightenment tradition: the idea that humans have certain fundamental and inalienable rights, simply in virtue of being human.

Nevertheless, if strong arguments can be offered in favour of human rights, before and after ecological considerations, there are also arguments that tell against. From its inception, the idea of human rights has been subjected to powerful sceptical arguments: from the scathing attacks launched against the French proclamations of the Rights of Man, at the time by Burke and Bentham, and later for different reasons by Marx, to the more recent criticisms of the UN declaration for its ethnocentrism, which are sustained to some extent by postmodernist critiques of universalistic ideas as such.[1] When human rights are viewed from a specifically ecological perspective, grounds for scepticism are renewed and augmented. For in view of the material constraints of the earth's finite carrying capacity, not *all* humans can plausibly be held, without qualification, to have all the human rights proclaimed as universal rights in declarations like that of the UN – since many rights have resource implications which count against their indefinite extension. Moreover, even if it can be argued that there are fundamental rights, and especially if these must now make reference to 'environmental quality', then there is also the question of whether *only* humans have them, since it may be argued that among 'resources' are included beings who themselves have rights. The range of questions, both practical and conceptual, concerning fundamental rights is thereby extended quite considerably.

In order to deal with these questions I shall begin this chapter by outlining what seems to me the rational core of the human rights discourse as such, showing, in the first section, how from traditional philosophical arguments for human rights a rationale can be distilled which is not intrinsically tied to the exploitation of nature: the rationale presupposed by any intelligible attribution of human rights, I shall suggest, is that there is a fundamental right of access to the means of life. I shall indicate how this is the case both for the traditional rights of man as proposed, for instance, in the Lockean tradition, and also for the more recently proposed social and economic rights. Then, with specific reference to the questions of equity, futurity and environmental quality, I indicate how the promotion of human rights can actually have advantages for the ecological cause. In the second section objections to this line of argument will be considered. One objection concerns the practicability, and in some ways also the desirability, of a universal right of access to the means of life. On the basis of the ecological consideration that the world's carrying capacity simply cannot support the demands placed on it by current, or imminent, levels of human population, it is objected that to guarantee even the most rudimentary rights to growing numbers of humans will simply prove impossible; indeed, to ward off a bigger problem in the future, it would be morally better not even to try. I examine replies to this argument which suggest there are reasons for thinking human rights may be part of the solution rather than of the problem, so that as long as doubt on this score remains, that objection is uncompelling as a moral argument. The other objection applies to the limiting of rights to humans only; hence the implications are considered of attempting to extend rights to beings other than humans, in particular to other animals. The difficulties involved in seeking to extend the application of rights in this way lead us to consider, thirdly, the appropriateness of continuing to think in terms of rights at all. Traditional forms of scepticism concerning human rights question whether the aims of social justice are best served by an orientation to rights; the question now arises, too, whether the interests of future generations and of non-humans are best served specifically by rights, rather than by being promoted in terms of some other ethical or political discourse. In the third section I argue that this radical line of criticism does place new requirements on the way rights are conceptualized, but does not require their abandonment. I show how a reconstructed conception of rights can meet the main points of the critique and also be compatible with ecological considerations. For human rights can be correlated with human *responsibilities* – responsibilities between humans, and also responsibilities regarding non-human beings and the environment – so that the aims of social justice are actually consonant with and promote ecological sensitivity.

4.1 The Liberal Tradition as a Basis for Rights of Equity, Futurity and Environment

In this section I show that the rationale presupposed by any intelligible attribution of human rights is that there is a fundamental right of access to the means of life. I shall indicate how this is the case both for the traditional rights of man as proposed, for instance, in the Lockean tradition, and also for so-called social and economic rights. Then, with specific reference to equity, futurity and environmental quality, I indicate how the promotion of human rights can actually have advantages for the ecological cause.

The Lockean argument

A particularly influential philosophical exposition of and justification for human rights is John Locke's account of natural rights in his *Second Treatise of Government*. This remains an appropriate starting point, not only because he elaborated at a historically propitious moment the idea that individuals have certain rights in virtue not of political or economic status but of simply being human, but also because he begins from a position where human beings are related first and foremost to their natural conditions of existence and only secondarily to one another. Furthermore, I seek to show, although Locke is generally taken to stand at the head of a tradition which is more to be associated with ecological indifference or malignity than with eco-friendliness,[2] there is in his theory a rationale of justice whose social and ecological implications have not much been appreciated by either his defenders or his critics.

As his starting point for talking about rights, Locke invites us to consider the condition of humans in a state of nature, that is, quite apart from any specific social or political arrangements which might prevail at a particular time or place: there is no hierarchy, and no right of any one to dominate another; humans live together according to the dictates of reason alone; this reason has them respect their reciprocal rights; the only purpose for which government is instituted, according to Locke, is to *protect* them in their natural rights. In these terms Locke articulates the basis of the modern view of humans as individual bearers of inalienable and imprescriptible rights. They have a natural right to self-preservation, and a right not to be interfered with. Rights to life and health follow from the definition of what it is to be human, and liberty is related to the pursuit of a truly human life too.

Locke also claims there is a natural right to possessions, but this, which is potentially at odds with ecological considerations, needs further explanation, since an inalienable right to essentially alienable goods does not follow quite so obviously. In Locke's view there must be such a right because although the world's bounties would originally have been at the disposition of all, it must be possible for individuals to appropriate them in order to make use of them. Locke believes he can establish a connection between external possessions and more intimate human goods, such as health and liberty, by claiming that 'every man has a "property" in his own "person".' From this it follows that the labour of his body is properly his; and, from this, that the fruits of that labour are too: 'Whatsoever, then, he removes out of the state that Nature hath provided and left it in, he hath mixed his labour with it, and joined to it something that is his own, and thereby makes it his property.'[3] Thus, if Locke's man picks an apple to satisfy his hunger, he has a right to enjoy that apple, and this implies a right to exclude others from the enjoyment of this apple. Locke believes this is the only justifiable view to take of the matter:

> Nobody can deny but the nourishment is his. I ask, then, when did they [the apples] begin to be his? when he digested? or when he ate? or when he boiled? or when he brought them home? or when he picked them up? And it is plain, if the first gathering made them not his, nothing else could.

Locke seals his case with a rhetorical flourish:

> Was it robbery thus to assume to himself what belonged to all in common? If such a consent as that was necessary, man had starved, notwithstanding the plenty God had given him.[4]

However, there would seem to be something a bit disingenuous about this. In particular, Locke suggests there is a seamless progression from nourishment back to gathering which is not at all obvious from the perspectives either of common sense or of ecology: for removing apples from the tree or field does not automatically mean they will enter the man's digestive system; there is no necessary connection between two such events at all. The starvation argument therefore does not suffice to make the claim that any apple a man picks is justly his. He might, after all, pick more apples than he could possibly eat. Now Locke acknowledges this possibility, but he does not see it as a reason to abandon the argument. Rather, he seeks to accommodate it by inserting a proviso:

> As much as any one can make use of to any advantage of life before it spoils, so much he may by his labour fix a property in. Whatever is beyond this is more than his share, and belongs to others.[5]

Yet although Locke presents this as a proviso, it actually provides a different principle of just acquisition. For it says that it is what one can *use* that fixes one's share of property: the 'labour mixing' principle thereby appears to be merely the mechanism by means of which one *acquires* what one is already *entitled* to on quite another basis – essentially, one of *need*. On Locke's own account, therefore, there would appear to be a right of access to the means of life, but not necessarily a right to property which exceeds this.

I highlight this point as it is in tension with the message Locke actually wishes to convey, which is that labour mixing can justify expanding one's entitlement to accumulate wealth beyond the limits of consumption of an individual human organism, to include private ownership of land and other major means of production. Locke only moves to this other argument, I now seek briefly to show, by abstracting from ecological considerations, and in two stages.

In the first place, in order to justify the accumulation of wealth, Locke has to find a way round the problem of spoilage, a way of bracketing out ecological considerations such as those which manifest themselves in the perishability of earthly goods. It is here that money is introduced in a key role.[6] Unlike the fruits of nature, money does not decay or perish. For practical purposes, therefore, there is no limit to the amount of money that can be accumulated under the 'no wastage' proviso. This means that an industrious individual can produce and appropriate increasing amounts of perishable goods, take them to market, and convert them into money which may then be amassed and invested in bigger productive operations still. Nevertheless, this argument severs the connection between accumulation and need, and therefore problematizes its justification, which can clearly not, in good faith, continue to make reference to the earlier consideration, 'lest he had starved'.

At this point, though, Locke offers a better justification, turning the wastage argument around to *favour* the industrious accumulator. It is precisely in the exercise of productive labour, he argues, that more of the earth's bounty becomes available for human use – bounty that would otherwise be wasted. He considers it 'a very modest computation to say, that of the products of the earth useful to the life of man, nine-tenths are the effects of labour'.[7] So given that the 'rational and industrious' valorize nature, they have a right to do so to the greatest extent they can: 'the exceeding of the bounds of his just property not lying in the largeness of his possession, but the perishing of anything uselessly in it'.[8] This right, though, depends on an assumption of abundance:

> this 'labour' being the unquestionable property of the labourer, no man but he can have a right to what that is once joined to, *at least where there is enough, and as good left in common for others.*[9]

Locke speaks here as if he considers it a contingent matter that as much and as good is left for others, but he does not consider the implications of matters being otherwise. He does grant that while his assumption – as much and as good is left – will have applied in the past, it does not apply any longer, at least in highly populated lands; but this does not matter, he believes, because the productivity of labour so increases man-made wealth that substitutes are amply available. He assumes, in other words, that there is always abundance – and this is the second, deeper, abstraction from ecological reality.

Thinking about justice and rights in an ecological era means proceeding without an assumption of natural abundance, and there is a question of whether without it appropriation can in fact be justified at all on Lockean grounds. It is possible to argue that if the condition that as much and as good is left for others does not hold now or at any particular time, it can *never* have held. The argument, as presented by Robert Nozick (for his own reasons), runs thus:

> Consider the first person Z for whom there is not enough and as good left to appropriate. The last person Y to appropriate left Z without his previous liberty to act on an object, and so worsened Z's situation. So Y's appropriation is not allowed under Locke's proviso. Therefore the next to last person X to appropriate left Y in a worse position, for X's act ended permissible appropriation. Therefore X's appropriation wasn't permissible

... And so on back to the first person A to appropriate a permanent property right.[10]

This is a particularly significant argument when one has in mind questions of sustainability and rights of future generations. Its implication is that no appropriation of natural goods can ever be justified unless they are both renewable and sufficiently plentiful for all. For one must have an eye to all future possible demands whose prospects of satisfaction could be worsened by our present actions.

A very interesting point to signal here, therefore, is that if the Lockean proviso is given a *stringent* interpretation, it would seem to support quite a radical ecological approach to justice whereby any individual or group would be entitled to satisfy their immediate needs, subject to their doing so with ecological sensitivity and regard to like needs of others, but not to pursue unlimited acquisition.[11] So taking the stringent interpretation makes it appear that Locke was an ecologist *malgré lui*.

However, this suggestion is problematic – Nozick himself was pointing up a problem, not making a proposal – and not just because the spirit of Locke's treatise clearly supports a less stringent, more flexible, interpretation (as I shall shortly discuss), but also because there is reason to question whether ecologists should actually support that stringent requirement. The radical ecological reading of Locke's proviso may actually not be conducive to the best interests of future generations, and may even be counterproductive to the ends of justice. If the present generation were to decide to make natural resources 'untouchable' this could be to the disadvantage of future generations; for although it may be claimed that by being frugal now we are leaving resources for future generations, this will not necessarily be the case if by preventing the development of man-made substitutes for natural wealth in the present, we are compromising their ability to provide for themselves in the future. Moreover, given that we have benefited from past developments which, arguably, have given us the power to make such great decisions autonomously today, we would be acting at best paternalistically by seeking to bind future generations to patterns of life they will not have had the opportunity to choose autonomously. My point, therefore, is that future generations themselves might *want* more than we think they should; and if their populations expand they are anyway likely to *need* to appropriate more. To seek to lay down their lifestyle or dictate their population in advance is a possible course of action for which reasons can be advanced, but – as we shall see in the next section – it is one which does not just place a proviso on human rights, but amounts to a fundamental challenge to the very idea of them.

Remaining for the time being with the hypothesis that fundamental human rights may be desirable and feasible, let us turn to consider a more flexible interpretation of the proviso. In view of the considerations just mentioned, it is arguable that one should be thinking in terms of leaving open *opportunities* to future generations rather than locking them into, say, an ascetic system, and denying them productive capacity that might be generated by transforming resources now. A less stringent interpretation of the proviso allows for substitution of indirect for direct access to means of life.[12] The reasoning might go as follows: suppose that in a hypothetical state of nature one man had land which he worked to yield one ton of potatoes per annum; on that land has since been built a factory now employing a greater number of people, including the land's original tenant, each of whom earns far more per annum than the cost of a ton of potatoes; all are better off; access to the means of life could be said to be enhanced by this arrangement. This, essentially, is the idea of the trickle-down effect whereby industrious entrepreneurs generate wealth which benefits everyone, even if in smaller proportions. However, it is important that *too* much flexibility is not allowed to creep into the interpretation of the proviso. The proviso places two significant limits on accumulation, and on production itself: it requires that the wealth created does actually trickle down and, indeed, that wealth is actually created. The implications of these two points are worth spelling out.

Firstly, a flexible reading of the proviso is no licence for *laissez-faire*, and it yields at most a very qualified justification for private property rights. Certainly, Lockean arguments have been used in support of private property rights, and Nozick summarizes a number of these:

> it increases the social product by putting means of production in the hands of those who can use them most efficiently (profitably); experimentation is encouraged, because with separate persons controlling resources, there is no one person or small group whom someone with a new idea must convince to try it out; private property enables people to decide on the pattern and types of risks they wish to bear, leading to specialized types of risk bearing; private property protects future persons by leading some to hold back resources from current consumption for future markets; it provides alternate sources of employment for unpopular persons who don't have to convince any one person or small group to hire them, and so on.[13]

It should be noticed, though, that most of the advantages claimed for private property pertain to increases in *aggregate* social wealth: none of those stated (apart from the rather dubious one about future generations) address questions of distribution or amount even to a claim that trickle down works. Yet trickle down can only be used as a justification for anything at all on condition that it actually works, and this does not happen automatically. Keekok Lee makes the point:

> Theorists, who advocate the trickle-down theory, are really advocating a particular type of politics to go with the growth, which makes it possible to transfer some of the wealth generated to the worse off . . . The trickle-down theory is, in other words, not so much an empirical thesis about wealth distribution as envisaged by its proponents, but a normative theory which makes sense, and works only, when it is underpinned by a particular type of policy prescription.[14]

The Lockean proviso therefore requires, if the more flexible interpretation is to be admitted, that trickle down be *made* to happen wherever some acquire exclusive rights to the detriment of others. This may go against the grain of libertarian interpretations of Locke; but this simply means that a libertarian position cannot consistently be maintained as an account of justice.

The second point to emphasize is that for wealth to trickle down, real wealth has to have been created in the first place. If ecological misgivings about the limits of substitutability of natural for man-made assets are heeded, then wealth must be understood as a real and sustainable increase in welfare, unaccompanied by excessive costs. This means accumulation has to be controlled in a context of ecological as well as equitable considerations. Ecological concern must be an integral part of a serious concern for social justice.

To sum up, then, Locke's conception of natural justice incorporates two main material criteria: one is the prima facie right of an individual to have access to the resources they need to sustain their own life; the other is the entitlement of an individual to full enjoyment of the fruits of their own labour. Although the latter entitlement has generally been most noted and discussed, we have seen that the concept of need plays a foundational role in Locke's account. This only gets shunted into a secondary or marginal position because of the assumption of abundance. Without that assumption, a theory of rights and justice, even of a broadly Lockean stamp, would have to reverse the priority and make the proviso the major principle, and entitlement subordinate to it.

Liberal rights and equity

A liberal approach to rights of equity and futurity would seek optimal balances within and between two conflicting sets of demand. With a view to the demands of futurity it would steer a mid-course between complete *laissez-faire* in the use of natural resources and stringent prohibitions on their use. Regarding the demands of equity, it would support a degree of wealth redistribution, but within limits: distribution cannot be oriented to the meeting of needs alone, for there would then be no guarantee of wealth generation, so a proportion must go to the industrious, regardless of the needs criterion. Conservation and distribution therefore represent two sets of constraint on the freedom of individuals to produce, consume and accumulate. Yet those freedoms remain of paramount importance to liberals. To strike an optimal balance between these conflicting demands is therefore imperative for liberalism. Rawls's theory of justice can be considered representative of the thrust of contemporary liberalism in that this optimal balance is what it is intended to achieve.

The principle of equity is fundamental to Rawls's theory. In contrast to libertarians like Nozick, he starts with a presumption of equality, which means that any departure from equality in the distribution of basic social goods – liberty and opportunity, income and wealth, and the bases of social respect – requires a justification.[15] But he does recognize that equality is not always necessarily advantageous, since it is possible to have unequal situations in which the worst off is better than anyone in an equal society. Hence equality can justly be departed from when everyone benefits – or, to put it another way, when trickle down works. His second principle of justice, accordingly, provides that inequalities can be justified when it is reasonable to expect they will work out to everyone's advantage. Rawls stresses, though, that *every* party must gain from any inequality, and excludes the possibility of justifying inequalities on the grounds that disadvantages of some are outweighed by greater advantages of others. In this he is unequivocally a defender of inviolable *rights* against any possible utilitarian calculation.

Nevertheless, whatever the desirability in principle of rights of equity, there are problems when these are understood as referring to substantive needs rather than merely formal equalities. Rights, essentially, are justified claims correlative to duties on the part of others;[16] yet the fact that one person *needs* something does not of itself or self-evidently imply that any other person has a duty – legal, moral or customary – to arrange for the satisfaction of that need. The mere existence or perception of a need does not alone suffice to generate any obligation. Other requirements include the need having such moral weight as to warrant placing constraints on others' behaviour; the persons to be bound by them being identifiable; and those persons being in a position to carry out the action/forbearance which is morally required.

Now it has sometimes been argued that meeting these conditions is more difficult for certain classes of rights than for others. Indeed, this problem is at the root of a long-standing division in the interpretation of which rights are genuinely human rights. On the one hand is the class of rights of non-interference which appear to be relatively unproblematic. Such rights – for instance, rights not to be tortured, not to be held in slavery, to worship whatever god one believes in, to marry whom one will, to think freely and express one's views, and so on – can in principle be held and respected by all. These are rights of individuals, essentially, to be left alone. There is no problem here of identifying who the duty bearers are because *everyone* has a duty not to interfere, bodily or morally, with any other. Moreover, they are 'non-zero-sum' goods: no matter how many people enjoy them, there is never any competition for resources involved. The enjoyment of these rights involves no trade-offs, in principle, with other people's rights or legitimate interests. All that is required of others is that they do not interfere with an individual's person and property: hence not only are the duties clear and the duty bearers identifiable, there need also be no problem of practicability. These rights of personal security and civil liberty make up the core of the liberal tradition, and are enshrined, for example, in the first twenty articles of the UN Declaration.

On the other hand, however, are rights which some theorists see as being qualitatively different: these are not simply rights of an individual not to be interfered with, but rights to be more actively done by in some way.[17] These are often referred to as social and economic rights; among them are a right to work, a right to education, a right to an adequate standard of living. Here it is not simply a case of individuals being left alone by other individuals or governments, for the *provision* of some substantive goods is also involved. Hence Maurice Cranston, for instance, argues that whilst such provision may be desirable, where it is possible, it is not appropriately spoken of as a universal human right. It is, he claims, conceptually mistaken to consider social and economic rights as human rights; moreover, attempting to portray them as such, he asserts, can only bring the whole discourse of human rights into disrepute – for whilst they may articulate desirable ideals, they are not and cannot be enforceable rights. His main argument is this:

The traditional 'political and civil rights' can ... be readily secured by legislation ... Since those rights are for the most part rights against government interference with a man's activities, a large part of the legislation needed has to do no more than restrain the government's own executive arm. This is no longer the case when we turn to the 'right to work', the 'right to social security', and so forth. For a government to provide social security it needs to do more than make laws; it has to have access to great capital wealth, and many governments in the world today are still poor.[18]

Cranston's argument against including social and economic rights among human rights has the virtue (if we may call it that) of presenting with brutal simplicity the bottom line of the view of human rights which actually underlies the foreign policy of Western governments.[19] On this view, the simple fact is that if, for example, you are one of the 480 million inhabitants of India you just cannot claim 'a standard of living adequate for the health and well-being of [yourself] and [your] family'[20] as a human right because your government does not have access to great capital wealth; even if you are one of those millions in the Third World (and not only there) who have been deprived of their erstwhile livelihood by the economic manoeuvres of the rich world's multinational companies you have no grounds to claim a right to work. So, Cranston argues, whilst social and economic rights 'may be the moral rights of some men' – those who live in affluent countries – they are not universal rights: while it may be desirable to extend them further, he says, 'this matter is correctly seen as a problem of *socialization* or *democratization* – that is, the extension of privileges and immunities – rather than as a problem about the universal rights of all men.'[21]

It is in fact true that social and economic rights come into existence through processes of socialization and democratization. Cranston's mistake, though, is to suppose that civil and political rights do not; on his view it would be inexplicable why, for instance, there were ever historical struggles for the abolition of slavery or the achievement of universal suffrage. In the last analysis, Cranston's argument amounts to an apologetic defence of some human rights against others on grounds which are merely arbitrary and ideological.

By contrast, it has been convincingly argued by Henry Shue that the division of human rights into civil/political and social/economic is intellectually bankrupt and misleading in a number of respects. For instance, he notes, some rights seem to be neither economic nor political in any very strict sense, and others – such as the right to form labour unions or the right to own private property – are both economic and political.

Moreover, not only can the protection of civil and political rights itself be very expensive in some circumstances – especially in societies under pressures arising from social and economic inequalities – but the removal of obstacles to social and economic independence can itself generate wealth.

But if the dichotomous distinction within human rights breaks down, it is not a case of inverting the priority between the two supposed kinds of rights. Rather, if priorities are to be assigned, a more appropriate criterion is that of basicness. Shue characterizes basic rights as 'everyone's minimum reasonable demands upon the rest of humanity': they are 'social guarantees against actual and threatened deprivations of at least some basic needs'.[22] Rights are basic in Shue's sense when the enjoyment of them is essential to the enjoyment of any other rights. He identifies three basic rights in this sense: rights to subsistence, security and liberty. His argument, essentially, is that in order to enjoy any other rights at all, an individual has to be physically secure, able to think, move and act freely, and have adequate nourishment and shelter. Unless these basic rights are guaranteed for all, there can be no genuinely universal human rights. A significant aspect of this approach is that the argument which establishes – against the dominant view of Western governments, as expressed by Cranston – that subsistence rights are basic in this sense, is the same as the reasoning which justifies treating security and liberty as basic. We see, then, that equity can and must be pursued as an essential aim of human rights.

Rights of future generations

To establish rights of future generations involves further complications. Can or should we meet their needs? Can or should we leave them alone? No straightforward answer can be given to such questions, for although we may suppose that any future generation will wish to arrive at an optimal balance of need and entitlement, productivity and conservation, we are not in a position to arrive at substantive decisions *for them* about the appropriate balance. To seek to do so would not be desirable, being a paternalistic encroachment on their autonomy; nor, more crucially, would it be possible, given our radical uncertainty about their available technologies, their populations and so on. On the other hand, though, we cannot proceed in total disregard of them; our acts and omissions will have effects on them, and we must seek to estimate these to the extent possible. If we assume that, other things being equal,[23] we have responsibilities to future persons akin to those we have to those living, then the answer to the general question would be that our obligation is to bequeath the best conditions possible for them to be in a position to make optimal decisions. This still involves a number of variables and unknowns, but it is an objective towards which there is some prospect of making headway. Again, Rawls provides a helpful framework within which to think about these issues. This time, though, we are concerned not so much with his principles themselves as with the procedures for arriving at them.

A reason why a number of commentators have considered Rawls's theory of justice a promising basis for theorizing the rights of future generations is that it is a *procedural* theory: it does not simply offer a definition of justice, but aims to account for the appropriate processes of reasoning and deliberating about justice which yield principles that would be settled on *by anyone* reasoning about justice. Because of the nature of these processes, interests of future generations can in principle make themselves heard on a par with interests of those alive. Rawls's proceduralism begins by identifying the conditions under which *just decisions* can and must be arrived at. In his ideal decision-making situation – the 'original position' – rationally self-motivated individuals debate what would be the basic structures of a society which would be as fair as possible for everyone within it. They do so behind a 'veil of ignorance', so although they are familiar with the basic facts of socio-economic life, they do not know what their own individual abilities, psychological propensities, material condition or position in that society will be. What is particularly relevant in the present context is that they will also be ignorant of the generation in which they live. They will therefore 'ask themselves how much they would be willing to save at each stage of advance [of the civilization] on the assumption that all other generations are to save at the same rates'.[24] They will work out a 'just savings rate' which improves the lot of each succeeding generation, without imposing undue hardship on any earlier generation. If Rawls's assumption here that societies will tend indefinitely to 'advance' is qualified so that not only the saving of benefits for future generations are considered, but also the need to save them from burdens and harms, then it seems that Rawls's procedure offers the constructive possibility of permitting the 'virtual participation', so to speak, of other generations in deliberations about resource use.

In a suitably qualified original position, as Bryan Norton has argued, rational choosers would opt for a midway position between stringency and exploitationism in the use of natural resources. An exploitationist or *laissez-faire* approach would not be chosen unless there was an assumption of abundance, such that resources for future generations would never run out; and it seems reasonable to assume that one of the facts of life with which persons in the original position are familiar is the finitude of earthly goods. Still, future shortages could be exaggerated, and continuing technological advances could create substitutes and hence man-made abundance; so although the assumption of abundance should be rejected, the substitutability of resources makes the question of exploitation a matter of degree, and so the choosers would not opt for an ultra-stringent position either, since this could yield an unnecessary amount of pain for too little gain.

Norton's own view is that consensus would settle on 'a society that imposes some pre-emptive constraints to protect biological diversity across generations'.[25] This would be consistent with a holistic Leopoldian approach which is wary of diminution of biological diversity over time. Within these constraints, though, each generation may choose its own strategy of resource use, which therefore minimizes the risk of paternalism in providing conditions for future generations. The advantage of adopting a Rawlsian approach in real-life contemporary debates, Norton believes, is that with the explicit thematizing of basic assumptions, discussion can focus on disagreements about matters of substance, and hence potentially anticipate increasing agreement.

Environmental rights

In talking about rights of future generations, one is already addressing matters of environmental concern. From the foregoing it will be evident that a sensitivity to the needs of future generations is bound up with sensitivity to transboundary obligations, to the global effects of local action, and to the need for assessing environmental impact and for preserving local environments. The question is whether it is appropriate to think of environmental concern in terms of human rights. Traditionally human rights were concerned only with human liberty and welfare, not with nature. By 1972, though, the United Nations Conference on the Human Environment in Stockholm declared as a first principle 'the fundamental right to freedom, equality, and adequate conditions of life, in an environment of a quality that permits a life of dignity and well-being'.[26] The language of rights in the context of environmental concern came up again, prominently, in the Brundtland Report. The first of the principles it proposes for international law is: 'All human beings have the fundamental right to an environment adequate for their health and well-being.'[27]

The right to an adequate environment now seems quite firmly on the agenda. The connection between environmental concern and the other concerns promoted in terms of human rights are becoming increasingly evident. It is thus particularly pertinent to note how the abuse, exploitation, and degradation of nature so often goes hand in hand with neglect or violation of the fundamental economic, social, or cultural rights of people. Thus William Aiken notes that in poor countries, in particular, environmentalism has become entwined with the struggle to ensure basic rights for the underprivileged and disenfranchised. He adds that the recognition of a right to an adequate environment may reveal other rights abuses which call for remediation: for instance there are cases of indigenous peoples, the destruction of whose environment 'entails the violation of their human rights as they lose their habitat and their means of sustenance, their social systems and their religious practices'.[28] Similarly, Ted Benton argues that the notion of environmental rights could be used to protect small, relatively self-sufficient communities with well-defined local ecological conditions of life.[29] Accordingly, he believes, environmental rights should extend to the preservation of the ecological integrity of a sufficient geographical terrain for the living of the social life of each subpopulation of our species.

Another reason for promoting environmental rights identified by Aiken is that 'it can prevent solving environmental problems in ways that merely shift the resultant environment damage to other peoples (e.g. exporting toxic waste), or to future peoples (e.g. inadequate storage of nuclear waste), since such action will violate their rights to an adequate environment.'[30] Under the rights approach, third parties who suffer the effects of others' actions may legitimately make claim to redress and compensation.

Finally, not to be disregarded are the pragmatic advantages of using a discourse of rights. Because it is familiar and well established, Aiken points out, 'we know how to proceed with this model of conflict resolution: establish priority rules, specify defeasibility and mitigatory conditions, create arbitration procedures and mechanisms, and then provide for appeal, redress, and compensation.'[31]

In short, there are reasons of both principle and practice to take an affirmative view of environmental rights.

Problems

The right to an adequate environment fits easily into traditional human rights concerns. As Aiken points out, this is simply to insert an environmental aspect into the familiar and time tested tradition of human rights by treating an adequate environmental quality as an entitlement of all persons. This, though, is itself an indication of the problems with which the rest of this chapter will be concerned. From an ecological perspective, it can be objected that while this right may appear to establish some special status for the environment, it does not really go beyond the view that the environment is just a resource which humans have a right to use for their benefit. Moreover, this emphasis on human welfare seems to be linked in practice to a continued commitment to the ideology of growth and progress. These considerations may be mitigated by the point that a truly *enlightened* conception of human interest would preserve the environment into the future: Norton's arguments for the rights of future generations would provide for this. However, these will not hold against more radical lines of objection which can be taken. One is that because the very *existence* of future generations is at issue, Norton's qualified Rawlsianism cannot assume that all generations are represented at the outset in the original position; more stringent constraints on present rights than he allows may therefore be justified. Another objection is that the makers and the beneficiaries of the 'rational decisions' being exclusively humans, the whole procedure is radically biased against non-humans from the outset: thus Rawlsianism, even as qualified by Norton, can be criticized for smuggling in substantive assumptions about who and what counts in the world in the guise of pure rational procedure. In fact, as we shall see in the next section, its presuppositions may be criticized not only on ecological, but also on social grounds: for although the connection between ecological harm and social injustice has been presented in this section as a reason for a rights approach, there is a well-established tradition of critical thought which views liberal rights as part of the problem rather than its solution.

4.2 Ecological Challenges to Human Rights

In this section I consider two lines of objection to the affirmative account of fundamental rights just outlined. They both can claim to derive from ecological considerations, and each in its way concerns the range of beings who are eligible to bear these rights. The force and direction of the two, though, are quite different. The basic problem underlying the first objection is that natural ecosystems have a limited carrying capacity which simply cannot support all the demands of a growing human population, and so cannot necessarily support all the rights they might want to claim either. The implications of this would be to reduce the role of fundamental rights in both ethical and ecological thought since the consistent pursuit of the full range of human rights, for all human beings, would be ecologically unsustainable and ultimately self-defeating. The second objection, by contrast, is that if humans are considered to have fundamental rights, then so too should non-humans – at least some of them. If humans have a right of access to the means of life, then perhaps other beings do too; indeed, one should consider whether among 'resources' there are not beings who might also have some claim of a right of access to the means of *their* life. This suggestion is examined and found quite compelling. It does appear to intensify the problem identified in the first objection, though, so that by extending the potential range of rights bearers even further the very notion of fundamental rights may be called into question. That question, though, will be reserved for the subsequent section.

Ecological constraints and neo-Malthusian objections

I have argued that all human rights, in crucial respects, must stand or fall together. The reasons why rights to freedom and subsistence might yet fall together have to do with questions of scarcity and natural limits. The concept of human rights outlined in the previous section has a fairly evident difficulty. There is claimed to be a universal human right of access to the means of life; but if the means of life are finite, then the number of beings they can support is finite. It may therefore be seriously misleading to speak of a universal right here. Thus a fundamental objection, if not immediately to human rights as such, at least to a too zealous pursuit of them, can be framed with reference to the ecological concept of 'carrying capacity', that is, the maximum population which can be supported on a given area of land of a given character. This idea informs the views of some highly influential 'ecological' writers.

For a classic statement of the problem we may turn to Garrett Hardin's much-discussed essay, 'The Tragedy of the Commons'. This essay allows us to see how perennial themes of social and political thought acquire a new poignancy in the context of ecological limits. Problems pertaining to the 'commons' are relevant to a range of ecological questions, and to questions of scarcity more generally. The tragedy of the commons is a parable depicting the situation of a medieval cattle herder who, along with his neighbours, has free access and equal rights to graze his cattle on commonly owned pasture. To begin with, the number of cattle is such that they consume the grass at the same rate as it grows, and everything is fine. The herder then reasons, though, that if he adds a further cow, then considerable benefits will accrue to him, while most of the costs will be spread over all the other herders and thereby appear negligible. It is therefore rational for him to do this. However, if it is rational for one herder to do this, it will be rational for each of the others to do the same, with the consequence that the commons becomes hopelessly overgrazed. What makes this a tragedy, Hardin says, is the *inevitability* of the destruction of communally owned resources if humans are left to act freely:

> Each man is locked into a system that compels him to increase his [use of the commons] without limit – in a world that is limited. Ruin is the destination to which all men rush, each pursuing his own best interest in a society that believes in the freedom of the commons. Freedom in a commons brings ruin to all.[32]

Now with the problem posed in these terms, the range of solutions Hardin is able to foresee is limited. He thinks the survival of the earth, in a condition capable of supporting confortable human life, depends on the emergence of a managerial elite armed with powers to regulate human behaviour in ways that would not be possible as long as individuals were left free and to their own devices. He does not believe a solution will be found in a democracy, where individual freedom prevails, since rational actors will act according to the same logic as the herdsman.[33] Democratically removable governments, moreover, are unlikely ever to take the serious long-term steps necessary if they have to seek re-election in the shorter term.

If Hardin sees no way of avoiding the tragedy of the commons which is compatible with freedom and democracy, nor is there one compatible with all the aspirations of human rights. Even the most rudimentary right of reproductive freedom must be called into question, Hardin believes. In fact, one of the first tasks of the managerial elite must be to restrict reproductive freedom.

Hardin is one of a number of theorists who think that the most fundamental cause of ecological crises is excessive growth of human populations. On this view, neither technological advances nor social transformations could ward off ecological crisis: this could only be averted by population control. There are influential writers – in affluent countries with stable populations, like the USA – who call for particularly tough measures, arguing that the population problem is so serious that governments which are unable or unwilling to take the necessary steps should be encouraged to do so, by others which are, with whatever inducements prove necessary. Thus Paul Ehrlich has argued that controls must be imposed at any cost:

> We must have population control at home, hopefully through a system of incentives or penalties, but by compulsion if voluntary methods fail ... We (i.e. the United States) must use our political power to push other countries into programs which continue agricultural development and population control.[34]

Ehrlich has been prepared to contemplate the use of economic and military power to this end; one weapon he has advocated is 'triage' – the granting of food aid 'not to the poorest nations but only to those with both an aggressive population policy and clear hope of obtaining food self-sufficiency'.[35] The application of such pressures is claimed to be supported not only by ecological, but also by ethical considerations.

There is a basic Malthusian argument subscribed to by writers like Hardin and Ehrlich which casts serious doubts not only on the workability of guaranteed universal subsistence rights, but also on the wisdom or desirability of them, on the grounds that taking steps to stave off starvation now will only result in a far greater starvation problem in the future.[36] The claiming of a universal human right to subsistence is therefore self-defeating, hence unrealizable, and so cannot be spoken of without wilful disingenuousness as a *right*. The basic argument is that it is not possible to guarantee everyone a right to subsistence – or hence even to life – if, quite simply, there are too many people for available resources. Such is the situation of the world today, it is held, and it can only get worse. Therefore a too zealous pursuit of subsistence rights in those areas where they are not currently enjoyed would be counterproductive: it would entail the survival of *more* people, and reproduction of *even more* people, who would eventually be unable to enjoy the right to subsistence. The conclusion of this reasoning is that it is not moral to store up this greater catastrophe for future generations, and its implication is that it is better to let some die off now to let nature restore a balance – thus avoiding that even more die later. The neo-Malthusian argument is that it is better to let nature take its course rather than seek to intervene.

Hardin believes it is questionable morality to increase the food supply given the unsustainable pressure this would directly and indirectly place on scarce natural resources. He further develops this theme with his idea of a 'lifeboat ethic'. This has been summarized by O'Riordan:

> allegorical lifeboats filled with the world's rich people are surrounded by the struggling poor who are desperately trying to clamber aboard. His

'ethics' pertain to how the rich behave. They cannot let everyone in because the lifeboats have a limited capacity; if they allow some people on board they remove the lifeboats' safety margin, and anyway they still have to choose by some means the fortunate few who are to be saved. To Hardin the only realistic solution is to ignore the pleas for aid and retain the spare capacity.[37]

A universal right to subsistence is thereby unequivocally ruled out. In fact, universal rights as such are ruled out either explicitly or implicitly, for Hardin's argument will not only bite against subsistence rights, but will have some chilling implications regarding civil and political rights too. So if, as I have argued, there is good reason to think that social/ economic and civil/political rights must stand together, the neo-Malthusians' arguments would have them fall.

Nevertheless, these arguments can be answered, and there remain reasons to believe that human rights may yet survive. If the need for population control is undeniable – since it is inconceivable that the world's population might continue to expand unchecked without sooner or later giving rise to catastrophe – there is still room for doubt not only whether neo-Malthusianism offers the morally most acceptable solution but even whether it would be practically the most effective. Considering first the morality, the justification for solutions like triage is put forward in terms of lifeboat ethics. If we grant for the moment the assumption that the world is like a lifeboat, in that it can only carry a certain number of people, there is the question of whom it is to carry and why. If it is to carry those who are already on board, then why them and not the others? The answer to this is straightforward: the selection of those on board is taken care of by the accident of being born in an affluent nation. There is no other morally relevant difference that has seriously been advanced.[38] Yet if there is no specifically *moral* reason, there are still questions that might be asked. For instance, if the cause of overloading a lifeboat is accumulation of excess *weight*, then there is a prima facie reason for thinking that differences of weight could have moral relevance. It could be argued that two morally equal individuals, who together weigh no more than a third morally equal individual, have twice the right of that single individual to be aboard. Indeed, if there were the strange situation where one individual weighed as much as 40 others, there would seem no reason to prefer the heavy individual, and some reason to prefer the 40. This is arguably precisely the situation of the real world's lifeboat: if wealthy populations consume as much as 40 times more resources per capita than poorer populations, then in effect each weighs 40 times more heavily on the earth-lifeboat.[39] There would be an argument for allowing more of the lighter people on board, or bringing coercive weight-reduction measures to bear on the others. This may not be a particularly good argument, but it does bring into sharp relief how Hardin's is even worse!

The moral privilege of those on board seems even less well-founded when their wealth and the others' poverty is viewed as to some extent a product of exploitative and oppressive relations in the past and the present. Neo-Malthusians, though, typically do not consider this at all.[40]

These considerations are intended to suggest not that there is no problem, but that the way it is characterized by neo-Malthusians is seriously inadequate. Alternative characterizations are possible, which take into account a fuller range of factors. For instance, there is strong evidence to suggest that population growth rates stabilize and may even decline in societies where there is a degree of *affluence* in the society; but whereas population growth is low, even tendentially negative, among affluent nations, it is high among the poor nations. This appears to be due to the fact that most of the reasons for having a large family have to do with a lack of economic security; once econonic pressures are removed, people prefer to have far fewer children. Henry Shue has pointed out that over-population is normally one part of a vicious circle also composed of poverty and malnutrition.[41] Given this, one might ask if it is really true that more extensive subsistence rights would fuel the problem. Certainly, in the present, the death rate would fall: but there are also reasons for believing that with a fall in the death rate, and with an increased sense of economic security, the pressures towards having large families would be reduced. It might well then be the case that improved access to means of life – that is, the substance of subsistence rights – could actually militate *against* the factors which encourage population growth. This hypothesis is lent further support when the situation of women is taken into consideration. It has been shown that there is a fairly simple and direct correlation between the degree of denial of their access to means of life and the rate at which they give birth. By denial of access to means of life we may understand not only the direct economic pressures just mentioned – which affect men too – but also the various kinds of heteronomy to which only women are subject: for example what Illich has called 'domestic enclosure', the pressures of the dominant culture or husband to produce more offspring than they would freely choose;[42] it also seems pertinent to include under the heading 'access to means of life' the access to control over the very reproduction of life, over one's own body. Birch and Cobb have gone so far as to suggest: 'If there were a serious commitment to justice for women, the problem of population would largely take care of itself.'[43] This may or may not be overstating the case, but there is a sufficient element of truth here to warrant advocating that serious commitment.

On the basis of these considerations it appears possible that social and economic, especially subsistence, rights, instead of being the problem, may actually be part of its solution.[44] We may have no way of ruling out the possibility of future overpopulation, but we can be reasonably assured that future generations will be better able to deal with such a threat – by controlling their birth rate – if they are not subject to conflicting economic pressures against doing so: if, that is, they have sufficient access to the means of life.

Given that the known facts do not definitively support the population objection, the moral options appear to be these: either to give a try to the extension of subsistence rights, seeking to spare existing populations from starvation and hoping that subsequent generations will also be spared; or else to refuse to give it a try on the grounds that the lesser evil now prevents the greater evil later. Given that the factual basis of the projections of an inevitable greater evil is anything but conclusive, it is in my view the greatest cynicism even to speak of (with or without intellectually sophisticated euphemisms) the present malnutrition of so many million human men, women and children as a lesser evil. In as much as the objection is presented as a moral argument it is, I think, quite evidently bankrupt.[45]

In so far, though, as population growth does indeed present a serious global problem, it needs above all to be properly understood. The neo-Malthusians who see population growth as an essential cause of contemporary ecological ills seem to disregard the fact that population growth itself has causes, and that these might usefully be addressed. Accordingly, rather than oscillating between empty moral exhortation and unjustified coercion, it could be helpful to follow Shue's advice and see population growth in context – rather more holistically – as part of a vicious circle driven by social and economic pressures. Here Marx's response to Malthus bears repeating. Where Malthus arithmetically relates a specific quantity of people to a specific quantity of resources, Marx affirms that the fact is:

that the quantity of grain available is completely irrelevant to the worker if he has no *employment*; that it is therefore the means of employment and not of subsistence which put him into the category of surplus population.[46]

Viewed in this light, it is arguable that the population question only becomes a moral issue at all if it is already assumed that there is a right of access to means of life.

With this reinforcement and expansion of human rights, however, the grounds of the second objection are intensified: if humans are according themselves more and more rights, overcoming various obstacles, what about the *other* beings who are squeezed out or treated as resources?

Rights of non-humans

By no means all radical ecologists raise principled objections to human rights as such. What many do argue, however, is that if human beings are considered as having rights, then so too should non-human beings. Certainly, the attribution of rights to animals, or plants, or even the land itself, will depend on the degree of 'ecological consciousness' of a society, and its readiness to redefine relations between humans and nature; but it is not inconceivable to speak of the juridical title of all manner of beings other than humans to be protected from humans.[47] Moreover, as Leopold pointed out, in the course of history there has been a continuous expansion in the categories of being deemed to be bearers of fundamental rights – slaves, women, children, Black people, mentally handicapped – all of whom were at some time denied moral citizenship. Of course, though, these categories all belong to the same species. The question I shall focus on here is how successfully rights can cross the species barrier, and for this reason I shall look primarily at the arguments concerning fundamental rights of animals.[48]

The case for animal rights has been set out fully and forcefully by Tom Regan. He believes that rights can be extended to (other) animals without any radical redefinition of what rights are. Thus whereas sometimes the idea of animal rights is used in a fairly loose sense, meaning only that animals should somehow count in human deliberations,[49] Regan aims to make a much tighter connection with fundamental human rights, to put animal liberation on a par with movements for human liberation. He sees the advocacy of animal rights as more radical than other forms of animal concern, and he spells out how it goes beyond them. For one thing, it has to go further than the aims of anti-cruelty movements which campaign against the inflicting of pain on animals. This is a necessary, but not a sufficient aim. One consideration is that unless pain were entirely obliterated, there would remain occasions when one being's pain needed to be weighed against another's, which would be likely to leave animals in a precarious position. Regan also highlights

how legislation that has been passed against animal cruelty has been
vitiated by definitions of cruelty in terms of unnecessary or unjustified
pain, inflicted wantonly or maliciously, thereby leaving too much scope
for people to claim necessity and justification for inflicting pain on other
animals. Moreover, cruelty is not the only problem: there is also an
absence of obligation to *promote the good* of other animals. He quotes St
Francis:

> Not to hurt our humble brethren is our first duty to them, but to stop there
> is not enough. We have a higher mission – to be of service to them
> wherever they require it.[50]

This, says Regan, captures the essential principle of those who stand for
animal welfare. Pro-welfarism can therefore be distinguished from anti-
cruelty. Yet if animal welfare means more than an end to cruelty, it too
has its limitations: for instance, its pursuit is consistent with utilizing
animals for human ends, and even killing them if, in life, they have fared
well.

Regan thus argues that there is a fundamental moral difference
between the advocacy of animal rights, on the one hand, and concerns
centred either on anti-cruelty or on welfare, on the other. The animal
rights position is distinctive, he says, in that individuals are never
morally expendable; they are regarded as having an inviolable right to be
treated with respect. He thus harnesses what is claimed as a great
strength of rights-based moralities in intrahuman contexts – the inalienable trumping power of the individual. For Regan, this moral position
issues in a radical challenge to existing human practices as they relate to
animals. For the aim must be not simply to ameliorate the conditions of
animals with which humans have dealings, but to liberate them from
human usage altogether: 'We are abolitionists,' says Regan, 'not
reformists.'[51]

There is a question, though, as to how compatible the aims of rights
and the aims of abolitionism really are. Robert Garner has discussed this
problem. On the one hand, he says, the fact that animal rights must trump
considerations of mere legality or property rights follows self-evidently
from their definition, and activists are therefore quite justified in taking
direct action – legal or illegal – against institutions which abuse animal
rights. On the other hand, though, he argues that there *is* also scope for
reform within prevailing laws which should not be ignored. In particular,
there is 'an opportunity for reformers gradually to extend the range of
activities which humans regard as unnecessary'.[52] Thus Garner places
weight on education and information, and emphasizes that activists must

continue to win over public opinion, 'since only when people's attitudes towards animals change, and this is reflected in their consumer and voting behaviour, will the greater protection for animals ... become a realistic proposition.'[53] He claims that 'the animal protection movement has achieved most in recent years when it has sought to challenge the importance (and sometimes the very existence) of the benefits it is claimed humans derive from making animals suffer rather than from the ethically-based denial that humans have a right to benefit from such suffering.'[54] This, of course, is the view of those who claim that what is necessary is the *enlightenment* of human self-interest – not its abnegation. Reformists may accordingly take encouragement from how a great many of the practices condemned by animal rightists are now recognized as superfluous to, or inconsistent with, genuine human interests. Public consensus in many places is already being mobilized, for instance, against the exploitation of animals in zoos, circuses and dolphinaria; against factory farming; against animal testing for cosmetics; against the fur industry; against hunting and culling wild creatures. However, this does not go as far as required by the rights view, which would prohibit as immoral not only practices like these, but also the using of animals for food and experimentation for vital human needs. The exploitation of animals, even when substantial human benefits do accrue, is inimical to those who hold a rights view. They make the principled objection that participating in reforms to ameliorate the conditions of animals is morally wrong because it gives implicit assent to practices which are in themselves immoral. Anything short of abolition is complicity.

Yet this yields the dilemma that abolitionism might require a sacrifice of some rights within the existing system in order to get a better system. A testing question then is, as Garner points out, whether it is justifiable, without knowing if the greater objective will be realized – nor, indeed, whether a strategy of gradual reform may not actually be the path to the eventual abolition of all exploitative practices – to allow greater suffering now, 'in the hope that it *may* yield long-term gain?'[55] There are evident parallels between this dilemma of animal liberation and dilemmas which have often been faced by those struggling in spheres of human liberation: whether radical and revolutionary aims are promoted or hindered by interim reform; whether immediate sacrifices, or even the use of unpleasant means, are justified by the ends. Hence questions arise as to whether the aims of animal liberation are in fact best served by an orientation specifically to *rights*.

This is a question examined by Ted Benton. Benton believes there is the basis of an ethical and political alliance between not only animal rightists and environmentalists, but also radicals in the sphere of *human* liberation; yet he also stresses that if the liberationary aims of animal rights are to be put on a par with struggles for women's rights, black people's rights and civil liberties more generally, then it will be necessary also to settle accounts with the well-entrenched *critique* of rights within radical human emancipatory movements. Thus a central question for Benton is why, on the one hand, radicals should be prepared to talk about animal rights when they have trouble even with the idea of *human* rights; on the other, it can be asked what the use is of rights for animals if rights are already of only limited use to humans. Benton points out that very often animals, like some human groups, are systematically disadvantaged by socio-economic structures of power such that even granting rights will not achieve substantive protection. It is social and economic relations which enable and foster abuse. An important point here is how the problem is a *structural* one of power and property relations. Animal rights abuses, like human rights abuses, tend not to be perpetrated by isolated individuals on other isolated individuals. Very often the individuals participating in an abusive practice are not individually culpable. In factory farming, for instance, 'the supplier of nutrients, the electrician, the veterinarian, and so on can all act with a good conscience about their individual contribution so long as the ethical legitimacy of the practice as a whole is not called into question.'[56] On the other hand, the victims of abuse are not always readily identifiable individuals. For example, humans alter other animals' habitats, both intentionally and unintentionally, knowingly and unknowingly; they also bring about more diffuse environmental changes which affect all species. Hence Benton is sceptical about how much use any appeal to rights could be in such circumstances. He notes that the rights discourse has prospects of success in some areas – for example, in protecting wild animals from hunters or protecting domestic pets from cruelty. But even in these cases the radical critique has a purchase. As regards wild animals, claiming these rights, under prevailing conditions, would lead to dismantling the security of their semi-wild habitat: hence the objective of protecting them would be better achieved by a 'broader strategy for large-scale shifts in patterns of land ownership', and so on. As regards pets, the effectiveness of rights is extremely limited by the privateness of any abuse – and Benton notes parallels here with domestic abuse of women and children. To counter this, he suggests, it would be hard to stop short of 'calling into question the institution of private property itself in relation to this class of being'.[57] Hence, it would seem that here, too, a transformation of the social relations of power and dependency which characterize the private, domestic sphere would be more effective than merely formal protections of rights. In the case of medical experimentation, commodity product testing and intensive farming methods, Benton argues, the need to foreground social-relational and economic conditions is even more clear-cut.

On Benton's view, the problem with the animal rights perspective is not that it purports to offer protection too widely, but rather that it is too restrictive in the purchase it gives to moral concern. For this reason, in seeking substantive rather than merely formal protections, he is prepared to restrict the discourse of animal rights more than Regan does. For example, because Benton's position recognizes their coevolution and interdependency with humans, the keeping of domestic animals does not necessarily violate conditions of their well-being. Hence 'liberation' is not always appropriate. 'The concern in such cases would be to ensure a proper moral regulation of those practices, rather than to seek their abolition.'[58] However, in cases where abolition is appropriate, then one must be *more* radical than Regan, and seek 'quite deep-level transformations of human social and economic arrangements, structures of power and patterns of land occupancy and use'.[59]

Benton has shown how animals may assume a place on environmentalist and radical political agendas. Moreover, his argument seriously challenges received wisdom. Hitherto a widespread view has been that if categories like rights are already problematic in their application to humans, then there is little sense in even trying to apply them to animals. Benton, essentially, overturns this logic: if such moral discourses are in fact problematic for humans, then their being difficult for animals too is not necessarily a reason for abandoning the attempt to apply them.

Problems with animal rights

There are, however, some objections that can be made to the extension of fundamental rights to animals, questioning their moral desirability, their practicability or their necessity.

One line of objection to animal rights takes issue with their desirability. It is sometimes pointed out, for instance, that there is a strongly rooted moral intuition in humans that others of their species are of greater value – all other things being equal, at least – than beings of other species. Moreover, even if it were possible to change this to grant equal rights to members of other species, there would not be any strong moral case for doing so, given that other species presumably give a similar priority to their own kind. To put animal rights on a par with struggles for women's rights, black people's rights or civil liberties, some argue, is morally offensive. In reply to this objection, it can be granted that some rights may override others, and that rights of humans may often override rights of non-humans, as long as the grounds for doing so are not speciesist – that is, not arbitrarily derived from species differences. There must always be the possibility, for any discourse of rights, of deciding priorities between potentially competing rights. Hence even Regan only claims that animal rights are prima facie, not absolute.[60]

Another objection to animal rights is that they are not practicable. For one thing, animals cannot claim rights on their own behalf. This can make a qualitative difference between campaigns for animal rights or liberation and the struggles of oppressed groups of humans. As Benton points out, whereas humans who suffer oppression are able themselves to articulate and press their own claims, there is an inescapable moment of paternalism in the attribution of rights to non-human animals.[61] Oppressed humans are able to correct any misconceptions on the part of their sympathizers about their aims; animals are generally not. Furthermore, the objectives of human struggles generally have to do with kinds of rights – civil, political, social, economic – which appear to be specific to human agents, and which non-human animals are intrinsically incapable of exercising. In reply, it can be pointed out that these problems also apply in varying degrees to the positing and claiming of rights for those humans – for example, children, mentally handicapped, temporarily incapacitated and others – who may not be able to claim rights for themselves. For this reason the objection is not specifically damaging to the case for rights of animals. Indeed, it may well be the case that these problems will be found in many of the situations where the need to claim rights – particularly basic rights – is most pressing.

This brings us to the objection that it is *unnecessary* to extend rights to non-humans. It can be argued that what really matters anyway is not so much that animals have acquired rights as that humans have taken on new duties; these duties can be specified without reference to rights of animals. It can be replied, though, that this objection, like the previous one, would be as applicable to human rights as to non-human rights: so if there are reasons in human cases for retaining a discourse specifically of rights – for instance, to mark where duties *need* to be, where they are perhaps not yet sufficient or sufficiently strong – then there may be similar reasons for keeping a discourse of animal rights.

Having defended human rights against neo-Malthusian objections, the thrust of the argument of the remainder of this section has favoured extending fundamental rights to non-humans too. It is certainly true that some features of moral rights are difficult to carry across the species divide; and the further one moves, the greater the difficulty becomes. For instance, the value of *autonomy*, a core value of the liberal rights discourse, is hard to square with animal rights: there is something paradoxical about trying to protect the autonomy of beings who are apparently unable to assert it. This in turn is connected with the problem, already discussed in chapter two, of epistemic limits: lacking the kind of communicative relation to non-human animals which is available in the human case, the reliability of our assessment of the subjective aspects of their well-being will always be open to question. As a consequence, there will always be the risk of causing harm or suffering by well-intended but insufficiently informed action. Nevertheless, epistemic limits are not fixed once and for all, and as they are gradually pushed back through the gaining of greater understanding of other species' needs, so the case for moral concern can be further extended. Moreover, as we have also noted, the position regarding animal rights is in important respects akin to the position of those human beings who cannot claim rights for themselves, such as children, the mentally handicapped, future generations. Such classes of humans, in various ways and for various reasons, are not in a position to enjoy rights whose exercise depends on a capacity for active citizenship or economic agency – but they nevertheless have *needs* which rights can protect. In fact, the point might be put more strongly than this: for even rights which relate not to any kind of 'recipience', but only to being left free from interference, cannot typically be secured by the rights bearers themselves. Moreover, most humans who find themselves in a position of needing to make a human rights *claim* may not be in a position to do so. Human rights are typically most at issue precisely in situations where those whose rights are being abused need to rely on others to make claims or call for action on their behalf. Hence, as I argued in the first section of this chapter, there are good reasons to think that all human rights will stand or fall together. There are now reasons for adding that certain animal rights may also stand or fall with them too.

But this raises the question of whether the discourse of rights is really the most appropriate moral discourse for protecting the interests of animals *or* humans.

4.3   Rights and Responsibilities

A major problem we have grappled with so far is that rights can pro-
liferate to such an extent as to risk becoming self-defeating, since the
more the discourse of rights is extended, to include more bearers and
more entitlements, the less effectual it may become. Thus there is the
'quantitative' problem of increasing conflicts between various rights,
their claimants and trustees, which leads to decreasing satisfaction of
their claims. But although this is a very real problem, it is one which, in
some degree, is endemic to the morality of rights as such: rights are
typically claimed in the face of competing claims, and the very logic of
rights is determined by this feature of the 'circumstances of justice'. So
the problem can be seen to constitute not so much an objection to rights
as a problem of priorities between claims to solve internally to the discourse. However, this response to the 'quantitative' problem brings into
view a further, and potentially more decisive, problem of a 'qualitative'
nature which concerns the moral discourse of rights as such. For it is
arguably also the case that the culture of rights – as essentially conflictual – is ethically impoverished and debilitating. There is a radical
tradition of rights criticism which sees the whole idea of rights and
justice as based upon, and inextricably implicated in, conflictual relationships which it can at most contain, but never resolve. That is to say, there
is a determinate type of social relation that takes a rights form, one
marked by competitive, atomistic, and egoistic individualism. Marx, for
instance, saw rights as based on and perpetuating 'the separation of man
from man'; this basic line of criticism has more recently assumed feminist, communitarian and other postmodern forms. If this is of concern at
the social and political level, it will have scarcely less worrying implications for animals or the environment: for if their interests have to be
expressed in the language of rights, then not only is this likely to leave
them in a disadvantaged position compared with human rights bearers,
but it is also arguable that this language, with its individualistic and
competitive features, is just not suitable to accommodate the sort of
holistic and long-term thinking that a true appreciation of their interests
requires. So even if one accepts the emancipatory impulse underlying the
discourse of fundamental rights, there are considerations from radical
socialist, feminist, postmodernist and ecological perspectives which lead
us to question whether rights is really the appropriate discourse in terms
of which to pursue it.

At this point, other options would be either to refrain from the discourse of rights altogether, or else to seek an improved conception of rights, one free of the specific features which critics find objectionable. In what follows I shall briefly examine arguments proposing the abandonment of rights and show that while their more extreme conclusions would give rise to more new problems than they solve, they do allow us to identify the requirements of an improved conception of rights. Accordingly, I shall then outline how a reconstructed conception of rights can meet the main points made by the radical critique and also be compatible with ecological considerations.

The radical critique of rights

The radical critique is based on evidence of inequalities centred on class, or race, or gender relations. Where such inequalities prevail, the discourse of rights and justice can be exposed as an ideology. It claims to offer objective principles which are just and fair, applying universally, and yet such claims are spurious and illusory. Moreover, it is 'a form of mystification which has a causal role in binding individuals to the very conditions of dependence and impoverishment from which it purports to offer emancipation'.[62]

There are, however, two ways of taking this critique. One is to see it as grounds for rejecting the discourse of rights and justice as such. On an influential reading of the orthodox canon, this would be Marx's view.[63] On this view, radical emancipatory aims cannot even be expressed in terms of justice and rights since those aims require the transcendence of the very conditions in which talk of justice and rights is necessary or possible. Nevertheless, this is a risky strategy, since one can remove the possibility of rights without removing their necessity, that is, the need people have for secure protection from various kinds of abuse. This is probably reason enough for holding on to a rights discourse. But if it is already utopian to suppose that the circumstances of justice – that is, limited resources and/or human sympathies – could be definitively overcome, this supposition is not so much utopian as plain untenable when ecological limits are also entered into consideration. Hence there is reason to take the view that human rights have something to offer yet, and so to see the role of critique to be to point up the limitations of specifically liberal-individualist interpretations of rights rather than reject rights as such. This is much the approach we have already seen taken by Benton regarding animal rights; and it is consonant with a reading of Marx which sees his critique as focused on the *restrictedness* of the liberal rights discourse, being limited in practice, as it was, to the representation of egoistic, paradigmatically bourgeois, interests, but not as implying an objection to the content of liberal rights and freedoms.[64] Nevertheless, to take this view is to share certain assumptions underlying liberal rights. In particular, there is the idea of human emancipation, in which individual self-realization is bound up with the idea of progress in history: this has itself become subject to criticism as an ideological illusion, part of a 'grand narrative' which, in this 'postmodern' world, has since been discredited.[65] The postmodernist spirit has sometimes found expression in new and revived forms of scepticism about rights and justice. A particularly relevant line of criticism has been made by those who have been grouped together as communitarians.[66]

Communitarians are sceptical about the validity of any universalistic moral discourse; they are even sceptical about the idea that humans can adopt a genuinely universalistic moral stance. This means that they take issue with the ideal of self-determination as it appears in a liberal theory like Rawls's. On Rawls's view, it is a feature of persons that, in order to be self-determining, they can stand apart from their current ends; they are not defined by their membership of any particular economic, religious, sexual, or recreational relationship; they can question and reject, enter and leave such relationships as they see fit. This view is encapsulated in Rawls's statement that 'the self is prior to the ends which are affirmed by it.'[67] Communitarians, however, believe this view is false in that it ignores how the self is embedded or situated in existing social practices, from which one cannot always stand apart. As Sandel puts it, in contrast to Rawls, 'the self is not prior to, but rather constituted by, its ends – we cannot distinguish "me" from "my ends" '.[68] Community values, he claims, are not simply ascribed to, but constitute the very identity of its members:

> For communitarians, the relevant question is not 'what should I be, what sort of life should I lead?' but 'Who am I?' The self 'comes by' its ends not 'by choice' but 'by discovery'.[69]

The challenge from this perspective for a discourse of fundamental rights arises because communitarians find implausible the idea that there are universal standards by which the practices of particular communities may sensibly be judged. Morality, they believe, is something which is rooted in the particular practices of actual communities; they are therefore sceptical of attempts to identify transcultural moral standards, in the absence of which the discourse of universal rights can have no force.

This is a point made by other cultural relativist critics of universalistic discourses in general, and of human rights in particular. Thus the UN Declaration, for instance, has been criticized by Pollis and Schwab as 'a Western construct with limited applicability' whose value assumptions are not genuinely universal.[70] Although this particular argument is advanced by radical critics of Western cultural imperialism, similar and related arguments can be traced back to the initial conservative reaction to rights proclamations in the eighteenth century[71] – a reaction whose political impetus would appear to be diametrically opposed to that of Pollis and Schwab. This points us to what is arguably a recurring problem with postmodernist forms of scepticism about universalistic discourses of rights: that either they offer no political alternative, or they turn dogmatic, thereby yielding non-novel solutions. Communitarianism, in particular, tends to be rather indeterminate as regards political consequences.

Nevertheless, the points about embodiedness and social embeddedness need to be taken into account, I believe, so it may be best to take communitarianism as providing a further rationale for an *immanent* critique of liberalism.[72] That is to say, one can maintain the moral value of individual autonomy but recognize that among the preconditions of realizing it is membership of a determinate community. In this way one can take the communitarians' main theoretical point whilst resisting the equivocal political stances it can lead them to adopt. Moreover, the value of community, though rightly emphasized against the individualistic excesses of liberalism, is not the only one, nor is it automatically or wholly good in itself. Indeed, it remains important to be aware of the respects in which rights claims have been made as claims *against* communities, for communities can also stifle, oppress and abuse.

This last point is one which some feminist theorists have been particularly concerned to develop in relation to communitarian philosophy, which they see as a perilous ally, not least because it tends to disregard gender-related problems with the norms and practices of traditional communities. More generally, when communitarians emphasize how 'we discover ourselves' in given communities, it should also be emphasized that one might then critically reflect on the self and community so discovered; in doing this, as Marilyn Friedman notes, 'one has probably at the same time already begun to question and distance oneself from aspects of one's "identity" in that community and, therefore, to have embarked on the path of personal redefinition.'[73] This suggests a more dialectical view of the relation between individuals and their communities whereby the question of which one pre-exists the other is superseded because each is recognized as to a great extent constituting the other.

Still, if feminist theorists distance themselves from communitarianism, they do not necessarily see this as a reason for returning to embrace a universalistic discourse of rights, and there remain distinctively feminist reasons for scepticism about such a discourse.[74] There are also constructive suggestions for an alternative sort of moral discourse. One alternative, which is also particularly relevant to ecological concerns, has been developed on the basis of Carol Gilligan's account of her investigations into moral development in children, and the critique which she was brought to mount against the influential account of moral development given by Laurence Kohlberg.[75] Kohlberg had identified a progression of stages which mark an increasing ability to engage in critical and post-conventional reasoning about right and wrong, to think systematically about the concepts of morality and law, to examine and challenge the logic of received moral truths. Gilligan noted how when faced with moral dilemmas designed to test their performance according to these criteria, girls seemed to do less well than boys. What she also observed, though, was that girls would tend to see a moral dilemma in the context of a temporal continuum of relationships rather than as a formal question of right, tending to see 'a world that coheres through connection rather than through systems of rules'. Gilligan suggests that this may be evidence not of an inability to think systematically about questions of right but of a less legalistic understanding of morality itself, and therefore of a different ability. In this way Gilligan claims to have identified two different trajectories of moral development to take the place of Kohlberg's single hierarchy: whereas boys seem to think quite easily in terms of rights, girls tend to see moral problems rather in terms of *responsibilities*.

This raises the question of whether the orientation to responsibilities may actually supply an alternative to the rights orientation. This prospect would be potentially rich in implications for an ecological perspective on justice, since an ecological perspective also sees 'a world that coheres through connection'. It too is dissatisfied with the 'right-bearing monads' of the dominant legalistic discourse which have the illusion of being independent and self-subsistent entities only because the real basis of their interdependencies is abstracted from. The responsibility orientation promises a suitably holistic perspective.

The imperative of responsibility

There are evident reasons for shifting the dominant moral discourse from an emphasis on rights to an emphasis on responsibilities. Such a shift seems to capture the key ecological intuition that it is necessary to change our basic attitude to the world from one which considers 'what we can get out of it' to one which considers 'what we can and must do for it'. It also provides a potentially useful focus for framing political demands. If the global system of production and consumption is becoming increasingly unsustainable, undermining its own basis, then the solution is to arrest and reverse the destructive trends; to do this requires identifying their causes, and this means identifying who is responsible for them. This brings us to the key point: if those who are de facto responsible are to be brought under rational control they must also be held responsible de jure. Hitherto, those with the most powerful and effective rights have often been those least required to shoulder responsibility for their actions. Indeed, they have been deemed to have right on their side, because not only are laws by and large supportive of their activities, but the economic freedom they enjoy is also supported by the ideology of moral freedom and individual rights; they are not responsible for effects of their actions on third parties, and the suggestion they should be is typically rebutted as a cost against their freedom. If primacy is attached not to individual liberty rights but to responsibility, then the onus of moral justification is shifted from those who would curtail economic freedom on to those who exercise it.

Some authors believe the concept of responsibility forms the core of a qualitatively new ethic. Hans Jonas, for instance, argues that the contemporary world faces a historically unprecedented situation for which no previous ethic is prepared.[76] Humans have developed the capacity to transform the natural world at such a rate and with such cumulative effects as to constitute a qualitatively new kind of human action; they have now put in question the continued existence of humanity itself. This means that technological practice can no longer be considered ethically neutral, and that humanity, collectively, has a qualitatively new obligation, namely, not only to consider the interests of future generations but to see to it that there will *be* future generations. The new ethic has to be an ethic of *responsibility*, argues Jonas, because our relation to the future is essentially an asymmetrical one; and, in contrast to rights–duties relations, which tend to involve a certain reciprocity, responsibility grasps this asymmetry. Responsibility, for Jonas, is proportionate to power: where one has the power to harm or benefit another being then one *should* care about the effects of exercising that power. In the human case the most basic imperative is that 'mankind should exist', an imperative Jonas believes is implied by the very existence of moral beings in the new circumstances. 'Put epigrammatically: the possibility of there being responsibility in the world, which is bound to the existence of men, is of all objects of responsibility the first.'[77] For the same reason, they have responsibility to promote value wherever they encounter it; and, on Jonas's account, value resides in any being that pursues its own ends. This can be established most easily for persons, but if it is taken to include natural goal-directed processes, then it holds also for all living beings, and, in fact, for the whole of nature.

However, while the imperative of responsibility may be compelling as a general idea, there are problems both with cashing it out as a guide to action and with grounding it. These arise even in relation to cases involving current generations of humans, as can be illustrated by reference to the micro-economic model, helpfully outlined by Shue,[78] of something that often occurs in underdeveloped regions: larger local farmers contract with agents of transnational companies to turn their land over from food production for the local community to cash crops for export; there follows an attendant fall in food supplies, a rise in food prices and eventually famine for the local community. If one then seeks to identify who is responsible for the famine one encounters the first difficulty that a degree of responsibility can be attributed at each link of a long chain which includes poor farmworkers, relatively well-off farmers, company agents, domestic politicians, international lawyers, multinational companies and their individual shareholders – including, for instance, fund managers for old-age pensioners – and Western governments which represent at least a part of whole populations. At each and every link of the chain there are agents who can be attributed a causal power which is necessary, though not alone sufficient, to bring about the undesired consequences. Thus in the final analysis responsibility seems to be completely dispersed and diffused. This problem is compounded by the second: the claim that causal agency coincides with some moral responsibility will not always be easy to establish. If all the parties involved are simply pursuing their own self-interest, legally and non-maliciously, then one cannot assume that any of them are wilful violators of the subsistence rights of the poorer villagers, and it is hard to see in what sense any of them can be held morally responsible for the end result. Thus it would seem to be neither realistic nor justifiable to seek immediately to translate causal responsibility into any kind of moral responsibility for the famine. Moreover, it is clearly not possible to assign responsibilities without at the same time providing a moral justification for doing so.

Nevertheless, from these difficulties of identifying who is responsible, and what exactly responsibility means, it does not follow that no one is responsible. Nor, though, would it be helpful, or justifiable, to hold that *all* are responsible, if that is taken to imply *equally* responsible. There are different kinds of responsibility which bear on the situation in different ways; so it is necessary to distinguish between them. As a first step toward doing so one might ask, at each link in the chain, who does what and why; and, perhaps more crucially, whether they could have done otherwise. The more alternative courses of action that are open, the stronger can be the attribution of responsibility: one could thereby invoke Jonas's principle that responsibility is a correlate of *power* – the power associated with freedom to act and to choose how to act. This criterion would allow us to draw some contrasts, for example whereas a plantation worker who actually uproots food crops and plants coffee, and so in purely physical terms plays a decisive causal role, in fact has an extremely restricted choice – she can either do her boss's bidding or starve –the multinational company, we may suppose, has a wider range of choices and could switch to a marginally less profitable commodity which did not involve such drastic costs in human terms. The de facto responsibility of the company then appears greater than that of the wage worker. This way of reasoning quickly brings us to the intuitively obvious conclusion that the company, unlike the wage labourer, 'could do otherwise'. Unfortunately, this swift conclusion is not necessarily satisfactory. For one thing, it is not strictly true that the company could have done otherwise and the wage worker not: on the one hand the worker could have chosen to starve; on the other, the employees and directors of the company might themselves be under constraints to avoid bankruptcy or being squeezed out of business. In identifying power in terms of a range of options we have also *evaluated* different options; and while placing a greater value on a wage worker's sustenance than on a company's profits may not be difficult to defend, the questions which will arise in relation to the agents who are situated between these two extremes will be more controversial.

There are a number of important points to be made here. One is that the identification of bearers of responsibility presupposes a theory of value in terms of which the relative acceptability of different courses of action or sacrifices can be assessed. The theory of value cannot be derived from the theory of responsibility. Jonas recognizes this; he seems less aware, however, of the attendant point that the need for a theory of right is also neither obviated nor supplied by a theory of responsibility.[79] This second point, then, is that responsibility does not replace but complements rights and social justice: as long as there are conflicting legitimate interests there will also be a need for a theory of justice. Familiar problems of rights and justice, especially those concerning the extent and distribution of the duties which are supposed to correlate with rights, are not obviated by an orientation to responsibilities but reproduced as the problem of assigning them. If an advantage of prioritizing responsibility is that it places limits on the extent of permissible human interventions in the natural world, it remains the case that responsibility must itself have limits – otherwise we would be left with a paralysing perspective of impotent but indefinitely responsible individuals. Identifying those limits means addressing the question of how normative responsibilities are to be shared out; which is itself a question of justice. A third point is that if 'we' find ourselves with a responsibility for solving problems in relation to the real world, including future generations and non-humans, we do not do so simply as single individuals. If a further advantage of prioritizing responsibility is that it foregrounds the context of relationships, this is lost if humanity's collective responsibility is seen as an aggregate of individuals' responsibilities. While causal responsibility may appear as a chain, a linear sequence or a set of linear sequences, a normative theory of responsibility needs to look at the context, the network of relationships, in which that causality operates. More precisely, this means appreciating how responsibility attaches to the individuals concerned not simply *qua* agents, but *qua* role bearers. Responsibility does not correlate immediately with the powers or capacities of individual agents, for the relevant powers do not attach directly to the agent: rather, they arise at specific places within a set of social relationships. One must therefore observe the distinction between individual actions and collective situated practices: the correlativity of power and responsibility is situational, and it is at this level that the imperative of responsibility must be formulated. Responsibility attaches to concrete differentiated roles, which means looking at situated practices rather than isolated actions, and seeing these in terms of a division of social labour. This, the social division of labour, is precisely what is missing from generalized accounts of collective responsibility (as it is from neo-Malthusian critiques of rights) which consider collective bads as if they arise as the result of a straightforward aggregate of individual actions within one homogeneous group. One defect of the rights orientation that an orientation to responsibilities was supposed to remedy was the idea of atomistic self-contained individuals: so it is clearly important to avoid reproducing that defect within a theory of responsibility. This leads to a further point: it is not just for empirical reasons that individual agents cannot be considered as bearing sole responsibility for their actions; there is the deeper consideration that individuals never act, formulate objectives, or even think as totally independent beings. This is not to say that they cannot act autonomously, but to draw a distinction between autonomous reasoning and solipsism. There are some respects in which others are always copresent in the formation of an individual's objectives. As Karl-Otto Apel emphasizes, even when one deliberates in 'solitude and freedom' one 'thinks with a *claim to intersubjective validity*',[80] and this not only in respect of the truth of one's thoughts but also in respect of their *meaning*. This is what makes it possible for an individual to speak about what 'we' know today, and, by implication, about 'our' responsibilities; but the knowledge and responsibilities presuppose the intersubjective discursive practices, and how well founded the knowledge and responsibilities are depends on the quality of those practices. This important point should not be lost sight of even when one speaks, in a general shorthand way, of 'our' responsibilities.

Apel thus situates the imperative of responsibility within the context of a discourse ethic.[81] He distinguishes two stages of ethical deliberation. At one level, 'the *ought*, in the sense stipulated by the ethic of discourse, can be derived . . . from the fact of always already having recognized the duties belonging to a member of the real as well as of the anticipated ideal community of communication.'[82] On the second level, the relation of responsibilities to abilities and powers must be concretely worked out by reference to the specialist knowledge of experts. In Apel's view, 'the proper task for philosophical ethics today lies less in proposing situational, material norms than in analyzing the normative conditions for organizing collective responsibility at the various possible levels of practical discourse.'[83] For it is scarcely possible, he believes, to *deduce* specific material norms from principles; rather, for these one should look to empirical experts, provided their contributions 'have first been achieved and put forward in the spirit of an ethic of responsibility'. Hence the first imperative is to secure the conditions of free discursive will formation.[84]

An advantage of this approach is that it clarifies, with its emphasis on two levels, how we can acknowledge the responsibility of humanity as a whole while also focusing on the point that specific responsibilities attach to specific places. But this also means that ethics cannot be reduced to the universalistic aspirations of discourse ethics. Normative questions remain to be addressed by us as participants on the basis of knowledge and understanding that comes from the world; and in the real world, where discursive procedures are imperfect, we still need to beware of the ideological limits of universalistic discourse. We have reason, too, to be sensitive to the standpoint of the 'concrete other' – the real, flesh and blood, socially situated being who is abstracted from in universalistic discourses oriented only to the 'generalized other'.[85] Thus, Benhabib's assessment of the political implications of Gilligan's distinction remains pertinent: 'the concrete other is a critical concept that designates the *ideological* limits of universalistic discourse. It signifies the *unthought*, the *unseen*, and the *unheard* in such theories.'[86] Nevertheless, to designate the ideological limits of universalistic discourse, as Benhabib also recognizes, is not simply to abandon all claims of universality, of rights: the standpoint of the concrete other does not preclude hate instead of love, or forms of prejudice such as racism or sexism.[87] In so far as there are generalizable interests, human rights will remain important to protect them, and, hopefully, to protect the space in which particular interests can flourish and be fulfilled. The perspectives of rights and responsibilities, of concrete and generalized other, then, are necessarily complementary.

Correlating rights with responsibilities

We have seen that radical criticisms of fundamental rights do not provide compelling reasons for abandoning that discourse altogether. Moreover, the concept of responsibility does not supplant it or provide a complete alternative. However, it can be used to contextualize rights and provide a key to mitigating the problem that allowing rights to burgeon involves a multiplication of right and duty relations beyond what may be sustainable, either ecologically or politically. So, having shown, in the first two sections, how an expansion of human rights discourse can be justified and defended, it remains to show how it can also appropriately be limited.

Two ways in which this *could* be done would be either to make rights less stringent or to restrict the range of possible bearers; but either of these options would undermine the discourse of rights which I wish to defend. A possible solution consistent with the aims of fundamental rights, though, is to see those rights as to some extent *conditional*; conditional, that is, on the corresponding recognition of certain responsibilities. This may seem to go against the principles of universality and inalienability, but in fact, I wish to argue, it is only to recognize that fundamental rights *do* always have certain preconditions anyway, even if these are not always acknowledged.

Fundamental rights are sometimes spoken of as attaching to individuals as some kind of property of those individuals, but this is an elementary mistake which has long been correctly pointed out by sceptics. The core of the legal positivist objection to natural rights, for instance, is that rights exist if and only if corresponding duties exist:[88] the truth of this objection derives from the fact that rights are not properties of persons but effects of *relations* between persons. Relations of rights and duties typically appear as external and atomistic relations between persons, but these relations themselves are only made possible by the social relations, the laws and political arrangements, which underpin them. So, if rights depend on the existence of duties, the existence of duties depends on appropriate social relations; we may add, furthermore, that social relations depend on ecological relations too. It is in the context of social and ecological relations that we have spoken of the imperative of responsibility applying; it is at this level, therefore, that a precondition of the realizability of fundamental rights resides. By invoking the imperative of responsibility, therefore, we are not inventing a new condition to place on 'inalienable' rights, but explicitly thematizing in a specific way a condition that was always already there.

Human rights cannot adequately be defined in terms of correlative duties of individuals. This can be illustrated by reference to the least controversial of human rights. If one individual is being tortured by another individual this would, in a civilized society, be considered a crime, not a human rights issue; the torturer would be arraigned not for a violation of the other person's rights but for a violation of their body. It becomes a human rights issue when the society falls short of civilized standards and does not pursue the torturer as a criminal. In fact, in the real world, human rights issues seldom involve isolated individuals: normally, deprivation of human rights, and struggles to secure them, occur in broader specific social contexts. This is to say not that the moral disposition and individual behaviour of torturers or other rights violators are of no account at all, but that they are of less relevance to the real problem than the normative standards generally enforced in their society. The whole society – including not only the torturers but also those who turn their backs, and even the good who in doing nothing allow evil to triumph – is in a very real sense responsible. This responsibility, though, as has already been discussed, is not spread equally over the society: for, as Jonas's principle holds, the greater the power the greater is the responsibility. The rights collectively available for equal recognition within any society will depend on how power operates in a society; unequal power will mean unequal responsibilities but equal rights.

To show in general terms how this idea of correlating responsibilities with rights may be cashed out in practice, it is useful to deploy the legal concept of a liability. A liability is not immediately a duty, but gives rise to a duty in specific circumstances. There is no need drastically to multiply duties when it is possible to transform the attribution of *liabilities*.[89] Instead of saying that the rights all individuals have are correlative to duties all have, which indeed would be too numerous to be enforceable, we need only speak about duties at all in situations where rights are actually under threat; duties need only come to bear on those in a position to do something, on those who are responsible for the threat. The point is, then, that factual responsibility be taken into account in the attribution of legal liabilities. This suggestion fits in with our intuition that we do not all have duties to all beings, since there is no way we could either carry them out or fail to; rather, we all have a liability to come under a duty in particular circumstances.

Those circumstances can be defined (at least in part) in terms of responsibility. One way responsibility can be understood is in terms of 'holding an office'. A person who holds an office in a particular institution may bear responsibility for a failing of a junior without necessarily being held *morally* responsible as an individual: the simple fact that, according to a formal description of her powers, she could have prevented the misdeed, is sufficient to make her responsible.[90] This bearing of responsibility is typically expressed not in terms of blame and punishment, but rather as the working of norms which define the office. The accepting of responsibility here typically yields the obligation to relinquish the post, for if one cannot maintain enforcement of ruling norms, one cannot retain the post. I see no reason in principle to prevent this institutional conception of responsibility being applied in other contexts. For instance, recalling a case considered earlier, it could be held that the parties to a cash crop contract occupy 'offices' to which responsibilities attach. Here I am speaking not only of the internal hierarchy of the transnational company, or of the relation of the landowner to his kin, but also of their place in their wider societies. We are accustomed to think of the parties to private contracts as free and independent agents; but we also need to remember what are the preconditions of their freedom and their contracts. If the institution of free contracts is maintained by a society for the sorts of reason identified by Locke, whose essential rationale as I argued in section 4.1 is that there is an equal right of access to the means of life, then a condition of entering into a contract, indeed a norm of the practice of contracting as such, ought to be that its effects should not run counter to the norm of a general right of access to the means of life. For this to be possible it is necessary that private contracts be seen as what they are: part of wider institutional and social practices, not isolated individual actions. Doing so allows us to pre-empt the foreseeable objection that if every time one enters a contract one finds oneself liable for all kinds of eventualities affecting third parties, there is an unacceptable cost against freedom: for the entering into a contract is not the exercise of pure freedom; rather, it is the exercise of legal power, and the exercise of a legal power is only possible because of certain legal rules governing the generation of powers. It is these rules and laws governing contracts which could and, I am suggesting, should be changed. Under existing private law the exercise of a legal power typically creates liabilities only towards second parties who enter into a contractual relation, this being defined as a private affair. My suggestion is that the power to enter into a contract, like the cash crop one for example, be accompanied by liability for certain foreseeable standard consequences to third parties.[91] Such a change does not involve an *a posteriori* curtailment of freedom, retroactively penalizing one party or the other for their actions, but an *a priori* clarification of legal *powers* and the conditions of their exercise.

This does not override rights of freedom; it extends them. In private law persons are individuated as free actors; the freedom of the legal actor, the one raising or defending claims, is prioritized: the freedom of the others is not entered into account. We should challenge this limit on the definition of the sphere of freedom, looking at the scope of powers and correlative liabilities not only of contracting parties, but also of those who are under a legal 'no power' or disability[92] – those whose freedom is adversely affected. The most basic aim of the demand is to give immunity from adverse changes. Indeed, the right not to be denied access to means of life can actually be understood as the statement of a claim to *immunity* against changes in legal relations which have adverse effects on third parties.[93] It seeks to overcome the institutionalized irresponsibility of private agents in overriding more equitable rights by transforming the sense of liability from the paradigm of private law, and bringing it closer to that of public responsibility. This, in fact, is to pursue an immanent critique of bourgeois law in the name of its own most progressive aspect – the rights of personality over and above private property rights.[94] For the very possibility of private legal relations presupposes that all persons are recognized as equal, in order to come into such relations: if law recognizes this, then it *could* also recognize that certain private transactions undermine freedom and equality of others.

So, this demand does not imply a drastic multiplication of duties, for in being framed at the level of liabilities it means that specific duties only arise in concrete contexts. This means thinking of human rights not as attaching to individual subjects as some kind of inherent property of theirs, but as arising, in determinate circumstances, out of relations of

what continental jurists call 'objective' right. In developing this conditioned account it is a case not of denying freedom as an end or a right,
but of using the idea of responsibility in order to reinterpret or recon-
textualize it. These rights are rights of humans against humans, not
against the rest of nature; the serious pursuit of these rights means a
serious engagement with human responsibilities.

Conclusion

In this chapter I have sought to elaborate and defend a conception of
rights and justice which is compatible with ecological aims and values.
In the last section I have shown that the various radical objections to
rights do not require us to abandon rights as such. They do, however,
present the challenge of rethinking the notion of rights in such a way as
to overcome the abstract individualist limits of the liberal discourse. This
means, firstly, reconceptualizing the 'persons' who are the bearers of
rights. The view of persons in the liberal tradition exemplified by Rawls
is one of abstract individuality of essentially disembodied and disassoci-
ated rational entities; in opposition to this the point is made, in broadly
similar or complementary terms by socialists, feminists and communitarians, that humans are, in Benton's words, 'necessarily embodied, and
are also to be conceptualized as "individuals-in-relationship" both to
other persons (and living beings) and to ecological conditions through
the medium of (highly variable) cultural forms.'[95] Contextualizing persons in this way means contextualizing their rights too. I have sought to
relate rights to responsibility; and to relate ecological responsibility, as
both causal and moral responsibility, to legal responsibility. By focusing
on the social and ecological preconditions of any discourse of rights I
have offered what I think is also a holistic view, and one which is
consistent with the broad critical realist perspective developed in earlier
chapters.

However, if what has been proposed in the book up to now is both
desirable and internally consistent, it remains to ask whether it is likely
to be achieved. A major aspect of this question concerns politics; indeed,
before the human species can become truly responsible for its interventions in the world, it will have to be constituted as a collective
agency. Traditional questions of politics are not obviated but given a new
urgency by ecological considerations.

5
Ecological Politics

The aim of this chapter is to determine whether there is, can be, or needs to be a distinctively ecological – or green – political philosophy. In asking what such a political philosophy might be like, one specific question which arises is whether green politics involves a break with the political values and forms hitherto associated with progressive politics as this has broadly come to be understood since the eighteenth century. For the most fundamental and universal of modern political ideals – central among these being liberty for individuals, democracy and equal political rights – are permeated by enlightenment values. Are these ideals consonant with ecological aims?

One answer to this question, from a green perspective, would be to affirm that, other things being equal, democracy and its attendant rights and liberties continue to be, in principle, a good thing – with political differences between various radical groupings concerning more the specific interpretation and policies to realize them than the validity of the fundamental values themselves. Hence green parties, for instance, invariably subscribe to these values in their manifestos.[1] But this answer is at best a partial one, for it begs the question: what if all other things are *not* equal? What, for example, if there is something inherent in the logic of democracy which tends to lead to ecological degradation? In earlier discussions, such as that centred on the 'tragedy of the commons', we have seen reasons for thinking there could be. Even if those reasons are not conclusive, and democracy is not inherently anti-ecological, it may still not necessarily be the best political form for pursuing ecological ends. A particular dilemma for green political thought, therefore, is that while its distinctiveness and polemical distance from other ideologies seems to lie precisely in its critical stance towards enlightenment ideals, it also seeks to maintain a commitment to political aims which embody just those ideals.

The main question for this chapter, then, concerns the relation of ecology to democracy. There are three basic ways of conceiving this relation: as one of indifference, as one of incompatibility, or as one of necessary connection. If the relation is one of indifference, then while democracy and ecology are not necessarily connected they may equally well not be incompatible; so if there are independent reasons for pursuing democratic politics this might seem to suffice as an answer to the question. Accordingly, the broad line of argument examined in the first section begins by showing that ecological values are not incompatible with and can indeed be found in democratic traditions and ideologies – such as liberalism and socialism – at least in as much as they converge on some form of social democracy; the question of whether they are *adequately* represented in social democratic political forms is then addressed with reference to the argument of Goodin which seeks to show not only that ideological alliances between green groupings and democratic parties are possible, but also that formal, strategic alliances are necessary, and, furthermore, that more radical alternatives are not realistic. This 'realist' position on green politics is, however, one which is criticized as too reformist by those who conceive of green politics more in terms of 'fundamental opposition' because it remains too closely tied to just those institutions and practices which are part and parcel of contemporary ecological and social problems. Accordingly, in the second section I examine claims of those radical greens who are sceptical as to whether a sufficient 'greening' of conventional politics is possible and who believe instead that ecological politics requires alternative institutions, practices and forms of association which embody both ecological values and the principle of democratic participation. In thus aiming for a more complete social transformation, they evidently see a strong connection between radical democratic and ecological aims – a connection often made through principles of decentralization and non-hierarchical organization. Yet there are problems and tensions within the radical position. For one thing, while in emphasizing the break with progressive traditions they would seem to weaken any presumption in favour of democracy, their alternative in fact invokes a stronger one; their appeal to decentralization, I observe, is equivocal. Another problem is that in attempting to develop an alternative politics untainted by what they see as defects of conventional politics, radical greens are liable to remain too far from real power, and they lack an adequate social theory of the basis from which it might be achieved. Nevertheless, their anticipatory strategies, suitably harnessed to realistic social and political theory, may, I believe, provide the basis for radical and effective politics. Hence in the third section I attempt to develop a distinctive position which is both realist and radical, and in which ecological considerations are used not simply to create an alternative conception of political practice, but to redefine the very notion of the political. Part of this involves showing how disputes between reformists and radicals take place *within* the ambit of democracy, because the dilemma for radical green politics is essentially a dilemma for radical democracy as such; I then give reasons for thinking that redefining radical democracy, even in terms simply of relations between *humans*, may in fact yield more ecological outcomes than attempts to theorize a purer 'ecocentric' politics. Hence rather than perpetuate dichotomous oppositions between reformist environmentalism and radical ecologism, I argue, many of them can be overcome by learning from debates between and within both reformist and radical camps. In doing so I point out respects in which democracy appears to be a necessary condition for effective ecological politics.

5.1   The Environmental Dimension of Emancipatory Politics

This section first examines reasons for thinking that traditional 'progressive' political ideologies associated with democratic values – liberalism and socialism in particular – can adequately accommodate the environmental dimension; it then turns to the question of political strategy and discusses the potential and limits of green reformism in this context.

At the outset it is worth noting that the relationship between green politics and forms of politics styled as progressive appears to be ambivalent. Certainly, if progress is understood in terms of economic advancement, and if environmental deterioration is accepted as a necessary price of economic advancement, then environmental concern must be anti-progressive. If it is noted, though, that the socially disadvantaged tend to bear the brunt of those deteriorating conditions, it could be considered progressive to improve conditions which are simultaneously social and ecological. Still, given that even here the real concern is not with the environment itself but with the plight of people who suffer from its deterioration, this can be deemed at best a shallow form of environmentalism rather than truly green. Accordingly, some greens insist their politics are 'neither left nor right', the reason being that specifically ecological values are inadequately represented anywhere along the traditional political spectrum.[2] Regimes of both right and left cause ecological devastation, and the traditional categorization of political differences reflects now outmoded divisions and masks tacit complicity *vis-à-vis* green issues. Nevertheless, if the left–right spectrum is not sufficient for locating the specificity of ecological concerns, many theorists of ecological politics nevertheless accept that it is still relevant in some ways, and some therefore advocate employing two axes in analysing political ideologies – one corresponding to the dimension of distribution and the other to that of ecology, or environment.[3] The left–right axis still holds good for dealing with distributional issues (social justice, welfare state etc.), and it is widely, if not universally, accepted that ecological politics tends towards the left in the distributional dimension;[4] but there is no necessary relationship, it is claimed, between one's position on ecological issues and one's position on distributional issues.

Now a central thrust of this book so far has been to argue that ecological questions neither can nor should be treated in isolation from distributive questions; and the way I've argued this, it would tend prima facie to favour a red–green position. But my argument is not formally incompatible with the proposition that positions at all coordinates of the two axes are possible. So although everr reformist arguments tend to yield positions at least slightly to the left on the distributive axis, this is conceivably a contingent matter of the social views that tend to prevail amongst people with environmental concerns today. In what follows, therefore, I am interested first to inquire what sort of connection there may be between green concerns and progressive social values.

Environmental concern in liberal and socialist traditions

Some environmentalist tendencies can be discerned within liberal thought. A number of writers have argued that if we separate the enlightenment ideals of liberalism – those of 'a society striving to ensure that all its members are equally free to realize their capabilities'[5] – from the attachment of economic liberalism to the capitalist market economy, then liberalism can claim common cause with environmentalism. Thus, for example, a number of writers have referred to J.S. Mill's advocacy of a steady-state economy:

> a stationary condition of capital and population implies no stationary state
> of human improvement. There would be as much scope as ever for all

kinds of mental culture, and moral and social progress; as much room for improving the Art of Living and much more likelihood of its being improved.[6]

Then there is the liberal rationale which we have already seen to underlie human rights: according to Dobson this is 'seen by many in the Green movement as the best way to generate a right for the environment and a consequent moral obligation for us to treat it with respect'.[7] That is a view endorsed by Paehlke: 'Environmentalism can be taken as an extension of liberalism in its claim that the basic rights established by liberalism belong also to future human generations and to other species.'[8] Dobson has gone so far as to assert:

Understanding the political and intellectual nature of Green politics means seeing that its political prescriptions are fundamentally left-liberal, and if a text, a speech or an interview on the politics of the environment sounds different from that then it is not green but something else.[9]

If this sort of claim is to be sustained, though, the emphasis should perhaps be placed on the *left* of left-liberal.[10] Green politics has to do with more than the advocacy of a steady-state economy: the aim cannot be a steady-state version of the status quo, if that is socially inequitable or oppressive. One needs to be realistic about the nature of capitalism and not assume its antagonisms will simply wither away, as J.S. Mill, for instance, appeared to. Moreover, one also needs to be alert to how economic liberalism, at least, is complicit in the generation of ecological problems. Environmentalism, then, may be consistent with ethical liberalism but not with economic liberalism. Some theorists argue that the consistent pursuit of the former leads in the direction of socialism.

Ecological themes can certainly be found in socialist traditions. We have frequently had occasion to note how the exploitation and ill-treatment of non-human nature goes hand in hand with the exploitation and oppression of human beings, and so it is not surprising that there have long been socialists who have made the connection. Among the precedents are some of the utopian socialists of the nineteenth century, and a good deal of the recent literature on ecological politics argues for a revival of the thought of the utopian socialists. For instance, Keekok Lee has found considerable merit in the thought of Fourier. Fourier's socialist utopia is oriented to the fulfilment of concrete human needs rather than to the expansion of the artificially created needs generated by the market economy. Human hostility to nature, both internal and external, is rooted in the hostility amongst human beings themselves, which is promoted, especially, in the competitiveness of the economic system which distorts the value of both humans and nature. Accordingly, for Fourier, the goal of ever-increasing possession and consumption of external goods is to be transformed into a liberating development of internal goods. Lee sums up Fourier's vision of socialism as 'one which is sufficient but frugal in material possession and consumption but paradoxically rich in spirit – in the possibilities of self-development'.[11] There is an evident anticipation here of the deep ecological recommendation to find ways of living which are 'simple in means, rich in ends'. Another utopian socialist who has inspired many greens is William Morris, who attempted to combine a simple egalitarian lifestyle with an ecological aesthetic, seeing 'the assertion and cultivation of the full variety of needs (needs for interesting work, more free time, safe and attractive domestic and public space, quiet and beautiful places in town and country) as the entire point of socialist transformation.'[12] Other prominent socialist theorists, like the early Rudolf Bahro and Raymond Williams, have invoked the ideas of the utopian socialists as a basis for the move from red to green. Interestingly, this convergence appears to be mutual, with a non-socialist green like Porritt writing: 'My own personal points of familiarity and very close connection with the left come from the early libertarian traditions, William Morris and so on, and from the anarchist tradition of left politics.'[13]

Nevertheless, Andrew Dobson has sounded a note of caution about reading too much into this, suggesting that it is 'evidence for the selective way in which both socialists and ecologists refer to the socialist tradition', and 'that claims for a convergence between socialism and ecology rest on the resurrection of a subordinate tradition within socialism'.[14] The implication here is that whilst sharing utopian aspirations is one thing, this should not allow one to be blinded to serious differences, which are especially marked in the cornucopian and productivist tendencies, of other, possibly more dominant, socialist traditions. An obvious and important reference point here is the work of Marx and Engels: although they too were appreciative of the social vision of the utopians, their thought is distinctive precisely at points where it takes issue with them, and is critical in ways which seem less ecologically sensitive, even anti-ecological. Yet as I have argued elsewhere, the pursuit of green concerns in general, and the revival of utopian socialism in particular, does not obviate Marx's critique of the latter.[15] Moreover, there may in fact be reasons for thinking that Marx's theory is *more* ecological than those of the utopians at a deeper level: as I argued in chapter 3, Marx's materialist conception of history, suitably reconstructed, offers part of an account of the human metabolism with nature, of the *mediations* between nature and human norms, which would be an indispensable foundation for any green political theory. Hence there are reasons for thinking that mainstream socialist thought, and not just a subordinate tradition of it, has very strong reasons for converging with ecological politics.[16]

But if that is the case in theory, Dobson is nevertheless right as regard socialist practice of the past century, which has paid scant heed to matters of ecological concern. In fact, the charge that greens can justifiably make against the left in general is that it has been slow and reluctant to recognize the irreducibility of such matters as a distinct and central political concern. This is not to say that the environment was not heeded at all: the often desperate environmental conditions of the working class had long been a major concern of socialists, but they were considered very much as just *part* of poor social and economic conditions in general, and hence as problems that socialism would resolve *en passant*, as it were. So when the new environmentalist voices began making themselves heard from the 1960s on, the left was initially not very receptive, for the new environmentalism was perceived as different from – indeed antagonistic to – that radical tradition. It seemed to them that just because environmental deterioration was now being noticed by the middle classes too it was being raised into a political issue – quite independently of the general working and living conditions of the working class. Hence environmental protests were dismissed as single-issue campaigns which were not connected to a broader social and political agenda. Not all on the left were so insensitive to green claims: Hans Magnus Enzensberger made a notable contribution in 1974, distinguishing between appropriate and inappropriate socialist responses to the environmentalist challenge.[17] Since then, growing numbers of socialists have gradually come round to the view that 'our forces belong together'.[18] But there has been an understandable preoccupation on the part of greens, even leftward-leaning ones, that this should not mean cooption, for there has also been a tendency of some socialists to seek to subsume ecological issues within a socialism which is reconstructed inadequately or not at all. Even socialists who take ecology seriously can be insensitive to the contribution of their potential partners. Dobson illustrates this with a quotation from Weston, who, he points out, is talking *past* the green movement when he writes

The problems with which most people are now faced are not related to 'nature' at all: they are related to poverty and the transfer of wealth and resources from the poor to an already wealthy minority of the Earth's population.[19]

This is to make an important point in an unhelpful, even misleading, way. I hope it has already been sufficiently argued in the course of this book that it would be a mistake to suppose ecological concerns can be *subsumed* under either liberal or socialist concerns – or any other ideology for that matter. There is a case for arguing, though, that ecological politics builds on liberal and socialist traditions,[20] and can be seen to participate in an evolving tradition of progressive politics. This would mean building on existing values and norms which exist in political culture and are to some extent already embodied in institutions, whilst recognizing that they are as yet imperfectly instantiated and that the institutionalized norms are to some extent ideological.

This takes us from questions of political ideologies and broad political aims to questions about the political forms and institutions necessary for realizing them. Up to now I have examined suggestions that green politics is not necessarily radically distinctive as regards its basic values and ultimate objectives, and discussed reasons for thinking alliances with ideologies of other political colourings are possible. I now turn to examine an argument that even distinctively green values do not translate into a distinctive politics; that their pursuit is compatible with, and perhaps even requires, the employment of conventional political forms.

Green reformism and political strategy

A thoroughgoing environmental reformism holds not only that ideological alliances are possible, but also that practical, strategic, alliances are necessary. The progressive tradition as characterized here is reformist in its qualified acceptance of, its willingness to work within, liberal democratic institutions and administrative states as these have evolved in the West. The question I consider in the remainder of this section is whether there are any good reasons why ecological politics should also subscribe to this reformist vision of politics.

Some reasons for taking a reformist view of ecological politics, seeking to use and reform existing political institutions rather than radically transform them, are connected with more general and familiar reasons for maintaining a political state. Robert Goodin, for example, emphasizes how the ecological problems to be confronted today are of global dimensions, and require the sort of concerted action world-wide which can only come about by strengthening the coordination between existing political institutions rather than seeking to undermine them.[21] In fact, Goodin sees the impetus of contemporary green movements as coming from the perception that purely local remedies will no longer suffice. The green slogan 'think globally, act locally' is vacuous without an account of how that concerted action is to be achieved, he argues, and the injunction to think globally may be given substantive content only on condition that one is prepared to square up to the implications this may have regarding state power. On a conventional view of politics, state power appears as an inescapable necessity for peaceful coexistence and the achievement of collective goals. Radical greens would resist this view; Goodin offers a useful analysis of the preconditions of that view and prospective alternatives.

He sketches four different models of how global coordination of environmental protection might be achieved. Two of these describe current realities; two correspond more closely to what radical greens desire. This analysis foregrounds some of the major issues separating reformists from radicals. The first model takes the basic logic underlying environmental disputes to be representable as a 'polluter's dilemma', a variant of the 'prisoner's dilemma' which embodies a similar logic of collective action to that discussed with reference to the tragedy of the commons in the previous chapter. Here, environmentally harmful practices like pollution are assumed to yield more benefits than costs to an individual enterprise, so that it is in their narrow economic self-interest to pollute. However, because each enterprise is worse off if all pollute than if none pollutes, each would be willing to accept the existence of anti-pollution regulations if that is the only way it can ensure others do not dump their waste on it. Yet because each enterprise would also avoid compliance if it could, such regulations require enforcement – of the sort which typically would be supplied by the state. The second model is essentially a variant of the first, amended to accommodate the point that in reality environmental protection can often be secured even without the cooperation of *all* the parties involved: 'Suppose the world's air, oceans or fisheries can afford for twenty nations to continue polluting. There will be a mad scramble in which each nation tries to lock itself inexorably into a policy of polluting, thereby forcing others to pay the costs of environmental protection that they have avoided.'[22] To the extent that either or both of these two models capture the logic of collective action actually operative in the real world, there would appear to be an inescapable need for centralized coordination backed by sanctions if environmental protection is to be secured. This would preclude radical green political solutions and make reformism the best possible hope.

However, as Goodin acknowledges, it may in fact be that not everyone manifests such beggar-my-neighbour attitudes. Hence a third model may be more appropriate. This would be based on the assumption that people might generally be prepared to behave *cooperatively*, provided that others do likewise. This possibility is captured in the assumptions of the 'assurance game', which differs from the prisoner's dilemma in one crucial respect: whereas the first choice of everyone with prisoner's dilemma preferences is to idle while others work, the first choice of everyone with assurance game preferences is to work while others work. On this assumption, so long as each is not being 'played for a sucker', cooperation is assured. On the face of it, this would provide a more promising model for environmental protection. It is also more consonant with enlightened self-interest, since it allows the satisfaction of a fuller range of human needs and values – such as those of cooperation, doing satisfying work and having a generally more hospitable environment, social and ecological – than is possible in pursuit of the mean and narrow self-interest characteristic of the prisoner's dilemma. Goodin does point out, though, that such cooperation as emerges on assurance game assumptions is likely to be fragile and would need to be further under-written – typically by the state and international treaties with teeth. Goodin therefore emphasizes that the assumptions underpinning this model do not support demands for a radical transformation of existing institutions: in particular, it does not 'provide any support for green suppositions that the needed coordination between decentralized juris-dictions will emerge naturally, if only the people within them "think globally", in an Assurance Game sense.'[23] So to the extent that this third model embodies assumptions which, though sanguine, are tolerably real-istic, it remains within the ambit of reformism.

It is the fourth model of coordination which would have to be sub-scribed to, Goodin argues, if the expectation of a radical green politics were to be fulfilled. On this model it is assumed either that no one will ever be tempted to take advantage of others or that no one would mind being taken advantage of; indeed, in the event of anyone doing less than their bit, others would always have to be assumed to be prepared to do extra to take up the slack. This would represent the strongest possible sense of thinking globally whereby one shapes one's preferences in accordance with global environmental demands, and these alone. This clearly presupposes a more radical departure from prevailing realities than does the assurance game. The latter merely requires people to be reciprocally reasonable, and can be grounded in the same way that a shift from crude immediate self-interest to enlightened self-interest can; the fourth model appears to presuppose not only a more radical conversion to green beliefs but also a widespread commitment to altruism. This is a highly speculative prospect far removed from any immediately foresee-able possibility, Goodin thinks.

Goodin's challenge to more radical greens, then, is to accept there is a need for the state, or else confess to beliefs which under existing conditions are liable to look distinctly implausible.

On his own view, however, it is not necessary to share radical beliefs to be green. Goodin's line of argument points in the direction of a reformism which, in green terminology, can be cast as realism as opposed to fundamental opposition.[24] In contrast to fundamentalists who insist on maintaining a radical opposition to those currently in power even if this means forfeiting the possibility of influencing them to some degree in the short term, realists are prepared to enter coalitions wherever this gives a chance of effecting genuinely green policies.

Goodin claims, in fact, that his argument provides philosophically grounded reasons why compromise and coalitions would be morally mandatory. These reasons depend on his specific way of conceiving the 'green theory of value' and its place in political morality.[25] On Goodin's account, the basic green value is naturalness, and good actions are those which maximize this value. It is the satisfactory consequences of environmental policy therefore with which greens are, or should be, most concerned. This means that his green theory of value is essentially con-sequentialist – that is, oriented to environmentally friendly outcomes rather than being concerned with people's motivations. On Goodin's account, therefore, it is not necessary to be radical to be green. This means that the assumptions required by radicalism – those underlying the fourth model of environmental coordination noted above – are not only implausible, they are in any case not necessary. Hence rather than make environmental protection attendant on moral and spiritual conversion of individuals, he believes that a commitment to the pursuit of green values means, first and foremost, a commitment to appropriate policies secured by robust laws with whatever sanctions are necessary to back them up. So the idea that the moral quality of actions matters is one which must take second place to a concern with green outcomes. The assump-tions of the fourth model capture what Goodin calls the 'green theory of action': but this, he argues, must always yield precedence to the green theory of value where they conflict since it is consequences that matter most. Realists, he says, like consequentialists more generally, would have us achieve as much good as possible in the circum-stances: they are pragmatists for whom half a loaf is better than no bread. Fundamentalists, by contrast, on Goodin's characterization of them, are less concerned to guide their actions by their foreseeable consequences than in deontological style: by what is right, what keeps their hands clean.

It remains to be seen, however, whether this characterization adequately captures what is at stake in the opposition. Before considering arguments from the other side, though, I shall finish off this section by considering some criticisms that can be made of those heard so far.

Limits of reformism

Goodin claims that his green theory of value unifies the entire green political programme, giving logical cohesion to the green agenda, so that it is 'illogical and inconsistent for other, more established parties to try picking and choosing some bits off that agenda, without accepting all the rest of its demands as well'.[26] Yet there is room to question how well this bold claim sits with the reformist politics which Goodin defends;[27] indeed, there are at least prima facie reasons for thinking that rather than save green values from cooption, Goodin's argument facilitates the process.

One reason is that real-life greens, as Goodin well knows, are concerned not only that ecologically sound environmental policies be pursued, but also that people might lead better lives; they do not assume the latter will simply follow from environmental regulations, but accept that it will require transformation of personal beliefs and behaviour. These further aims are categorized by Goodin as questions of agency which, in cases where they conflict with questions of value, must always cede priority. Yet this dichotomy invokes a conception of means and ends as radically separate which greens would typically wish to transcend. It can in fact be criticized on both pragmatic and principled grounds.

Goodin gives pragmatic reasons for considering questions of agency and lifestyle as secondary to the pursuit of policy outcomes. Yet there is good reason to believe that ecologically sound outcomes will also require a more thoroughgoing conversion to ecological principles of action, since not all human interactions are governed, or governable, by policy-makers. Therefore activities governed by a theory of agency, or even lifestyle principles, can themselves have instrumental effects which, cumulatively and in the long term, may be very significant. Goodin would of course grant that these may be pursued as *means* to ends; yet the agents might also pursue them as ends in themselves; so there is the paradox that while Goodin's position owes much of its robustness to its claimed pragmatic purchase on real motivations, in order to prioritize an orientation to outcomes in individual practices he would precisely have to disregard those real motivations which have to do with leading better, greener lives. Yet it may in fact be more realistic to expect individuals to pursue lifestyle changes which they perceive to be in their own interest than to support global policies whose scope and implications they may scarcely comprehend.

Still, there remains Goodin's point that an aggregate of individual actions could anyway only have useful outcomes *if they were coordinated*, and there are the difficulties we have already seen with achieving this. Yet Goodin's challenge might not be unanswerable. The hypothesis I have invoked is that at least some significant outcomes can be achieved from an aggregate of spontaneous or informally coordinated action; and although this need not be vulnerable to Goodin's critique of the altruistic model of coordination, since the individual action can be pursued for self-interested reasons, it does look potentially vulnerable to other criticisms he makes. He criticizes alternatives to centralized advanced planning: on the one hand, the kind of coordination provided by market forces, he rightly argues, is not a serious contender to provide *environmental* outcomes; on the other hand, the idea that organization might arise 'naturally', on analogy with the sorts of coordination found in the order of nature, involves some assumptions about social mechanisms which are at best unproven and at worst implausible. However, there is a third possibility: neither the blind operation of natural selection nor its market analogue, but that of coordination arising as the outcome of dialogical learning processes and discursive democracy. Whereas Goodin sees coordination as a *strategic* matter, it could alternatively be viewed as a matter of *communicative action*,[28] and this would mean giving a central place to democratic procedures.

Goodin's theory of value, however, is so stated as to have no particular implications as regards political forms or ideologies; it does not even rule out authoritarian solutions. In fact, Goodin draws a rigid line between green values and values of democracy. 'To advocate democracy is to advocate procedures, to advocate environmentalism is to advocate substantive outcomes: what guarantee can we have that the former procedures will yield the latter sorts of outcomes?'[29] Goodin is certainly right to raise this question, for greens typically tend merely to *assume* that the two sets of desirable things will go together, even in the absence of independent reason other than the wish that it be so. However, if they err on the side of wishful thinking, Goodin leaps to the opposite conclusion:

For now, pending demonstration of some such necessary linkage, we must
conclude that the green theory of agency is a separate issue from the green
theory of value that truly lies at the core of the green political
agenda.[30]

Pending demonstration, I think, we would do better to reserve judgement
on the question.

In fact, it could be argued that precisely the existence of uncertainty
makes procedures more rather than less important. One reason is that
what counts as an ecological problem in the first place will depend to
some non-negligible extent on the specific knowledge and interests
which go into comprehending it as a problem, and even assuming goodwill and disinterested pursuit of truth there is the likelihood that
knowledge may be uncertain; being as realistic as Goodin elsewhere
claims to be, though, there is the further likelihood that knowledge may
be contested on the basis of various interests other than the pure pursuit
of truth. Given the likelihood of uncertainty and disagreement about
knowledge of means, let alone ends, it would therefore seem important
that a degree of democracy be allowed into scientific processes in general; and this point would apply *a fortiori* to processes of policy-making.
This implies at least some degree of specific preference for procedures –
namely, for procedures which leave a maximum openness to the revision
of means and even ends in the light of new knowledge and understanding. Whether improved social learning levels will also improve concern
for the environment, or whether radical democracy will also be ecological, is of course still something of an open question. But that is all I
have sought to argue so far – that it is a question to investigate (see
section 5.3) rather than one referring to a possibility that can be ruled out
in advance, in the absence of affirmative evidence, as Goodin claims.

The point of principle to emerge from all this, therefore, is that there
are questions of agency bound up in the very formulation of ends and the
means used to pursue them.

To sum up. Reformism of the sort discussed here fails to do justice to
the promise of green political thought in at least two key respects. Firstly,
if green politics is 'neither right nor left', this cannot be because it simply
remains neutral on conventional questions of distribution, welfare, social
justice etc. If the slogan is to have any real and morally defensible
meaning, it will not imply indifference to such questions; rather, it will
have to imply that the very preconditions of the dichotomy are to be
transcended, and this may well require radical, agency-oriented struggle.
Secondly, the greens' motto, 'think globally, act locally' may yet have

more meaning than Goodin has adduced. Far while a consideration in favour of his position is that large-scale problems are going to require large-scale solutions, a countervailing consideration is that large-scale problems need to be broken down at source: thus, everyone who benefits from the despoliation of the planet must take some degree of responsibility for it. This suggestion is not without its difficulties – some of which I discussed in the preceding chapter – but I believe it is worth trying to work through them. Radical greens emphasize the importance of acting locally as well as thinking globally, which gives political expression to the philosophical end (or value) of overcoming the separation of ends (or values) from means (or agency), and the justification it allows of means by ends. Hence in contrast to a reformist approach which would keep them separate, the next section inquires whether a more radical integrated green political theory is possible.

5.2   Ecologism as a Political Ideology

Implicit in green fundamentalism and radical ecologism is the idea that there is a distinctively green political philosophy which owes little to or even represents a radical break with the dominant political ideologies of modern societies. This idea is connected with the general concern of radical ecologists to locate green politics in a critical relation to the rationality and values of the enlightenment. Various aspects of this general project have already been examined in the course of this book. In this section I shall chiefly be concerned with the question of political forms and institutions.

A claim that there is a specifically green political ideology has been advanced by a number of writers. One of the more systematic arguments to this effect comes from Dobson who claims that ecologism constitutes a political ideology in its own right. Dobson's presentation of specifically green political thought is organized around a central distinction between ecologism and environmentalism. 'Ecologism', he says, 'seeks radically to call into question a whole series of political, economic and social practices in a way that environmentalism does not.'[31] Whereas environmentalism may be compatible with any number of political forms, and may also encourage technocratic solutions to ecological crises, ecologism is to be contrasted on both points: it advocates institutions which embody and guarantee egalitarian and participatory politics; and its practices must be based on ecologically sensitive techniques and values. Hence, Dobson argues, whereas environmentalism can be

coopted with relative ease into more traditional political ideologies, ecologism represents a distinct and new radical political ideology. This is the
case, he claims, because it contains a description of the political and
social world, a programme for political change, and a picture of the kind
of society that political ecologists think we ought to inhabit – the sustainable society. In what follows I shall briefly examine some of the key
elements of this ideology and, working back from the utopia, via strategy, to assumptions about the nature of social and political reality, see
how well they hang together.

Ecological utopia and the politics of the good society

There is a view of the good society which, according to Dobson, is
distinctively green and cannot readily be identified in any traditional
political ideology. Although the literature on ecological utopias offers
some contrasting visions of the kind of social and political life to be
aimed at,[32] there are certain fairly common features; and if we concentrate specifically on those aspects bearing on questions of political
organization there is something approaching consensus. Given the key
values of an ecological society it appears, in particular, that its political
organization would have to be non-hierarchical and decentralized. In
what follows I shall briefly note why decentralization is thought desirable
and how it is claimed to be connected with ecology.

The desirability of decentralization has been argued for across the
range of green politics. From early inspirational ecological figures like
Roszak and Schumacher in the 1970s, through the more robust political
programming of the German Greens in the 1980s, to the green political
theorists of the 1990s, a constant theme has been that political power
should be located at the lowest level practicable.

Among the major reasons why decentralization is so important is that
it means hierarchies are broken down and people are empowered by
being members of small political communities. The root ideas here are
that people must feel a part of their community in order to participate
meaningfully; to do so they must be able to meet face to face, confident
that their participation might make some material difference; moreover,
they must be able to comprehend what is actually going on in their
community well enough to estimate how different policies might affect
it; finally they must be able to survey the community as a whole, not just
their own corner of it, if they are to judge the general good rather than
pursue narrow sectional interests.[33] In these respects, of course, the ideal
of decentralization is not novel or peculiar to ecological politics. It also

figures in certain branches of liberal, socialist and communist politics; more particularly though, it embodies concerns which are very much those of anarchist traditions. It is therefore not surprising that a strong current of opinion maintains that ecological politics must in fact be a form of anarchism. Certainly, from a historical perspective, it seems to be the case that the most searching ecological questions were raised – long before questions of environment and ecology were of widespread public concern – by anarchists more than by thinkers of other political colours.[34] In more contemporary debates too, Eckersley, for instance, sees concerns with ecology and decentralization as combined in 'eco-anarchism', and she takes seriously the claim 'not only that anarchism is the political philosophy that is most compatible with an ecological perspective but also that anarchism is grounded in, or otherwise draws its inspiration from, ecology'.[35]

This claim was already forcefully advanced in Murray Bookchin's seminal writings of the 1960s which argue that ecological and anarchist principles are mutually reinforcing. Bookchin believes there is no hierarchy in nature and that a society free of hierarchy is a precondition for putting ecological principles into practice; decentralization is therefore not only desirable but even necessary for human survival. Specifically ecological reasons why decentralization is necessary have to do with how centralization reverses the direction of organic evolution and causes ecological imbalance. Bookchin believes the 'validity of the decentralist case can be demonstrated for nearly all the "logistical" problems of our time';[36] for instance, he argues, sustainable agriculture and the use of energy resources as well as the fight against pollution require a far-reaching decentralization of society and a truly regional concept of social organization. This also means that metropolitan areas need to be broken down so that a 'new type of community, carefully tailored to the characteristics and resources of a region, must replace the sprawling urban belts that are emerging today'.[37] Bookchin thereby invokes what he calls a 'true regionalism' as an antidote to the ecologically destructive concentrations of economic and political power which characterize the modern world.

More recently this idea of 'true regionalism' has been worked up into the influential idea of 'bioregionalism', in which the aim of decentralization receives an even more distinctively green colouring. A bioregion, on the definition given by Kirkpatrick Sale, 'is a part of the earth's surface whose rough boundaries are determined by natural rather than human dictates, distinguishable from other areas by attributes of flora, fauna, water, climate, soils and land-forms, and the human settlements and

cultures those attributes have given rise to.'[38] The boundaries of a bioregion should be drawn so as to encapsulate certain self-contained
physical and biological processes of nature, such as airsheds and water-
sheds. The term 'bioregion', though, has been used to refer not only to
the place but also to ways of living in that place. Living bioregionally
means living with the resources which are found within one's own territory, or, more accurately, becoming aware of the ecological relationships
that operate within and around it so that humans see themselves, in
Leopoldian fashion, as members of a biotic community rather than its
exploiters. Within bioregions people would live in communities, which
Sale sees as the basic units of the ecological world: these 'more-or-less
intimate groupings' of somewhere between 1000 and 10,000 people
would be the primary locus of decision-making.[39] They would seek to
minimize resource use, emphasize conservation and recycling, avoid pollution and waste. The aim of all this is to achieve sustainability through
self-sufficiency. This involves reducing both the spiritual and material
distance between humans and the land they live on:

> We must somehow live as close to it [the land] as possible, be in touch
> with its particular soils, its waters, its winds; we must learn its ways, its
> capacities, its limits; we must make its rhythms our patterns, its laws our
> guide, its fruits our bounty.[40]

The guiding principle of bioregionalism, and of green politics in general,
according to Dobson, 'is that the "natural" world should determine the
political, economic and social life of communities'.[41] Thus Sale, for
instance, believes that 'by a diligent study of nature we can guide ourselves in constructing human settlements and systems'.[42]

Certainly, one must always be duly cautious on the question of what is
to be learnt from nature, and criticisms that can be made of bioregionalism will be considered at the end of this section, but I believe that the
broad principles underlying an ecological utopia constitute an ideal
worth striving for. To live in communities whose economies and politics
are of human scale, whose principles embody the aim of living in a
closer relation to nature, and where belonging is a relation of reciprocity
and membership rather than ownership, are desirable ends. The question
to consider next is that of strategies for attempting to achieve a society
embodying these principles.

Strategies for getting there: green parties and alternatives

Whatever the desirability of the green utopia, whatever its internal
coherence and its consistency with ecological realities, there remains the

question of if and how it might be achieved. This is to raise the question of what forms and strategies of politics are appropriate in the here and now; it is also to raise the question of how greens can exercise power, what sort of power is possible for them, and what sort is consistent with their ends. New sorts of answer to these questions have to be sought because, viewed from a radical green perspective, political power in the contemporary world is fatally compromised. More often than not it is grounded in vested interests which are unecological or give low priority to ecological values. Certainly, to the extent that modern political systems support and are supported by capitalist economies they reproduce the characteristic ecological shortcomings of compulsively pursuing economic growth, discounting the future and, in allowing market forces full rein, having no mechanisms for dealing with the problems they generate.[43] Hence it is arguable that the liberal democracies tend to share capitalism's own defects. On the other hand, more centralized alternatives have defects which are no less serious. The manifest failure of central planning to cope with ecological problems in actually and formerly existing socialist states, for example, may very well be due to inherent features of that form of organization: in particular, those at the centre will often not have the political will, and almost certainly not have the ability, to respond with sufficient sensitivity to the complex and novel problems that continually arise.[44]

Green politics aspires to new political forms which are more sensitive to both human and ecological needs than are those oriented either to the free market or to centralized organization. A distinctive feature of green politics being its basis in grassroots social movements which are committed to extra-parliamentary, non-conventional and decentralized forms of political action, it aims to organize these into a force for change. Pursuit of this aim does involve potentially conflicting demands, though. The imperative of decentralization means seeking to develop a genuinely participatory polity which provides for a grassroots democracy that will remain true to the aims of the various constituent new social movements. Another imperative, however, is that of actually transferring power, and if this is not to be sought through violent revolution (and no greens to my knowledge think it should be) then it will mean working within and against existing institutions, attempting to render them more democratic, that is, more participatory and genuinely transparent.

The need for strategies to mediate between these potentially conflicting demands has been the *raison d'être* for the formation of green political parties. The idea of a 'new kind of party' which would seek to bring the influence of new social movements to bear on the existing machinery of power was summed up by Petra Kelly of *die Grünen*: 'We can no longer rely on the established parties . . . and we can no longer depend entirely on the extra-parliamentary road. The system is bankrupt, but a new force has to be created both inside and outside parliament.'[45] When *die Grünen* won seats in the Bundestag they saw this as part of a dual strategy which they described with the metaphor of 'two legs': one leg moving freely through the parliamentary institutions but the other having a firm foot in the extra-parliamentary movement.

This dual strategy of green party politics needs to be looked at in two dimensions: the role of oppositional groupings within and against the state; and the internal organization of a green party itself.

A constructive role for green representatives in parliament, as outlined by Joachim Hirsch, includes offering careful criticism of the administration's bills and countering them with concrete alternatives. Such critical labours aim at uncovering distortions and the systematic exclusion of certain issues. The objective, though, is not just to force concessions, but also to stimulate political development within the opposition movements themselves. This, he argues, establishes political and social legitimacy and demonstrates that there is *no* area where the opposition is not present. Parliamentary activity is thus seen as creating legal, organizational and financial conditions for developing and strengthening practical measures for changing society.[46] It provides a *support* for the political praxis whose real basis and vital context remains outside, with the movements. On the other hand, however, there remains the question of whether the greens' achievements within parliament will not be of too piecemeal and pragmatic a nature really to satisfy demands, pointing to the need for a more radical transformation of the political system itself. This in turn raises questions about the role of the Green *party* as a mediator of grassroots politics. As Hülsberg notes, there appears to be a contradiction between the anti-institutional character of the new social movements on the one hand, and their coagulability into a political party on the other. Moreover, it also seems to be the case that green parties virtually everywhere (perhaps like any political grouping with radical aims) tend to be wracked by internal strife, with a central line of tension invariably being that between accepting the demands of party discipline and the need for leadership, and allowing a genuine voice for the grassroots membership.

A central question, therefore, is whether green parties, through innovations in their internal organization, can overcome these contradictions and tensions. *Die Grünen* set out to develop a new type of party organization, the fundamental idea of which was continuous control over all officials and elected representatives in parliament and their recallability at any time. As stated in their programme of 1983, they sought to establish a party which was half citizens' initiative and half party. Rank and file democracy was supposed to be guaranteed by a number of means including a system of rotation in the Praesidium. Nevertheless, in practice, the weight tended to shift in favour of the parliamentary party. So whilst the German Greens went into parliament with the aim of changing the system, the system also changed them, as one by one the measures designed to ensure grassroots control were dropped.[47] One cannot, of course, conclude from this example, or even from the lack of counter-examples, that these kinds of measures designed to ensure democratic party structures will necessarily fail. On the other hand, though, nor should this perhaps be seen simply as a story of a careerist or corrupt centre disregarding the views or wishes of the grassroots. It does in fact appear that some of the problems are intrinsic to the project of grassroots democracy itself.

Political analysts have identified basic problems which appear to be intrinsic to grassroots democracy. For one thing, the openness of all meetings to ordinary members means that rank and file democracy easily degenerates into endless discussion: the more people who take part in meetings, and the more that meetings strive for unanimity, the longer it takes to reach any decision, which makes for inefficiency. This inefficiency is only compounded by the principle of rotation in office which, argues Goodin, generally means more in costs (in terms of lost expertise and effectiveness) than in benefits (which he sees as amounting to little more than the self-satisfaction of maintaining the principle of rotation itself).[48] Worse still, though, is how the green vision of grassroots democracy threatens to undercut the democratic character of the process it was intended to ensure: because no decision will be taken until nearly everyone has been talked around, observes Goodin, 'green theorists guarantee that only a small and unrepresentative sample of party members will be left in the room by the time the final decision is taken.'[49] Moreover, this open structure means whoever is there can vote for whatever measures they wish without having to bear any direct responsibility for the consequences. These problems are not peculiar to *green* theories of grassroots democracies, Goodin notes, but nor do the latter have any novel answers to offer.

In practice, parties like *die Grünen* have responded to these problems by developing a kind of professionalism with informal leadership structures. In doing so they have been taken to confirm a widely recognized tendency of parties in general to succumb to what has been called the 'iron law of oligarchy', whereby they end up being run by small groups of unrepresentative leaders.[50] From the perspective of someone like Goodin, this may be no bad thing; for radical greens, however, it points up the question of whether engagement in conventional politics is consistent with green objectives at all, and whether a single green party is even necessary or desirable. Certainly, in the light of these problems it does appear that the ideal of the green party being a radically different sort of party, a non-party party, might not be workable. Hence the choice may be the starker one of either accepting the role of a more or less conventional party *or* returning to strategies of more fundamental opposition – of strategies, in other words, of a movement *rather than* a party.

If it is the case, as Dobson suggests, that the institutions of representative democracy are effectively designed to preclude the possibility of massive regular participation, then the pursuit of participatory politics will demand the radical restructuring, or even abolition, of existing institutions.[51] Arguably, then, to be consistent, fundamentalists should abandon the party altogether.[52] And even though others may grant a residual case for considering participation in parliamentary politics as necessary or useful, there is agreement among greens that parliamentary politics is not sufficient to bring about the kind of change they seek.

So we turn to consider alternative green politics – that is, practices over and above those associated with parliamentary activity, with local government, or with political parties. Under the general heading of alternative politics may be included citizens' initiatives, networking, changes in individual and family lifestyle, peace camps, cooperatives, and communities experimenting with ecological lifestyles such as rural self-sufficiency farms or city farms. These are generally localized and particularistic types of activity, aimed not at seizing levers of existing power but at creating a new society in the interstices of the old. Something distinctive about these types of practice, therefore, is that they are to some extent pursued as ends or goods in themselves, and not only as means to separate goals. To some extent they constitute an attempt to create a radical alternative ecological culture in the here-and-now, an anticipatory practice in a quite different spirit from a reformism which would allow the use of any means necessary in the pursuit of green policy outcomes.

Accordingly a good deal of importance has been placed within green movements on the strategy of seeking social and political change by means of a change in one's lifestyle. Schumacher concluded his book, *Small is Beautiful*, with words whose spirit is a notable influence in green politics: 'Everywhere people ask: "What can I actually *do*"? The answer is as simple as it is disconcerting: we can, each of us, work to put our own inner house in order.'[53] A guiding lifestyle value has been captured by Bill Devall in the slogan 'simple in means, rich in ends'.[54] And as Arne Naess argues, this aim is not to be confounded with appeals to be Spartan, austere, or self-denying, for in one's lifestyle one can appreciate opulence, richness, luxury, and affluence so long as these are defined in terms of quality of life rather than standard of living. On this view of it, the politics of lifestyle would follow quite directly from the ecologically enlightened conception of the good life which was described in chapter 3. It would also have a greater importance than allowed it by reformists like Goodin. Arne Naess offers reasons for a different order of priorities: 'Attempts at a change in lifestyle cannot wait for the implementation of policies which render such change more or less required. The demand for "a new system" *first* is misguided and can lead to passivity.'[55] Of course, as Naess also notes, changes in lifestyle alone are unlikely to be sufficient, and must therefore proceed simultaneously with more directly political changes. The point is, though, that they are necessary.

Examples of the kinds of practice envisaged as lifestyle would be, according to Dobson, 'care with the things you buy, the things you say, where you invest your money, the way you treat people, the transport you use and so on'.[56] Lifestyles may incorporate ends which are communicative, educational, exemplary, or even involve direct action. Naess describes how they can operate as part of a cultural renewal: 'The movement encourages the reduction of individual total consumption, and will through information, increased awareness, and mutual influence attempt to free the individual and society from the consumer pressures which make it very difficult for politicians to support better policies and a healthier society.'[57]

It should be noted, though, that a good deal of the emphasis is placed on the power of *consumers*, and, as Dobson points out, there are pros and cons with this: 'The positive aspect of this strategy is that some individuals do indeed end up living sounder, more ecological lives ... The disadvantage, though, is that the world around goes on much as before, unGreened and unsustainable.'[58] Dobson notes that the consumer strategy may even be counterproductive at a deeper level of green analysis: for one thing, 'there are masses of people who are disenfranchised from this exercise of power by virtue of not having the money to spend in the first place'; and, for another, 'the underlying aim of this green consumerism is to *reform* rather than fundamentally restructure our patterns of consumption.' But although these are valid criticisms of consumerist strategies, it is nevertheless arguable that lifestyle is not reducible without remainder to these especially when it is oriented to new forms of production and exchange. A second line of criticism, though, is potentially more serious: such strategies do not take account of the problem of political power, argues Dobson, 'they mostly reject the idea that bringing about change is a properly "political" affair – they do not hold that Green change is principally a matter of occupying positions of political power and shifting the levers in the right direction.'[59] However, without denying that there are always likely to be individual lifestylers who are too naïve about political realities, I think this line of criticism risks missing the potentially radical force of alternative politics, for it is liable to beg the very question of principle which is central to any grassroots form of politics – namely, that of identifying, or even creating, new points of leverage and positions of political power. It is worth appreciating that lifestyle change can be of positive value not only to those individuals who end up living sounder, more ecological lives, nor just because it provides examples that others might be encouraged to follow, but also, and maybe more importantly, because it can highlight – as has already been the case for some time in feminist practice – that many aspects of daily life can indeed be considered 'properly political'. In this way, lifestyle changes can be seen as part of a broader strategy to transform and enrich the very concept of the political, and thereby to increase the sense, and reality, of empowerment of those hitherto excluded from politics in its mainstream definition.

Still, I speak of lifestyle as part of a broader strategy, for even if political change can start with a change in individual consciousness, it clearly does not end there. If a major question with lifestyle change is how the individualism on which it is based will convert into the communitarianism which is central to the ecological utopia, then it may in fact be, as Dobson says, more sensible to subscribe to forms of political action that are already communitarian. What he refers to as community strategies would be an improvement on lifestyle strategies 'because they are already a practice of the future in a more complete sense than that allowed by changes in individual behaviour patterns. They are more clearly an alternative to existing norms and practices, and, to the extent that they work, they show that it is possible to live differently – even sustainably.'[60] One notable proponent of this sort of strategy is Rudolf Bahro, who speaks of creating alternative 'basic communes' in which people opt for non-industrial lifestyles outside conventional patterns of employment and consumption. These would be 'liberated zones' oriented to genuine human needs and fulfilment. They would be self-sufficient communities of around 3000 people 'which would agree on a mode of simple, non-expanded reproduction of their material basis'.[61] Robyn Eckersley locates Bahro's suggestion in the tradition of monasticism, and summarizes its appeal:

> this tradition has shown that it is possible to create relatively self-sufficient and stable domestic economies from very small and humble beginnings. Moreover, it is a tradition that fosters a community that is 'simple in means and rich in ends,' provides an economics of permanence, offers egalitarian fellowship, and is able to synthesize qualities that have become polarized in modern life such as the personal/social and the practical/spiritual.[62]

The pursuit of community strategy also harmonizes with the aim of bio-regional politics, already discussed above, to achieve communal autarky, that is, the self-sufficiency and independence of constituent communities.

There are, however, questions as to how well community strategies will serve the ends of either the good life or justice. On the one hand, the quality of life in communities will not necessarily be an improvement in all respects on life in more anomic societies. For instance, as Naess has noted, communities have a potential for oppressiveness, a pressure towards conformity, which reduces both personal initiative and self-determination.[63] This is echoed by Gorz, who writes in quite a contrasting spirit to Bahro: 'communal autarky always has an impoverishing effect: the more self-sufficient and numerically limited a community is, the smaller the range of activities and choices it can offer to its members. If it has no opening to exogenous activity, knowledge and production, the community becomes a prison.'[64] On the other hand, connected to these concerns about the parochialism and personalism of community life, there are also concerns to do with justice, both retributive and distributive. One of these is the question of how recalcitrant members of the community are to be dealt with: Edward Goldsmith has suggested that 'crime' might be controlled 'through the medium of public opinion' by subjecting the offender to 'ridicule', but, as Dobson rightly points out, there is good reason to worry about this sort of suggestion,[65] and to prefer the impersonal impartiality of more formal systems of justice. On the distributive side, another set of questions concerns intercommunal or interregional justice and the problems of disparities of resources between regions which are differently endowed. If the principle of independence and self-sufficiency is paramount, then it can always be invoked by the better endowed as a reason for their non-beholdenness to the less well endowed.

If community strategies in and of themselves do not necessarily meet the desiderata either of good life or of justice, it is also a moot point how ecological they are: for it would not seem to be quite consonant with ecological principles to suppose that any region, let alone community, is wholly independent of others and therefore able to be entirely self-sufficient. Indeed, if communal decentralization means a more uniform distribution of human settlement, there are ecological arguments against it: for instance, as Paehlke points out, 'urban settlements are a less eco-logically stressful and more energy efficient way of accommodating large numbers of people on the land than dispersing the human population more thinly and widely throughout existing wilderness and rural areas.'[66]

These observations lead us to appreciate that there are both social and ecological limits to how far decentralist strategies in general, whether communal or individualistic, can successfully be pressed. The appro-priateness of decentralization as either strategy or objective depends at least in part on assumptions which are made about the nature of people and their relations. It presupposes people can and will work together cooperatively without a need for coercion from above or even coordina-tion from a centre. This in turn presupposes that a consensus can normally be arrived at, and that therefore there are no irreconcilably conflicting interests between or among individuals, communities and regions, or related problems such as that of chronic discrimination against permanent minorities.[67] In short, purely decentralist strategies are ultimately dependent on extremely sanguine assumptions about human cooperativeness, yet as has already been said, there are good reasons for caution about this sort of assumption. These reasons are compounded when such assumptions are claimed to derive support from ecological considerations. When the idea that nature knows best, and that we should therefore follow nature, is appealed to as a political principle, it should be remembered that nature teaches notoriously equivocal lessons: decentralists are impressed by the lack of hierarchy in nature, but social Darwinists, for instance, read quite other messages in nature. In the light of these considerations, finally, one should be extremely wary that if, as Sale suggests, it is not necessarily the case that each bioregional society 'will construct itself upon the values of democracy, equality, liberty, freedom, justice, and other suchlike desiderata',[68] then this may well be a good reason for wanting to maintain or develop some overarching institutions which *do* embody these values.

I should emphasize that these criticisms of decentralization apply to the carrying of it to an extreme; they do not require us to deny it as an important political principle. Kemp and Wall try to put the matter in perspective:

> Critics of decentralization argue that tight national control and strong central powers are needed in case local communities decide to dump PCBs in their drinking water or build nuclear power stations, but a far more real danger is that strong central government, supported by big business, distant from its electorate and protected by laws of official secrecy, will create pollution on a national scale . . . The ecological dangers of centralization are proven and dangerous; the positive contribution decentralization could make to a cleaner environment and a better democracy are clear.[69]

Limitations to ecologism

The conceptions of politics examined in this section do not add up to a fully coherent alternative to business as usual. Yet if the pursuit of green politics in its more radical forms is rife with paradoxes and contradictions, this in itself need not constitute an objection, since they have arisen as a response to a reality which itself is rife with contradictions; what it does mean though, is that contradictions need to be worked through rather than peremptorily foreclosed. To preserve the cutting edge of radical green ideas, it is necessary to find ways of bringing them to bear on existing power relations. Effective strategies depend not only on utopian goals, but also on a theory of the given: it is necessary to understand existing power relations and forces for change. In this section we have examined two of the three elements identified by Dobson as the constituents of an ecological political ideology – utopia and strategy – and in both cases have found significant problems. These problems can be related to an underlying question – which has to do with the third constituent of ecologism as an ideology – namely, whether there really is or could be a distinctively green understanding of social and political reality. In previous chapters we have already noted reasons for being cautious about how much of such an understanding to expect from ecology. My final argument, accordingly, will be that green political theory involves the pursuit not of absolute novelty in conceptualizing society and politics but of a thoroughgoing critique of dominant conceptions of the political in the light of ecological considerations.

5.3   Towards a Green Political Theory: Radical Democracy, Ecology and Concrete Utopia

If ecological politics has to be radical to be ecological (versus environmentalism), it also has to be realistic (versus ecologism). The challenge for a green political theory is to avoid the fallacies of ecologism without lapsing back into the complacencies which are attendant on a reformist environmentalism. In other words, it is not an appropriate aim simply to supplant conventional politics by ecologism, but nor can all conventional views be taken at face value or their assumptions taken over unchallenged. It is necessary to understand the social mediations of eco-logical and political questions, to get a critical purchase on the society out of which the politics emerges and upon which it needs to have impact.

In this section I wish to show that radical political aims can be pursued to a significant extent through an immanent critique of existing institu-tionalized norms, by pushing the values that can be justified as far as possible and challenging those which may have had some historically contingent or socially particularistic rationale that does not, or no longer, commands universal assent. This very way of casting the project of radi-cal politics does raise fundamental questions, though. In particular there is the question of whether it should really be seeking universal assent. This, as I argue in the opening subsection, is to bring into focus a central and perennial dilemma of democracy, and one which is particularly acute where there are aspirations for a *radical* democracy. This dilemma, essentially, is a conflict between the demands of pluralism on the one hand, and those pertaining to a more universalistic notion of the common good on the other. I indicate why radical political aims in general and ecological radicality in particular appear to be at odds with democracy in this respect, and ask whether they can be reconciled. I shall suggest that reconciliation is possible through a redefinition of the political itself. A question this leaves is whether there is any good reason to think radical democratic processes would embody ecological values. I argue that there are good reasons for so thinking, because there is a significant con-vergence between the aims of radical ecology and radical democracy.

The dilemma of radical democracy: pluralism and the common good

The dilemma for radical democracy appears when one considers the question of whether one can generally assume that people are the best judges of their own best interests and of how those interests may best be pursued. One might expect a proponent of radical democracy to give an affirmative answer to both of these questions as to do so would be expressive of quintessentially democratic beliefs. In fact, though, a consistent radical democrat has to be very circumspect about doing so since for democracy to be *radical* it has to be theoretically informed by ideology critique, that is, by an awareness of how people's perceptions of their own interests, and perhaps of social reality more generally, may be systematically distorted in and through ideology. Without this awareness, what appears to be democratic process could in fact be systematically biased. If this is the case, then there must be doubts whether people at large are always the best judges even of their own interests, let alone of the best policies to pursue.

One way of viewing the dilemma of radical democracy, then, is to see the demands of radicalism as militating against democracy. History supplies abundant instances of this appearing to happen: when a radical vanguard puts itself at the head of the demos, this can all too often be the first step towards a totalitarian dictatorship. The idea that radicals know better is a problem that can arise with radical ecologists too: given that people's understanding of ecological questions may not extend beyond the effects these have on their own immediate interests and may not reach out to underlying causes, radical ecologists may similarly be tempted into the role of experts, and at least adopt a counterproductive 'greener than thou' attitude, even if they are not in a position to impose decisions in a more totalitarian fashion.[70]

Environmental reformism, by contrast, can move closer to a classical liberal position which could be claimed to undercut the problem here: if one drops the radical requirement and the assumptions of ideology critique, democracy may appear in a less problematic light. Thus, according to the classical theorists of liberal democracy it can straightforwardly be asserted that there is no one who knows what is for your interest so well as you yourself. This makes matters simpler. Democracy can be viewed as a mechanism which allows people to say what they want, and thereupon supplies those wants in an optimal fashion.[71] The underlying assumption here is what Offe and Wiesenthal refer to as the 'liberal equation', that is, the belief that an individual's interest is simply what one says it is.[72] This means that democracy can function in much the way that a market does, as a supply and demand of political goods, with politicians supplying and voters demanding.

A major problem with this particular sort of liberal 'solution', though, when viewed from a radical perspective, is that the model of democracy it provides for is not fully democratic. If democracy is taken to mean rule of the people, and to embody popular sovereignty, it cannot be likened to a market. In a market the consumers are not sovereign, despite certain illusory appearances, and this is not least because a market itself only exists in a wider context of social, economic and cultural practices. Democracy is not about consumers making choices between a narrow range of pre-packaged commodities, but about people taking responsibility for their own lives and taking decisions in the full range of their activities. In other words, true democracy must be a more *participatory* democracy. This means more than voting at periodic intervals: it means having a say about the *agenda* of politics; ultimately it means that democracy entails not simply a mechanism for electing leaders, but rather a fuller and richer form of associative life. On this view democracy is also about promoting a better life, which, like ecology, implies a commitment to the pursuit of some substantive ends as being intrinsically better than others. It also thereby implies a shared conception of the common good.

This rejection of the liberal solution, though, brings us back to the dilemma of radical democracy; for the attempt to pursue a unified conception of the good life, in a society where individuals have a plurality of conceptions of what is actually good, risks imposing on them moral values against their will. This can lead not only to imposing policies on people 'for their own good' but also to claiming that any protests they might make are merely indicative of 'false consciousness' about their true interests. Even when such claims might have some truth, the *making* of them is hard to reconcile with democracy, since the result is liable to be criticized as at best paternalistic and at worst totalitarian. So the aims of participatory democracy – which on the face of it appear to be emancipatory and progressive – imply some idea of a common good, the pursuit of which can be criticized in the name of pluralism. If the very idea of radical democracy includes *both* participation and pluralism, then the dilemma is how to preserve pluralism, but without relativism.

If this is a dilemma for radical democratic politics in general, it is also a dilemma for radical ecological politics in particular. For on the one hand, to the extent that ecological politics makes reference to ecological truths, it will not be relativist: an ecological perspective will not be neutral with respect to one ecological policy compared with another. Hence on this score the aim would be, as our understanding of ecology improves, to incorporate ecological insights in a conception of a common good. On the other hand, though, if ecological understanding cannot be assumed to be neutral, nor will it generally be sufficiently full and

unequivocal to determine appropriate policy. Hence a plurality of perceptions remains possible, appropriate and largely unavoidable. In this
context, then, to advocate pluralism without relativism indicates the
imperative of being consistent with what we know of ecology but without overstretching our knowledge.

Reconceptualizing the political

If the dilemma of radical democracy is to be overcome, then the aim of
participation must be shown somehow to be compatible with pluralism.
In order to do this both need to be reconceptualized. This in turn will
yield a conception of the political itself which differs from that of liberalism. For if the aims of participation appear to be incompatible with
pluralism this is to some extent due to certain specifically liberal assumptions about the meaning of pluralism which can in fact be challenged.
From a liberal perspective, the objection to denying the equation of
people's interests with what they think or say they are is that this appears
at the same time to be denying basic respect for people's autonomy: what
needs to be shown, therefore, is how respect for autonomy can be promoted without assuming that an empiricist account of people's interests
will necessarily be reliable. The key is to focus on the question of *conditions* which are favourable for the development and exercise of
autonomy. The radical argument seeks to show that liberals accept or
promote conditions which on a deeper analysis are actually *unfavourable*
for it.

The conditions for securing and promoting individual autonomy on the
liberal view are a strong but morally neutral state which governs by the
rule of law. Hence moral pluralism is in fact underpinned by legal
'monism': no particular interpretation of the good life is imposed on
individuals, but the requirements of justice, peace and public order are
non-negotiable. The benefit of this is that individuals are free to decide
for themselves what they think is good, with what is *just* being laid down
by the law which thereby guarantees the free space within which those
personal opinions can be held. Hence liberals demand neutrality on the
part of public institutions *vis-à-vis* questions of morality so as to respect
individual autonomy.[73]

However, this assumes that which matters are of public concern and
which are not is already settled. State neutrality, therefore, must be seen
in the context of a set of prior divisions: ethical life is already bifurcated
into questions of goodness and justice, morality and legality, matters of
private and matters of public concern. But one can ask how these particu-

lar divisions themselves arise and are justified. The divisions have come
into being in the course of a determinate history of social struggles
and contain within them the result of historical power compromises.
Benhabib illustrates this by observing how, before the emergence of
strong working-class movements and the welfare state, questions relating
to the health of workers were frequently construed by employers as
'trade secrets' and 'business privacy'; as a result of political struggle,
however, such matters were transformed into issues of 'public concern'.
More generally, she argues, all struggles against oppression in the modern world 'begin by redefining what had previously been considered
"private", non-public and non-political issues as matters of public concern, as issues of justice, as sites of power which need discursive
legitimation.'[74] This, of course, is exactly what is involved in ecological
struggle too. In this respect, Benhabib observes, the women's movement,
the peace movement, the ecology movements, and the new ethnic identity movements all follow a similar logic: they all refuse to take given
distinctions at face value or to accept them as immutable.

Regarding the justification of these historically contingent distinctions,
radicals can then ask, for instance, whether the state is really neutral, and
on what grounds it can be claimed that some particular values are nego-
tiable and others are not. The ethical strengths of the liberal view lie in
its non-coerciveness and its refusal, in contrast to undemocratic forms of
radicalism, to impute 'true' interests which are supposedly obscured by
'false' consciousness. Its weakness though is that, in refusing to criticize
empirical appearances, it is effectively endorsing the status quo; and if
the status quo is coercive, then it is complicit in coercion anyway.[75] On
a liberal interpretation of it, therefore, pluralism is not necessarily a
solution to the evils associated with an orientation to the common good.
The radical logic implies that questions of values and neutrality must be
kept open to renegotiation. This means not so much denying the core
values of liberalism as immanently criticizing the limitedness of their
application. As Benhabib writes, the search for a just, stable and tolerant
political order has 'led to an excessive focus in contemporary liberalism
upon the limits and justification of state power and other public agencies
to the neglect of other dimensions of political life, like life in political
associations, movements, citizens' groups, town meetings, and public
fora.'[76] Once the concept of the political is expanded, the meaning of
political participation is also transformed – from an activity that is only
possible in a narrowly defined political realm into activities which are
pursued in social and cultural spheres as well.[77] The aim of politics
becomes not merely that of seeking a compromise between separate,

privately formed interests of individuals, but that of creating and maintaining autonomous public spaces in which collective interests can be dialogically defined. These public spaces would make possible

> the creation of procedures whereby those affected by general social norms and by collective political decisions can have a say in their formulation, stipulation and adoption . . . The public sphere comes into existence whenever and wherever all affected by general social and political norms of action engage in a practical discourse, evaluating their validity. In effect, there may be as many publics as there are controversial general debates about the validity of norms.[78]

This is not to deny the principle of pluralism but to radicalize it. This is to appeal to a communicative model of democracy which goes beyond the liberal in not presupposing any fixed distinctions between what is properly political and what is not. Everything is yet to decide: 'citizens must feel free to introduce . . . any and all moral arguments into the conversational field.'[79]

However, this radicalization of pluralism might seem to compound the original problem by increasing rather than reducing the scope for divergent views about the good life. The important point to note, though, is that a communicative model of democracy, like the discourse ethics in which it is ultimately grounded (see section 4.3), operates at two levels: on one there is a commitment to discursive democratic procedures which itself is non-negotiable, while on another what people substantively decide while using those procedures is not laid down in advance. The idea of the public sphere as a regulative idea implies criteria and standards of what Habermas calls communicative rationality: the rationality of action oriented to reaching a consensual understanding, as opposed to strategic forms of action which do not attempt more than to achieve compromises between irreducibly separate and conflicting individual goals. Securing the *conditions* for discursive will formation implies substantive imperatives generated directly from the higher level – for instance, conditions of equality and non-coerciveness which make *effective* participation possible – and this goes well beyond the formal liberties of a liberalism whose admittance of a free market in ideas is little disposed to encourage an intersubjective appreciation of how that freedom conceals real imbalances of power and inadequacy of reasons. In short, the conception of politics sketched here is oriented to communicative as opposed to merely strategic forms of action; it involves a commitment to consensus as opposed to mere compromise; it implies procedures but also commitment to substantive preconditions of their actualization; in sum, it promises to mediate the conflicting pressures which yield the dilemma of radical democracy. The next question to address is whether there is any good reason to suppose that decisions arrived at through radical democratic processes would embody ecological values.

Is radical democracy ecological?

So far in this section I have sought to establish that democracy can be radical and remain democratic. The question now – the one I resisted Goodin's attempt to foreclose (section 5.1) – is whether it would also be *ecological*.

As John Dryzek recognizes, one may ask whether individuals engaged in discursive practices might nevertheless not 'reflectively and competently choose to downgrade environmental concerns in comparison with (say) economic prosperity or social integration'.[80] His reply is that discursive democratization is indeed ecologically rational, particularly from the point of view of sensitivity to feedback signals, complexity, generalizability and compliance; moreover, it promotes 'sensitivity to signs of disequilibrium in human–nature interactions because their *sine qua non* of extensive competent participation means that a wide variety of voices can be raised on behalf of a wide variety of concerns.'[81] The fact that discursive democracy gives voice to a wide variety of concerns, Dryzek argues, makes it a particularly effective way of dealing with the complexity which typifies ecological problems. 'The interactions between the multiple facets of a problem which define its complexity can be matched by joint, cooperative problem-solving among the individuals concerned with these multiple facets.'[82]

I think this is a strong argument, and shall now show how the politics of discursive democracy can meet objections from both environmental reformists and ecological radicals on their own territory because this approach is no less realistic than that of the former and no less ecological than that of the latter.

One criticism from reformists would be to recall Goodin's observation that practical attempts to make green political procedures radically democratic have tended to produce a lot of long and exhausting talk, with the productivity of any outcome being in more or less inverse proportion to the democratic quality of the process by which it was arrived at. If this is the case, then discursive democracy would seem to promise more of the same. In reply to this objection, however, it may be argued that the unfortunate features of the phenomenon described are precisely respects in which it *deviates* from the principles of discursive democracy. As Dryzek puts it:

> To the extent participants in interactions are committed to the principles of communicative rationality, and so renounce strategy, deception, distortion, and manipulation, then the possibility of felicitous understanding across the individuals who represent the diverse facets of complex problems becomes conceivable.[83]

Hence discursive democracy captures a situation quite unlike the one where real-life greens have particular axes to grind and are impervious to opposite points of view. In this, it is of course somewhat utopian; and as Dryzek himself says, the achievement of communicative rationality can only be a matter of degree, not an absolute accomplishment. The point is, though, that a high degree of priority should be accorded to this particular goal, that of achieving unconstrained discourse. If greens take seriously their ideas of improving the world also through improving themselves then they perhaps should be committed to just these aims.

A further objection is that people involved in green politics should be talking about questions of substance and arriving at recommendations for policy, not focusing all their attention on procedural and self-reflective matters. Thus Goodin, for instance, argues that the best decision will be that which most completely realizes green ends: between such matters of substance and matters of procedure, however, there is no necessary connection. In reply it can first be acknowledged that substantive decisions must of course be reached, and so there is no disagreement on this point; what is at issue, however, is the question of whether it particularly matters *how* they are arrived at. To put it crudely, for Dryzek it does and for Goodin it does not. I think the position I am associating with Goodin is wrong for the following reasons. He does not actually ask how his green theory of value is arrived at as a theory people might subscribe to: what he does is present an argument, monologically, to explain why he thinks the theory is a good and compelling one. Now it may well be that in actual forums where green political ideas are discussed, some people will disagree with his arguments and dissent from his conclusions: but unless there are procedures for coming to reasoned agreement no effective policy will necessarily be arrived at, or the one arrived at may not be the one for which the best reasons can be advanced. Even if everyone should accept Goodin's theory of value, there will remain the question of how policies can be derived from the principles of the value theory: Goodin himself would not, I think, wish to claim policies can be derived infallibly, if indeed they can be derived at all, from a theory of desirable consequences. So even if one shares Goodin's primary concern with consequences, the means of arriving at decisions about how to achieve them *do* matter. To deny this is to take an unecological view – effectively licensing one to cut with a blunt instrument through the complexities of problems to reach a decision, come what may, with no way of knowing in advance whether the decision is a particularly good one. There are good reasons for believing that real efficiency in the pursuit of ends will be promoted by establishing good procedures for discussion, not by curtailing it. Hence I believe it is pragmatically as well as ethically important that democratic procedures are built into policy formation.

On this basis it can be argued that discursive democracy goes *deeper* than any green theory of value, since the ends are not derived from a theory of value; rather, any theory of value has first to be arrived at democratically. But even if this claim were accepted, the problem then would be that this could be criticized as an *anthropocentric* sort of depth by contrast to ecocentrism. From a radical ecologistic perspective there are reasons of principle for focusing criticism on how discursive democracy accords more priority to human relations than to green values. Part of a reply to this argument would be that nothing about discursive democracy is intrinsically opposed to ecocentrism; in fact, the whole point of discursive democracy is that any stand on substantive questions can and must be arrived at by the participants in discourse, and if ecological crises are as serious as expert opinion says they are, then in conditions of discursive democracy those expert voices will be given appropriate weight in deliberations, and therefore what they say will be acted upon. However, this reply may not suffice for radical ecologists because the 'appropriate weight' may be appropriate for humans only; so the problem remains, as Dobson has noted, that even when the public sphere has been invigorated as described, 'there is no guarantee that the free and equal conversations that ensue will grant a more valued status to the non-human world than it has at present'.[84] Greens, he says, will want stronger guarantees than this. If one is to reply to this, however, one has to pose the question of what constitutes a guarantee. If what is sought is an improvement in humans' treatment of non-humans this will certainly not be guaranteed by rhetorically asserting the intrinsic value of nature or the values of deep ecology if those values do not permeate the actual practices of humans; only if sufficient humans actively identify with the plight of others could we begin to think of guarantees. Ecological ethics may offer good reasons for protecting and preserving non-human beings; it does not guarantee humans will accept them, let alone act on them. So thinking politically, as opposed to reasoning about ethics, the question of guarantees scarcely arises as yet; what exists is the prospect of struggle. If ecological politics is seen in the context of other historical struggles of various oppressed groups of humans this is appropriate because of the continuities between the forms of exploitation and domination; it is also likely to be effective because it can tap into existing forces and build on ethical reserves already achieved. These advantages are likely to be sacrificed by a rhetorical insistence on an ecocentrism which represents a radical break with all previous human ethics and politics. Moreover, realizing these advantages need not imply a pragmatic compromise with principle. Humans themselves are, after all, a part of nature; the better they deal with their specific concerns the better they will have to grasp the concerns of nature too, and perhaps recover a vocation 'to be the voice of all that is dumb, to endow nature with an organ for making known her sufferings'.[85] As Max Horkheimer sums it up: 'Distorted though the great ideals of civilization – justice, equality, freedom – may be, they are nature's protestations against her plight, the only formulated testimonies we possess.'[86]

I would add to this that only in a culture where humans are accustomed to listen to one another will there be any real prospect of heeding nature's protestations too. In this respect, discursive democracy is a necessary condition for systematically realizing ecological values.

The politics of concrete utopia

Of course, real politics involves real struggles: discursive democracy is not only a strategy, it is also an objective which yet needs to be achieved. Moreover, while it gives political form to specific struggles it does not automatically ensure their success, and their success will involve achievements which are not reducible without remainder to democratization. This means that, especially while processes of discursive democracy are only partially instantiated, there remains a place for political practices guided by other substantive objectives. As Barbara Holland-Cunz says, 'we need imaginative forms, inspirations, pictures, mental images, utopian ideas and conceptions to give us strength and direction when working for a new society's new relationship with nature.'[87] Here an element of utopianism is appropriately invoked: but if this is to serve as a guide to action, rather than as merely the articulation of an unrealizable aspiration, then its place needs to be carefully delimited. Here it will be helpful to refer to Ernst Bloch's idea of the politics of 'concrete utopia.'

Concrete utopia is a term which has to some extent entered the green vernacular, particularly in Germany. In its original formulation,[88] the idea of *concrete* utopia is to be distinguished, on the one hand, from the drawing up of blueprints for an ideal society, which would be 'abstract utopias': it refers to anticipatory practices in the here-and-now, involving, as John Ely notes, 'the self-conscious and largely "voluntary" development of alternative forms and counter-institutions'.[89] On the other hand, though, it is not reducible to the unmediated opposition of alternative lifestyles alone: the inspiration for the idea as formulated by Bloch comes from the young Marx's formulation of *immanent* critique as the clarification of that towards which the world is already striving: 'we do not anticipate the world with our dogmas but instead attempt to discover the new world through the critique of the old . . . the critic can take his cue from every existing form of theoretical and practical consciousness and from this ideal and final goal implicit in the *actual* forms of existing reality he can deduce a true reality.'[90] For Bloch, concrete rather than abstract utopia is to be discovered in the not yet actual but objectively real possibilities of the world.[91] Thus Benhabib describes the task of the critic as showing that 'the given is not a mere fact, that to understand it to be actuality is also to criticize it by showing what it could be but is not'.[92] The more general political objective, consonant with this, depends on 'the knowledge of a self-transforming present, not an ideal future'.[93] It is a 'politics of fulfilment' in as much as it is directed to the realization of promises immanent in existing institutions and normative structures.

Nevertheless, one still needs to be alert to the risk of being utopian in a sense vulnerable to criticism as unrealistic. Steven Lukes, for instance, has suggested that it may be unfounded optimism to suppose that the result of forces already at work within social reality will be the realization of the ultimate objective. Marx and Engels themselves, he writes, were rash in assuming that 'humankind only sets itself such tasks as it can solve', supposing thereby that success in the task of building socialism was somehow historically guaranteed.[94] The same point can be made with regard to the idea that if humans get sufficiently enlightened about their own ecological conditions of existence, about their dependence – not only material, but also psychological, aesthetic, spiritual – on nature, they will develop practices which respect it. There is no guarantee that such enlightenment will come about, or, if it did, whether it would be objectively *possible* to act on it whilst also fulfilling all human needs. A politics of fulfilment, therefore, may not suffice; and taken alone could encourage complacency about the enormity of the real task. In this context, indeed, it is appropriate to reflect, with Benhabib, on the fate of radical politics in the twentieth century:

> The course of European history after the beginning of the twentieth century left little hope that the Enlightenment could fulfil its own *promesse du bonheur*. Critical theory lamented the dialectic of an Enlightenment condemned to leave its own promises unfulfilled. The project of emancipation was increasingly viewed not as the fulfilment, but as the transfiguration of the Enlightenment legacy.[95]

It is unlikely to suffice simply to take over and redeem promises of earlier generations; qualitatively new imperatives are also called for.

Benhabib therefore suggests it is necessary to recognize that the politics of fulfilment is one of two contrasting visions of politics, the other being the politics of transfiguration:

> The politics of fulfilment envisages that the society of the future attains more adequately what present society has left unaccomplished. It is the culmination of the implicit logic of the present. The politics of transfiguration emphasizes the emergence of qualitatively new needs, social relations, and modes of association, which burst open the utopian potential within the old.[96]

The politics of fulfilment seeks to realize the universalist promise of bourgeois revolutions: justice, equality, civil rights, democracy and publicity are goals not to be abandoned, but yet to be fully achieved. The politics of transfiguration, on the other hand, is oriented to the formation of a community of needs and solidarity and '*qualitatively transformed relations to inner and outer nature*'.[97]

What Benhabib describes here is precisely what was characterized as a tension within green political thought at the outset of this chapter: a concern, on the one hand, with universalist principles of justice; and, on the other, with substantive relations between humans and the rest of nature. Whereas reformism appreciates the achievements embodied in existing society and values, 'pure green' concerns are typically presented in terms of a transfiguration of present society and values. Yet if there is a tension between the two orientations, Benhabib emphasizes, 'a critical social theory is only rich enough to address us in the present, insofar as it can do justice to both moments'.[98] It would therefore be a mistake to think pure green utopianism should prevail over universalistic norms; it would be equally mistaken to suppose the contrary. Benhabib continues in a fashion which well captures the situation of radical politics:

The community of needs and solidarity is created in the interstices of
society by those new social movements, which on the one hand fight to
extend the universalist promise of objective spirit – justice and entitlements – and on the other seek to combine the logic of justice with that of
friendship.[99]

That friendship should be extended to our fellow beings on this planet –
human and non-human – should scarcely need emphasizing; that the
conditions for the flourishing of such relationships need care and cultivation perhaps does. In ecological politics it cannot be forgotten that
relations of justice and democracy are as vital, but also as fragile, as any
ecosystem.

Conclusion

This chapter began with the question of whether there might be a distinctively green political philosophy. My conclusion is that there can be,
but that it must be distinguished not by what it excludes, but by what it
includes – by how it enriches and expands the horizons of previous
political philosophies.

Afterword
Ecological Enlightenment

It has been my aim in this book to demonstrate the possibility of constructive dialogue between those of deep green convictions and those who, even when sympathetic to the former's intuitions and value orientation, are sceptical of many of their claims and the reasoning underlying them. In particular, I have wanted to show that ecological enlightenment is not a contradiction in terms. My arguments to that end will be judged on their merits. In these closing remarks I should like just to illustrate why I believe that much of the dispute and polemic is expressive not so much of insoluble contradictions as of differences of perspective. The illustration, for me, has quite personal resonances. On the one hand, I empathize with Arne Naess's description of ecological philosophy:

> Green philosophy or the philosophy of the deep ecology movement is largely an articulation of the implicit philosophy of 5 year old children who have access to at least a minimum of animals, plants, and natural places. These children experience animals as beings like themselves in basic respects. They have joys and sorrows, interests, needs, loves and hates. Even flowers and places are alive to them, thriving or having a bad time. The personal identity of the small child has environmental factors. They are part of himself or herself, the personal, social and natural self being one and indivisible.
>
> Philosophers of the deep ecology movement may be said to be people who have never found biological, political or other arguments to undermine those attitudes implicit in childhood.[1]

There would seem to be a marked contrast here with the philosophy of the Enlightenment as proclaimed by Kant when he spoke of enlightenment as precisely the attaining of maturity, of leaving childhood

behind. Yet what he emphasizes is the emancipation from *self-imposed*
immaturity. I could scarcely find a better description than this of the
essence of the ethical and existential requirement for moving from the
crassly nihilistic and self-destructive consumerism of contemporary
Western culture into a mature and responsible ecological era. Therefore
preserving the spontaneous wisdom Naess finds in childhood is quite
compatible with, and may well be a precondition of, overcoming
maturity.

Of course, it may be observed that the Kantian is, at root, as naïve as
the deep ecologist – maybe more so than the average child! Ecology and
enlightenment, invoked as symbols, both stand for optimism; and the
latent danger within optimism is that it can degenerate into complacency
and hubris. So if in this book I have sought to emphasize the potential for
constructive alliance between environmentalism and ecologism, reformism and radicalism, it should not be forgotten that the more powerful
forces remain at present ranged against this alliance – but that, I believe,
is all the more reason for trying to build it.

Notes

Introduction: Environmental Values in Social and Political Thought

1 World Commission on Environment and Development, chaired by Gro Harlem Brundtland, *Our Common Future*.
2 M. Saloman et al., '*Appel de Heidelberg*'.
3 Vandana Shiva, *Staying Alive*, p. xiv.
4 Ibid., p. 233.
5 Robyn Eckersley, *Environmentalism and Political Theory*.
6 T. O'Riordan, *Environmentalism*.

Chapter 1   Ecology and Enlightenment

1 Robert P. McIntosh, *The Background of Ecology* p. 1.
2 Max Horkheimer and Theodor Adorno, *Dialectic of Enlightenment*, p. 3.
3 McIntosh, *The Background of Ecology*, pp. 1–2.
4 This suggestion is taken from Nicolson, in ibid., p. 16.
5 For a general characterization of the historical Enlightenment see N. Hampson, *The Enlightenment*; Peter Gay, *The Enlightenment, An Interpretation* (2 Vols).
6 Isaiah Berlin, 'Two Concepts of Liberty', pp. 56–7.
7 Some commentators would consider Bacon and Descartes as already thinkers of the Enlightenment. Accepting the Enlightenment's own estimate that its view of science is epitomized in Newton, they depart from the tendency of the majority of eighteenth-century thinkers to pit Newton against Descartes: thus, for instance, Fritjof Capra, *The Turning Point*, speaks of 'Cartesian-Newtonian science'; see also Peter A. Schouls, *Descartes and the Enlightenment* and Jonathan Rée, *Descartes*. I signal this issue because whatever the continuities in the development of scientific thought from Descartes to Kant, there are significant philosophical differences which I shall want to emphasize.

8 Capra, *The Turning Point*, p. 44.

9 Descartes quoted in ibid., p. 45.

10 In ibid., p. 47.

11 Ibid.

12 Ibid., p. 46

13 For an accessible introduction to the character of critical philosophy see J.G. Murphy, *Kant: The Philosophy of Right*, pp. 26–38.

14 See Kant's discussion of 'The Paralogisms of Pure Reason' in his *Critique of Pure Reason*, pp. 328–83.

15 In his *Critique of Judgment* Kant writes that an organism is 'an organized natural product in which every part is reciprocally both end and means'; it is a natural end with 'intrinsic natural perfection and a self-propagating formative power' that cannot be explained in mechanistic terms. 'Strictly speaking, therefore, the organization of nature has nothing analogous to any causality known to us ... Organisms are, therefore, the only beings in nature that, considered in their separate existence and apart from any relation to other things, cannot be thought possible except as ends of nature ... Thus they supply natural science with the basis for a teleology' (pp. 310–24).

16 Hampson has described Kant as 'the philosopher who summed up the achievement of the Enlightenment, defined the frontiers of empirical knowledge and established for pure reason and for ethics realms of their own beyond the mere appearances of the world of phenomena' (*The Enlightenment*, p. 196).

17 Kant, *The Moral Law*, pp. 60–1.

18 Kant, 'An Answer to the Question: What Is Enlightenment?', p. 41.

19 Kant, *Critique of Judgment*, p. 349.

20 Gay, *The Enlightenment, An Interpretation*, p. 141.

21 Kant, 'An Answer to the Question: What Is Enlightenment?', p. 44.

22 For an overview of the various declarations see J. Kleinig, 'Human Rights, Legal Rights and Social Change'. It will be noticed that it was not yet self-evident that women might have inalienable rights too. Cf. A.J. Arnaud and E. Kingdom, *Women's Rights and the Rights of Man*.

23 McIntosh, *The Background of Ecology*, p. 26.

24 McIntosh, 'The Background and Some Current Problems of Theoretical Ecology', pp. 219–20.

25 Donald Worster, *Nature's Economy*, p. 33; also R.C. Stauffer, according to Pascal Acot, *Storia dell'ecologia*, p. 19, sees Linnean thought as the birthplace of ecology.

26 Worster, *Nature's Economy*, p. 35.

27 Acot, *Storia dell'ecologia*, p. 43 (my trans.).

28 Cf. McIntosh, *The Background of Ecology*, p. 14, where he quotes Glacken's remark that virtually every great thinker of the last two or three millennia has had something to say on this theme, which is one that permeates mythology, history, literature and art: a continuing problem, therefore, 'is discerning the relation of ecology to this ubiquitous interest'.

29 Daniel Simberloff, 'A Succession of Paradigms in Ecology', p. 13.

30 Worster, *Nature's Economy*, p. 210.

31 Cf. McIntosh, 'Some Problems of Theoretical Ecology', pp. 209–10; Clements's concepts were influential for J.C. Smuts, *Holism*.

32 Simberloff, 'A Succession of Paradigms in Ecology', p. 20.

33 Quoted in Worster, *Nature's Economy*, p. 301.

34 Ibid., p. 302. For an introduction to the basics of ecosystems see Eugene Odum, *Ecology and Our Endangered Life-Support Systems*, especially chapter 3.
35 Worster, *Nature's Economy*, p. 302.
36 Eugene P. Odum, *Ecology and Our Endangered Life-Support Systems*, chapter 2.
37 Worster, *Nature's Economy*, p. 302.
38 McIntosh, 'Some Problems of Theoretical Ecology', p. 243 (my emphasis).
39 Marcello Cini, 'Science and Sustainable Society', p. 41.
40 Cini, ibid., mentions that the work of the meteorologist Edward Lorenz in 1963 provided the point of departure for this development; Cini and others give an overview of the sorts of phenomena involved in Gianfranco Bangone et al., *Gli ordini del caos*.
41 Cini, 'Science and Sustainable Society', pp. 42–4, cites the work of biologist Stephen Gould, biophysicist Mario Ageno, and cyberneticist von Forster in this connection.
42 J. Baird Callicott, 'The Metaphysical Implications of Ecology', p. 302.
43 Ibid., p. 303.
44 Cf. also C. Birch and J.C. Cobb, *The Liberation of Life*.
45 Morowitz quoted in Callicott, 'The Metaphysical Implications of Ecology', p. 309.
46 Ibid., p. 313.
47 Ibid., p. 311.
48 McIntosh, *The Background of Ecology*, p. 1.
49 Anthropologists have also recorded practices which we might with some justification abhor: see Tim Ingold, 'In Search of the Noble Savage', *Horizon*, BBC2, 27 January 1992). So one needs to be open to learning from other cultures whilst guarding against a romanticized view of them. To take another instance, Frederick W. Turner writes of the emergence of a new stereotype of the North American Indian as the 'original ecologist', 'the original communist with a small "c"', 'non-competitive' and 'a natural democrat'; 'The Indian, because he was pre-scientific, had a profound wisdom about the workings of the world and the universe; he divined essential rhythms which allowed him to live a happy, harmonious existence destroyed forever by the coming of the white man.' I would endorse Turner's comment about this: 'Two things are true of all stereotypes. One is that they fulfill some needs of the makers; and the other is that they are partially correct' (*The Portable North American Indian Reader*, p. 10).
50 Quoted in R. Grove-White and O. O'Donovan, 'An Alternative Approach', p. 73.
51 A notable example is Martin Heidegger who in *Being and Time* speaks of human beings, 'thrown' in the world, finding themselves being-there [*Da-sein*], and being there with-others, and for-others; this finding is not simply intellectual apprehension, but is characterized above all by *care*, an ontologically rooted concern and attentiveness. *Dasein* is intrinsically permeated by world and others and implicitly the anticipation of an authentic co-being as ethical life in the original sense of *ethos*, 'dwelling there'. Richly suggestive as this is, however, the Heideggerian mode of philosophy is ethically equivocal: cf. e.g. R.J. Bernstein, 'Heidegger on Humanism', pp. 104–5. David Harvey, 'The Nature of Environment', has recently observed that Heidegger 'offers considerable sustenance to contemporary ecological thinking', and I think he is right to draw the parallels he does, though he gives no references to self-consciously Heideggerian ecologists. Given that Heidegger also appeared to offer considerable sustenance to those who once promoted an ideology of blood and

soil, I think it would be a good thing for the ideas here to be given a fuller airing than they have hitherto received.

52 J.E. Lovelock, *Gaia: A New Look at Life on Earth*.

53 For an overview of how this question divides environmental ethicists see, for instance, J. Baird Callicott, 'Animal Liberation: A Triangular Affair', and the reply by Edward Johnson, 'Animal Liberation versus the Land Ethic'.

54 Quoted in McIntosh, *The Background of Ecology*, p. 25.

55 Holmes Rolston, 'Is There an Ecological Ethic?', p. 94. The naturalistic fallacy, so named by G.E. Moore, can arise when one fails to appreciate the observation made by David Hume that statements about what *is* the case are qualitatively different from statements about what *ought* to be. For a relevant discussion see Callicott, 'Hume's *Is/Ought* Dichotomy and the Relation of Ecology to Leopold's Land Ethic'.

56 Quoted in Rolston, 'Is There an Ecological Ethic?', p. 97.

57 Ibid., p. 98.

58 Aldo Leopold, 'The Land Ethic', pp. 224–5.

59 Rolston, 'Is There an Ecological Ethic?', p. 98; that he apparently observes no distinction between community and ecosystem is probably not important in this context.

60 Ibid., p. 99.

61 Ibid.

62 Ibid., p. 101.

63 See Rolston, 'Are Values in Nature Subjective or Objective?'

64 Ibid., p. 129.

65 Ibid.

66 Ibid., p. 130.

67 Ibid., p. 132.

68 Cf. Thomas S. Kuhn, *The Structure of Scientific Revolutions*.

69 The factors that go into the construction include some which, relative to the practice of the science, are pre-scientific. Science can be subject to external influences in various ways. A particularly obvious way is via funding: the flourishing of ecosystems theory, for instance, has been attributed by some of its critics not so much to its intrinsic scientific value as to the fact that research in that area attracts more money. To determine which are the factors that determine funding decisions would require entering the province of the social sciences. There one is liable to encounter not only hard material interests at work, but also more nebulous notions bound up with values and beliefs – even myth, superstition and religion. Moreover, these factors are liable to influence scientific activities in more subtle ways than through paypackets. For scientists themselves are not disembodied minds but real beings with social and ecological conditionings whose effects on their ratiocinations may or may not be transparent to them.

70 The point of departure for this approach has already been suggested by Worster in his preface to the 1985 edition of *Nature's Economy*, p. xi.

71 This is arguably a feature of enlightenment thought as such. Apparently it was a commonplace of the eighteenth-century Enlightenment to consider philosophy itself as the 'organised habit of criticism'; and this view could be traced back to classical antiquity where criticism was already a 'solvent of custom, accepted explanations, and traditional institutions' (see Gay, *The Enlightenment: An Interpretation*, e.g. p. 121). I emphasize this point to counter the view of enlightenment as committed to a particular positive conception of the human relation to nature as one of domination.

72 Hegel, *Phenomenology of Spirit*, p. 46.
73 This way of putting it, and the summary which immediately follows, are from C. Taylor and A. Montefiore, 'From an Analytical Perspective', an introductory essay to Garbis Kortian, *Metacritique*', p. 7.
74 Herbert Marcuse, *Reason and Revolution*, p. 43.
75 Ibid., pp. 24–5.
76 See Seyla Benhabib, *Critique, Norm, and Utopia*, p. 48.
77 Karl Marx, 'A Contribution to the Critique of Hegel's Philosophy of Right', p. 252.
78 For instance, William Leiss, *The Domination of Nature*. An appreciation of the Frankfurt School also informs the work of Murray Bookchin; more recently, Robyn Eckersley has re-emphasized their potential contribution, in *Environmentalism and Political Theory*, chapter 5.
79 Eckersley, *Environmentalism and Political Theory*, p. 101.
80 On the one hand, there is the impeccable enlightenment pedigree of the goal she has described; on the other, although she writes 'the hope for a reconciliation of the negative dialectics of Enlightenment that would liberate both human and nonhuman nature, speaks directly to ecocentric concerns' (ibid., p. 100), it is not clear what she understands by negative dialectics or their reconciliation.
81 Benhabib, *Critique, Norm, and Utopia*, p. 164.
82 Ibid., p. 173.
83 Ibid., pp. 166ff.
84 See e.g. Jürgen Habermas, *The Theory of Communicative Action* and *Moral Consciousness and Communicative Action*.
85 The heart of Habermas's philosophy is captured in this passage from *Communication and the Evolution of Society*, p. 97: 'In action oriented to reaching understanding, validity claims are "always already" implicitly raised. These universal claims (to the comprehensibility of the symbolic expression, the truth of the propositional content, the truthfulness of the intentional expression, and the rightness of the speech act with respect to existing norms and values) are set in the general structures of possible communication. In these validity claims communication theory can locate a gentle but obstinate, a never silent although seldom redeemed claim to reason, a claim that must be recognized *de facto* whenever and wherever there is to be consensual action. If this is idealism, then idealism belongs in a most natural way to the conditions of reproduction of a species that must preserve its life through labor and interaction.'
86 Habermas, *Moral Consciousness and Communicative Action*, p. 66.
87 Andrew Dobson, 'Critical Theory and Green Politics', p. 198.
88 C. Fred Alford, *Science and the Revenge of Nature*, p. 77.
89 Habermas, 'A Reply to my Critics', pp. 243–4. Alford, ibid., pp. 148ff examines reasons for Habermas's claim and finds them wanting; however, a point I would stress here is that these criticisms do not show Habermas to *preclude* the development of new attitudes.
90 Habermas, *The Theory of Communicative Action*, vol. 1, p. 238.
91 Habermas, 'A Reply to My Critics', p. 245.
92 Ibid., p. 243.
93 Stephen K. White, *The Recent Work of Jürgen Habermas*, p. 138. Moreover, as Habermas himself notes, compassion and solidarity – with non-humans as well as humans – do 'appear in a discourse ethic that is consistently thought through to the end, at least as limit concepts' ('A Reply to My Critics', p. 246).
94 See e.g. Thomas McCarthy, 'Reflections on Rationalization'.

95 Habermas, *Moral Consciousness and Communicative Action*, p. 17. It throws up some of the fundamental problems philosophy has to deal with, though: philosophy is 'rooted in the urge to see social practices of justification as more than just such practices', and that is why philosophy is linked to an emancipatory interest in critical theory.
96 Eckersley, *Environmentalism and Political Theory*, pp. 111–12.
97 John Dryzek, 'Green Reason'.
98 Roy Bhaskar, *Reclaiming Reality*, pp. 187–9.
99 Peter Dickens, *Society and Nature*, p. xv.
100 Bhaskar, *Reclaiming Reality*, p. 6.
101 Ibid.
102 Ibid., p. 67.
103 Ibid.
104 Dickens, *Society and Nature*, p. 182.
105 Cf. ibid., pp. 182–3.
106 Bhaskar, *Reclaiming Reality*, p. 185.
107 Ibid., p. 186.
108 Ibid., p. 187.

Chapter 2   The Ethics of Ecological Humanism

1 Erich Fromm, *Man for Himself*, p. 39.
2 Ibid., p. 40.
3 Cf. Erich Fromm, *To Have or To Be*, p. 17.
4 Fromm, *Man for Himself*, p. 128.
5 Cf. ibid., pp. 131ff.
6 Ibid., p. 136.
7 James O'Connor, 'Ideologies of Human Nature', p. 7.
8 Ibid., p. 9.
9 Cf. R. and V. Routley, 'Against the Inevitability of Human Chauvinism'. The term 'speciesism', originally coined by Richard Ryder on analogy with 'racism' and 'sexism', refers to the discrimination against other species on the basis of morally irrelevant differences.
10 Cf. K.E. Goodpaster, 'From Egoism to Environmentalism'.
11 Bryan G. Norton, 'Environmental Ethics and Weak Anthropocentrism', distinguishes weak, or as I call it moderate, from strong anthropocentrism on the basis of a distinction between felt and considered preferences; this effectively corresponds to my distinction between unreflective and enlightened self-interest. The latter is argued to be sufficient to establish an environmental ethic *without* subscribing or appealing to the intrinsic value of non-human beings; it provides a basis for criticism of value systems which are purely exploitative of nature. Cf. e.g. Janna Thompson, 'Preservation of Wilderness and the Good Life', who offers a related argument; and John Passmore, *Man's Responsibility for Nature*, especially pp. 101ff.
12 Even anti-anthropocentric theorists generally grant that only humans are the addressees of moral discourse or moral agents; an exception is Lawrence E. Johnson, *A Morally Deep World*.
13 Cf. G.J. Warnock, *The Object of Morality*, chapter 9; W.K. Frankena, 'Ethics and the Environment'.
14 H. Rolston, 'Is There an Ecological Ethic?', p. 103 (Rolston here is discussing the views of René Dubos).

15 Dubos quoted in ibid., p. 104.
16 Norton, 'Environmental Ethics and Weak Anthropocentrism', p. 136.
17 Indeed, moderate anthropocentrists may well share such beliefs. This is, I believe, an important point which is surprisingly often missed by critics of anthropocentrism who claim people do precisely *deny* it when in fact they simply claim it cannot consistently be attributed. In 'Kant and the Moral Considerability of Non-Rational Beings' I try to show that scepticism about our *ability* to know what intrinsic value non-human beings might have should not be confused with an *unwillingness* to show them moral consideration. Cf. also Robert Elliot, 'Ecology and the Ethics of Environmental Restoration', which argues that non-anthropocentric normative ethics is impossible, and John O'Neill, 'Varieties of Intrinsic Value', which reiterates the independence of meta-ethics and normative ethics in the context of environmental ethics.
18 Robin Attfield, *A Theory of Value and Obligation*, p. 31. On defining intrinsic value see ibid., chapter 2, and O'Neill, 'Varieties of Intrinsic Value'.
19 Norton, 'Environmental Ethics and Weak Anthropocentrism', p. 138.
20 Paul W. Taylor, 'The Ethics of Respect for Nature', p. 198.
21 Cf. the views of Hare and of Feinberg which are critically discussed in Robin Attfield, 'The Good of Trees'.
22 Attfield, 'The Good of Trees', p. 37.
23 Cf. ibid., pp. 38 ff.
24 Attfield, *A Theory of Value and Obligation*, p. 18; Attfield is here endorsing the view of K.E. Goodpaster in 'On Being Morally Considerable'.
25 Cf. Richard Sylvan, 'A Critique of Deep Ecology', part I, p. 8; Attfield replies in 'Sylvan, Fox and Deep Ecology'.
26 Taylor, 'The Ethics of Respect for Nature', p. 201.
27 Ibid., p. 206.
28 Cf. Robin Attfield, *The Ethics of Environmental Concern*, p. 208.
29 Cf. Janna Thompson, 'A Refutation of Environmental Ethics'.
30 Taylor, 'The Ethics of Respect for Nature', p. 210.
31 Indeed, it might be noted that even Kant described them as such. See the passage quoted at note 15 to chapter 1, which is taken from Kant's *Critique of Judgment*, pp. 310–24.
32 Taylor, 'The Ethics of Respect for Nature', p. 217.
33 Thompson, 'A Refutation of Environmental Ethics', p. 150.
34 Ibid.
35 For a fuller view of what is at stake here one might make reference to a further, related, criticism Thompson has made of Taylor, whose claim that all and only individual organisms have inherent worth she thinks is hard to sustain: 'Why can't we say, for example, that hearts, lungs, livers and kidneys have intrinsic value and thus deserve in themselves to be objects of our moral concern? Once we come to appreciate how a kidney or some other internal organ develops within the embryo, how it functions and maintains itself, what makes it flourish and what harms it, then surely as in the case of the butterfly or the bacteria we have to recognize that it has a good of its own ... This can be determined independently to the same extent that the good of a wood-boring insect can be determined independently of the good of the tree it feeds on or that the good of intestinal bacteria can be defined independently of the good of the intestine or the good of the creature who has the intestine ... For the same reason, it seems that we also ought to say that individual leaves, buds, and bits of bark have a good of their own and are equally candidates for having intrinsic value. And what will stop us from saying that a piece of skin, a bodily cell, or a DNA

molecule has a good of its own?' (ibid., pp. 152–3). Attfield, taking Taylor's side in *The Ethics of Environmental Concern*, responds to this line of argument with 'the good of an organ is dependent on that of the organism to which it belongs ... in a way which has no analogue where the good in question is the good of individual living creatures' (p. 206). Hence there *are* criteria for picking out relevant individuals; whether they would be acceptable to a holist or a sceptic, though, is another question.

36 Robin Attfield, 'The Comprehensive Ecology Movement', usefully distinguishes a number of different versions of the greater value assumption, and recommends amending that cited with the qualification 'at least for normal members of respective species'. Interestingly, it is actually a moot point whether moderate anthropocentrists need to make this assumption.

37 Sylvan, 'A Critique of Deep Ecology', Part I, p. 2.

38 Arne Naess, 'The Shallow and the Deep, Long-Range Ecology Movement', p. 96.

39 Attfield, 'Sylvan, Fox and Deep Ecology', p. 24.

40 Arne Naess, *Ecology, Community and Lifestyle*, p. 167.

41 See Warwick Fox, 'Approaching Deep Ecology: A Response to Richard Sylvan's Critique of Deep Ecology', especially pp. 29–52.

42 Goodpaster, 'From Egoism to Environmentalism', p. 29.

43 Aldo Leopold, 'The Land Ethic', pp. 224–5.

44 J.Baird Callicott, 'Animal Liberation: A Triangular Affair', p. 320.

45 Quoted in Callicott, 'The Metaphysical Implications of Ecology', p. 310.

46 Ibid., p. 314.

47 Ibid., p. 315.

48 Ibid., p. 316; very similar argumentation is also set out in Rolston, 'Is There an Ecological Ethic?', pp. 104–5.

49 Cf. Freya Mathews, *The Ecological Self*.

50 Robyn Eckersley, *Environmentalism and Political Theory*, p. 78.

51 Ibid., p. 63.

52 Goodpaster, 'On Being Morally Considerable', p. 30.

53 This section incorporates, with revisions, some parts of my 'Ecology and Human Emancipation'. An earlier version was discussed at a workshop of the Radical Philosophy Conference at the Polytechnic of Central London in November 1990, and I should like to acknowledge the contribution of the participants at the workshop; I am especially grateful to Ted Benton for his detailed comments on the text of the earlier version.

54 The ideas in this sentence are presented in extremely compressed form – and as such may appear to beg a number of questions. For one thing, the meaning of 'sustainability' may be more complex and problematic than is apparent here: see e.g. Michael Redclift, *Sustainable Development*. For another, I have used the idea of 'nature-transformative activities' in a very broad sense, where a more differentiated account of the kinds of practical relation between humans and nature would use the term in a narrower sense: see e.g. Ted Benton's 'Marxism and Natural Limits', where the term 'transformative' is reserved for activities which tend not to be ecologically benign, whilst for more sustainable activities other descriptions such as 'eco-regulation' are employed; and Linda Nicholson's 'Feminism and Marx: Integrating Kinship with the Economic', which further distinguishes various kinds of productive and reproductive activity. However, my theoretical aim here is limited to marking a straightforward distinction, also drawn by Benton in 'Ecology, Socialism, and the Mastery of Nature: A Reply to Reiner Grundmann', between the 'Promethean project,

on the one hand, and the much more readily defensible notion of mastery of, or control over our human *interchange* with nature, on the other'.

55 An example of this would be the building of a nuclear power station whose waste at the time of building we do not know how to deal with, but we build it anyway on the assumption that we will find a way of sorting it out. The Promethean assumption was virtually taken as axiomatic within orthodox Marxism, but it is now generally recognized, at least by ecological socialists, to be untenable. Reiner Grundmann, though, in 'The Ecological Challenge to Marxism', effectively reaffirms that assumption (see p. 108). Thus whereas Benton rejects humanism along with Prometheanism, Grundmann appears to think it necessary to defend Prometheanism in order to save humanism. I am here seeking to offer an alternative to both these positions by distinguishing humanism from Prometheanism.

56 In practice, of course, it may be very difficult to draw a hard and fast line between sustainable and unsustainable practices, for the amount of ecological knowledge required would be formidable. However, between the two *aims* there is a very clear distinction – and so there is good reason to think that the trajectories of practices guided by these aims will be different.

57 Karl Marx, 'Economic and Philosophical Manuscripts (1844)', p. 329.

58 Richard Lichtman, 'The Production of Human Nature by Means of Human Nature', p. 18.

59 Ibid., p. 22.

60 Ibid., pp. 24–5.

61 Ibid., p. 23.

62 Ibid., pp. 25–6.

63 Ibid., p. 26.

64 Ibid., p. 45.

65 Ibid., p. 50.

66 Ibid., p. 50.

67 Ibid., p. 25.

68 Ted Benton, 'On the Limits of Malleability', p. 69.

69 Ibid., p. 70.

70 Ted Benton, 'Humanism = Speciesism? Marx on Humans and Animals', p. 13.

71 Ibid., p. 14.

72 Ibid., p. 13.

73 Ibid. In his recent book, *Natural Relations*, Benton further develops this suggestion; see also my discussion in section 4.2.

74 Ibid., p. 15.

75 Ibid., emphasis in the original.

76 Benton does not pursue this question further in the article under discussion. Nevertheless, in his conclusion he affirms his belief that 'Explanatory strategies in relation to such supervenient needs would be to make them intelligible in terms of the (ontologically) more fundamental common needs' (p. 15). He claims that this broad naturalistic approach would provide the beginnings of a methodological defence for some already existing explanatory strategies and offer a promising direction for future developments. He cites, for instance, Gould's notion 'that biological modifications which *are* adaptive may bring in their wake a train of consequences which are *non*-adaptive is an important concept for this strategy' (ibid.). However, as I go on to argue in the text, I think Benton's uptake of this point might involve some confusion of needs with powers.

77 Benton, 'On the Limits of Malleability', p. 69.

78 Richard Lichtman, 'Response to Comments', pp. 73–4.

79 Ibid.
80 For this reason Lichtman sees the treatment of this question as a *subordinate* moment in the delineation of human nature. As Lichtman observes regarding the contention that nature grounds value: 'In truth, the opposite is closer to the truth: know what is good and you will better know what *human* nature is, since to be human is to be capable of recognizing and realizing value. Value determines what is human in human nature, and which needs are therefore worthy of being realized and which are not' (ibid., pp. 73–4).
81 One could speak of autonomy as a basic human need, as do L. Doyal and I. Gough, *A Theory of Human Need*, as long as one recognizes with them that this need is irreducible to needs of physical well-being.

Chapter 3   Environmental Economics, Sustainable Development and Political Ecology

1 For an overview of ecological problems, see e.g. John Passmore, *Man's Responsibility for Nature*; R.J. Johnston, *Environmental Problems*.
2 The term was also used by Aristotle to describe 'the arrangement of domestic activities most conducive to affectionate and harmonious relations within the family' (quoted in T. O'Riordan, *Environmentalism*, p. 85).
3 Donald Worster, *Nature's Economy*, develops this idea at length; for further critical discussion see section 1.2.
4 Herman E. Daly and John B. Cobb, *For the Common Good*, p. 138.
5 Ibid., p. 139.
6 Keynes quoted in O'Riordan, *Environmentalism*, pp. 49–50.
7 Keynes quoted in ibid., p. 50.
8 E.F. Schumacher, *Small is Beautiful*, p. 26.
9 'The antics of stock exchanges are a mystery to most people, but in reality stocks are little more than assumptions of growth on paper. Most North American cities pay their bills by means of bonds – credit notes granted by banks on the anticipation of continued urban affluence' (O'Riordan, *Environmentalism*, p. 86). See also Shiva's observations reported in section 3.2.
10 Michael Jacobs, 'Growth Can Be Green', p. 5. This is a point frequently insisted on by greens: see e.g. P. Kemp and D. Wall, *A Green Manifesto for the 1990s*, chapter 5; also Daly and Cobb, *For the Common Good*, chapter 3.
11 As understood, for instance, in Kemp and Wall, *A Green Manifesto for the 1990s*, p. 75.
12 Jacobs, 'Growth Can Be Green', p. 5.
13 David Pearce et al., *Blueprint for a Green Economy*, p. 19.
14 Cf. e.g. Victor Anderson, *Alternative Economic Indicators*.
15 Pearce et al., *Blueprint for a Green Economy*, p. 29.
16 Ibid., pp. 29–30.
17 'A society which does not maintain or improve its real income per capita is unlikely to be "developing"' (ibid., p. 30). The assumption that the well-being of the poor necessarily means increase in *income* is one which on a more radical view would need questioning, as we shall see below. It should also be noted, though, that Pearce et al. at the same time observe: 'But if it achieves growth at the expense of the other components of development it cannot be said to be developing either.'
18 A selection of definitions is given in the appendix in ibid.

19 From Brundtland in ibid., p. 34.

20 See ibid., pp. 37ff.

21 Alan Holland, 'Natural Capital', p. 171.

22 For a useful critical discussion of cost–benefit analysis see John O'Neill, *Ecology, Policy and Politics*, chapters 4 and 5.

23 Pearce et al., *Blueprint 2*, preface. They add: 'Moreover it offers the prospect of doing it all rather more efficiently than traditional approaches based on "command and control".'

24 Pearce et al., *Blueprint for a Green Economy*, p. 52.

25 Pearce et al., *Blueprint 2*, p. 2.

26 See e.g. R. Grove-White and O. O'Donovan, 'An Alternative Approach', p. 79.

27 Pearce et al., *Blueprint for a Green Economy*, p. 54.

28 See O'Neill, *Ecology, Policy and Politics*, chapter 7.

29 R. Attfield and K. Dell (eds), *Values, Conflict and the Environment*, p. 29.

30 Ibid., p. 30.

31 O'Neill, *Ecology, Policy and Politics*, p. 107.

32 Holland, 'Natural Capital', p. 172.

33 Grove-White and O'Donovan, 'An Alternative Approach', p. 75.

34 Pearce et al., *Blueprint for a Green Economy*, p. 75.

35 Ibid., pp. 76–7.

36 Vandana Shiva, *Staying Alive*, p. xiv.

37 Ibid., p. 221.

38 Ibid., p. 219.

39 Ibid., p. 84.

40 Ibid., p. 3.

41 Cf. also Marshall Sahlins, *Stone Age Economics*.

42 See e.g. Ted Trainer, *Developed to Death*; Michael Redclift, *Development and the Environmental Crisis*; and the various works by Susan George in the bibliography.

43 Shiva, *Staying Alive*, p. xvii.

44 Ibid., p. 44.

45 Ibid., p. 224.

46 Andrew Dobson, *Green Political Thought*, pp. 6–7.

47 Porritt and Winner quoted in ibid., p. 7.

48 Aldo Leopold, 'The Land Ethic', p. 203.

49 Ibid., p. 202.

50 Ibid., p. 205.

51 Goldsmith quoted in Thijs de la Court, *Beyond Brundtland*, p. 130.

52 Ibid.

53 Quoted in ibid., p. 129.

54 Ibid., pp. 129–30.

55 Giorgio Nebbia, 'La bioeconomia', p. 80 (my translation). It will be noted that Nebbia rightly speaks of material flows as well as energy flows; I acknowledge this since in the text I shall be following Martinez-Alier's focus on theorists who concentrate on energy flows. The classic text of bioeconomics is Nicholas Georgescu–Roegen, *The Entropy Law and the Economic Process*.

56 Juan Martinez-Alier, *Ecological Economics*, p. 127n.

57 Ibid., p. 135.

58 Ibid., p. 130.

59 Daly and Cobb, *For the Common Good*, p. 195.

60 Eugene P. Odum, *Ecology and Our Endangered Life-Support Systems*, chapter 4.

61 Daly and Cobb, *For the Common Good*, p. 11.
62 K. Lee, *Social Philosophy and Ecological Scarcity*, pp. 74–5.
63 See Daly and Cobb, *For the Common Good*, chapter 10.
64 Martinez-Alier, *Ecological Economics*, p. 136.
65 Fred Hirsch, *Social Limits to Growth*.
66 Ivan Illich, *Tools for Conviviality*, p. 52.
67 Ibid., p. 54.
68 In view of how the term 'ecologism' is sometimes used as an affirmative designation referring to deep green values and attitudes (cf. e.g. Dobson, *Green Political Thought*, passim), it is interesting to note that the founder of deep ecology, Arne Naess, actually defines ecologism as the fallacy of 'excessive universalisation or generalisation of ecological concepts and theories' (*Ecology, Community and Lifestyle*, p. 39).
69 Martinez-Alier, *Ecological Economics*, p. xxiv. In similar vein, he also observes: 'While the patterns of migration of animals can probably be explained to a great extent by ecologists (who else?), the preventing of Mexicans from entering the United States, and the export of oil from Mexico to the United States, are social, political phenomena. The openness of Saudi Arabia and Iran to visiting oil tankers, even the relative isolation of the Tsembaga-Maring or the Kung San in the 1960s, are facts of human history which energetics and biology do not explain' (p. 11).
70 Ibid., p. 15.
71 Ibid., p. 11.
72 Ibid., p. 11.
73 This section incorporates, with some revisions, 'The Meaning of Political Ecology' Earlier drafts were presented at the Political Thought Conference, New College, Oxford, January 1991, and at a seminar of the series 'Socialism and Ecology', run by David McLellan and Sean Sayers, at Canterbury in October 1991: I am very grateful for the helpful comments of participants on both occasions.
74 This concept is quite often referred to in the literature. Böhme and Schramm, for instance, see it as an indispensible heuristic and metatheoretical concept: 'It continually forces reflection back to the material basis, to the concrete interaction between humans and nature ... embracing not only productive appropriation of nature, but also the consumptive relation of humans to nature; of not just intentional engagement with nature, but also unintended effects' (G. Böhme and E. Schramm, foreword to *Soziale Naturwissenschaft: Wege zu einer Erweiterung der Ökologie*, p. 8, my translation).
75 See Alfred Schmidt, *The Concept of Nature in Marx*. Martinez-Alier has commented that although the concept was used non-metaphorically by Marx and Engels, they thought only in terms of the exchange of *matter*, without recognizing the importance of energy exchanges: this was drawn to their attention by Podolinsky, and Martinez-Alier sees their inadequate response as a crucial missed opportunity in the dialogue between Marxism and ecology (Martinez-Alier, *Ecological Economics*, especially chapter 14).
76 The exploitation of nature, like the idea of natural capital mentioned elsewhere, is the sort of concept which it would be a central task of political ecology to critically examine.
77 A forum for this project is the journal *Capitalism, Nature, Socialism*: it is seen as involving not only an ecological interrogation of the work of Marx and Engels, but also a re-evaluation of radical thinkers (e.g. anarchists and utopian socialists) previously marginalized by orthodox Marxism.

78 James O'Connor, 'Capitalism, Nature, Socialism: A Theoretical Introduction'.

79 On the one hand, according to O'Connor, ibid., it can theorize how traditional economic crises of overproduction now yield ecological and social crises: global capitalism attempts to rescue itself from its deepening crisis by cutting costs (hence allowing a deterioration of environmental quality), or raising the rate of exploitation of labour (hence furthering new and deeper inequalities in distribution of wealth and income world-wide). On the other hand, there is a feedback mechanism between ecological crisis and economic crisis: the barriers to capitalist accumulation which Marx called conditions of production in general, and external conditions (i.e. nature), in particular, take the form of economic crisis – a self-induced crisis from the cost side.

80 'Perhaps we can surmise that feminism, environmental movements, etc. are "pushing" capital and state into more social forms of the reproduction of production conditions. As labor exploitation . . . engendered a labor movement which during particular times and places turned itself into a "social barrier" to capital, nature exploitation . . . engenders an environmental movement . . . which may also constitute a "social barrier" to capital.' (ibid., p. 31). Since conditions of production can be both limiting and enabling, the political aims of ecological movements may be seen, O'Connor argues, in terms of struggles for either the protection or the restructuring of production conditions.

81 Linda Nicholson, 'Feminism and Marx'.

82 S. Benhabib and D. Cornell, 'Beyond the Politics of Gender'.

83 Quoted in Nicholson, 'Feminism and Marx', p. 24.

84 Valerie Bryson, *Feminist Political Theory*, pp. 208–9. The concept of reproduction itself is highly contested, so that any specific usage will require theoretical clarification. Even basic definitions need work: some of the unhelpful connotations that can attach to the term are illustrated in C. Delphy and D. Leonard, *Familiar Exploitation*, e.g. p. 58; a number of other senses are distinguished in a preliminary way in Marilyn Waring, *Counting for Nothing*, pp. 22–4.

85 Among the writers Bryson is referring to here are Susan Griffin, *Woman and Nature*, and Andrée Collard, *Rape of the Wild*. To some extent this is the view Shiva proposes, as we saw in the previous section. It must be emphasized, though, that not all ecofeminist theory can be characterized in this way, as neo-romantic or biologistic. Others, particularly materialist ecofeminists, 'are engaged in a subtle deconstruction of the patriarchal "Mother Nature" ideology while yet trying to re-theorize our human embeddedness in what is called "nature"' (Ariel Salleh, 'Discussion: Eco-Socialism/Eco-Feminism').

86 Bryson, *Feminist Political Theory*, p. 211.

87 Kate Soper, 'Discussion: Eco-Feminism and Eco-Socialism', p. 113.

88 Ibid., p. 112.

89 The approach to economics of Waring, *Counting for Nothing*, exemplifies what I have in mind here.

90 The argument of this chapter may also be set in the context of the ecological reconstruction of enlightenment values. The theorists examined in section 3.1 can be seen as continuing the enlightenment tradition not only in their rationality (which retains elements of a rationality of domination), but also in their optimism – which, from the standpoint of those in section 3.2, appears as a misplaced confidence. The position developed in section 3.3 corrects this: it takes enlightenment as *critique*, and re-emphasizes the way in which, like ecology, it is a *project*.

Chapter 4   Rights and Justice in Ecological Perspective

1 For abridged versions of the arguments of Burke, Bentham and Marx, with comment, see J. Waldron, *Nonsense upon Stilts*; for criticisms of ethnocentrism in human rights see A. Pollis and P. Schwab, *Human Rights: Cultural and Ideological Perspectives*; for a concise statement of postmodern critiques of universalism see J.-F. Lyotard, *The Postmodern Condition*.

2 Cf. e.g. William Ophuls, *Ecology and the Politics of Scarcity*; Keekok Lee, *Social Philosophy and Ecological Scarcity*; also Robyn Eckersley, *Environmentalism and Political Theory*, pp. 15–17 and 23–5.

3 John Locke, *Second Treatise of Government*, p. 131.

4 Ibid., p. 130.

5 Ibid., p. 131.

6 I am here adapting a line of argument already presented by C.B. Macpherson: see e.g. *The Political Theory of Possessive Individualism*.

7 Locke, *Second Treatise of Government*, p. 130.

8 Ibid., p. 139.

9 Ibid., p. 130 (my emphasis).

10 Robert Nozick, *Anarchy, State and Utopia*, p. 176.

11 See Wolfgang Sachs, 'The Discovery of Poverty', where he distinguishes frugality from destitution and scarcity.

12 Note that the less stringent interpretation is not necessarily a less stringent requirement. If what has to be preserved is the position of others, as opposed to the stock of natural resources, there may be more opportunities for substitution, but there could also be more obligations to create substitutes, and these could be increasingly onerous as ecological problems intensify.

13 Nozick, *Anarchy, State and Utopia*, p. 177.

14 Keekok Lee, *Social Philosophy and Ecological Scarcity*, pp. 285–6.

15 John Rawls presents his full-blown theory in *A Theory of Justice*; its arguments were introduced in articles including 'Justice as Fairness' and 'Distributive Justice'.

16 Wesley N. Hohfeld, *Fundamental Legal Conceptions*.

17 D.D. Raphael, 'Human Rights, Old and New', calls these 'rights of recipience' to highlight the point that they normally involve the transfer of resources from duty bearers to rights bearers.

18 Maurice Cranston, 'Human Rights, Real and Supposed', pp. 50–1.

19 Cf. Henry Shue, *Basic Rights*.

20 UN Declaration, Article 25.

21 Cranston, 'Human Rights, Real and Supposed', p. 53.

22 Shue, *Basic Rights*, p. 18.

23 Of course not all things *are* equal, and there are peculiar difficulties in establishing rights of people who do not yet exist; however I do not believe any of these difficulties strike at the heart of the principle here. For a defence of speaking of rights of future generations against five frequently heard objections see Ernest Partridge, 'On the Rights of Future Generations'.

24 Rawls, *A Theory of Justice*, p. 187.

25 Bryan G. Norton, 'Intergenerational Equity and Environmental Decisions', p. 155.

26 Quoted in William Aiken, 'Human Rights in an Ecological Era', p. 193.

27 World Commission on Environment and Development, *Our Common Future*, p. 348.

28 Group of 100 quoted in Aiken, 'Human Rights in an Ecological Era', p. 98.

29 Ted Benton, *Natural Relations*, p. 175.
30 Aiken, 'Human Rights in an Ecological Era', pp. 198–9.
31 Ibid., p. 199.
32 Quoted in T. O'Riordan, *Environmentalism*, p. 29.
33 Cf. also Mancur Olson, *The Logic of Collective Action*.
34 Quoted in O'Riordan, *Environmentalism*, p. 67.
35 Robert Paehlke, *Environmentalism and the Future of Progressive Politics*, p. 56.
36 See Shue, *Basic Rights*, chapter 4, for further discussion.
37 O'Riordan, *Environmentalism*, p. 30.
38 Though see Hardin's thesis concerning the 'self-selection of the conscienceless', discussed in ibid., pp. 34–5.
39 The figure of 40 is chosen just to give some sense of the scale of the disparity in overall patterns of resource use. For some resources there may be less of a difference between rich and poor. For others there is a far greater difference: in energy use, for instance, there was a ratio of 430 to 1 between the US and low-income countries according to the World Bank in 1986, cited in Ted Trainer, *Developed to Death*, p. 13.
40 Note the contrast, on this point, with libertarians like Nozick who would at least support rectification of injustices where these could be established.
41 Cf. Shue, *Basic Rights*, p. 101; he gives references to the relevant studies.
42 Ivan Illich, *Shadow Work*, pp. 107–9.
43 Charles Birch and John B. Cobb, *The Liberation of Life*, p. 315. They refer to one study which states that in Thailand 'women were asked what they consider the ideal number of children. In every case, they would have preferred fewer children.' Another considers that 'the social indicator that correlates most closely with declines in fertility appears to be education for women, particularly the attainment of literacy.' They also note something interesting about the totalitarian solution – compulsory birth control – adopted by China: 'Its slowed population growth is achieved more by changing the role of women than by direct pressure against having children.' The same is even more true in Western democracies (p. 314).
44 Cf. Shue, *Basic Rights*, p. 102.
45 'Any form of the population objection must assume that the existing distribution of wealth and income is morally beyond challenge ... To attempt to settle the argument by merely declaring certain countries to be overpopulated is in effect to declare some of their people to be "excess" – extra people with no business to be there. And this is to smuggle in a judgement about justice disguised as a fact about demography. To see the strength of the implicit and unargued moral assumption, one need only ask: why is it they who have no right to be there (consuming scarce food, energy, etc.) and not I who have no right to be here (consuming scarce food, energy, etc. – at much higher rates)?' (ibid., pp. 109–10).
46 Karl Marx, *Grundrisse*, p. 607.
47 Although the extension of rights across different species will give rise to certain problems which do not arise within human rights, it can be argued that any being which can be said, for instance, to have 'interests', could be the bearer of rights protecting those interests. Moreover, Christopher Stone has argued in 'Should Trees Have Standing?' that legally enforceable rights for all kinds of beings other than humans – including forests, oceans and rivers – appear to be practicable. This means, of course, that the ability to *claim* – or therefore to waive – a right, in the first person, is not essential to the definition of a rights bearer.
48 Establishing that animals may have rights need not bring with it a positive commitment to the thesis that non-sentient nature has moral rights. However, because most

of the difficulties usually mentioned set in at the species barrier, I shall use the limited available space to concentrate on the question of whether these can be overcome.

49 For example, Peter Singer, *Animal Liberation*, uses utilitarian rather than rights-based theory, but is prepared to accept the rhetorical value of rights; Richard Ryder, editing *Animal Welfare and the Environment*, says he sees no difference between animal rights and animal welfare.

50 Quoted in Tom Regan, 'Animal Rights: What's in a Name?', p. 52.

51 Ibid., p. 55.

52 Robert Garner, *Animals, Politics and Morality*, p. 246.

53 Ibid., p. 251.

54 Ibid., p. 7.

55 Ibid., p. 248.

56 Benton, *Natural Relations*, p. 196.

57 Ibid., p. 148.

58 Ibid., p. 211.

59 Ibid.

60 Cf. Tom Regan's discussion in *The Case for Animal Rights*, pp. 324f.

61 Ted Benton notes that vicarious action may be inadequate: 'while paternalistic or vicarious action on behalf of oppressed human groups may often be a necessary element or moment in such campaigns, it is hard to imagine such a campaign ever generating the moral momentum for success without the eventual active identification and involvement of the oppressed groups themselves.' Moreover, it may be inappropriate: 'when this phase in a liberation struggle is reached the autonomous definitions sought by the oppressed for themselves are often markedly different from those anticipated by their sympathizers, frequently to the point of sharp mutual alienation' (*Natural Relations*, p. 93).

62 Ibid., p. 144; see also Steven Lukes, 'Can a Marxist Believe in Human Rights?'

63 See Lukes, ibid.; for an elaboration of this view see E.B. Pashukanis, *Law and Marxism*.

64 Cf. Russell Keat, 'Liberal Rights and Socialism'; Ernst Bloch, *Naturrecht und menschliche Würde*, chapters 19–21.

65 See e.g. Lyotard, *The Postmodern Condition*.

66 The works most often discussed under this heading are: Michael Sandel, *Liberalism and the Limits of Justice*; Alasdair MacIntyre, *After Virtue*; Charles Taylor, *Hegel and Modern Society*; Michael Walzer, *Spheres of Justice*. For commentaries see Will Kymlicka, *Contemporary Political Philosophy*, chapter 6; Simon Caney, 'Liberalism and Communitarianism'; S. Mulhall and A. Swift, *Liberals and Communitarians*.

67 Rawls, *A Theory of Justice*, p. 560.

68 Sandel quoted in Will Kymlicka, *Comtemporary Political Philosophy*, p. 211.

69 Ibid., p. 213.

70 See their essay with this title and other contributions to Pollis and Schwab, *Human Rights: Cultural and Ideological Perspectives*.

71 cf. Waldron, *Nonsense upon Stilts*.

72 This is what I take to be shown by the arguments of, for instance, Chandran Kukathas and Philip Pettit, *Rawls*, pp. 103ff; or Kymlicka, *Contemporary Political Philosophy*, p. 206.

73 Marilyn Friedman, 'Feminism and Modern Friendship', p. 158.

74 For a range of perspectives on this question see e.g. Cass R. Sunstein, *Feminism and Political Theory*.

75 Carol Gilligan, *In a Different Voice*.

76 Hans Jonas, *The Imperative of Responsibility*.

77 Ibid., p. 99.
78 Shue, *Basic Rights*, pp. 41ff; see also S. George, *How the Other Half Dies*, *passim*.
79 See the critique in Karl-Otto Apel, 'The Problem of a Macroethic of Responsibility to the Future'.
80 Ibid., p. 21.
81 See Karl-Otto Apel, 'The Ecological Crisis as a Problem for Discourse Ethics'.
82 Apel, 'The Problem of a Macroethic of Responsibility', p. 32.
83 Ibid., p. 33.
84 This is a point developed by Habermas, and one which is further discussed in chapters 1 and 5.
85 See Seyla Benhabib, 'The Generalized and the Concrete Other'.
86 Ibid., p. 416.
87 Ibid., p. 415.
88 The rest of the positivist position is that duties exist only if sanctions for their non-fulfilment exist, and that sanctions exist only if there exists a state, as monopoly of legitimate use of force: hence there can exist no rights in the absence of enforced law; hence there are no pre-legal fundamental rights. However, if there can be sanctions other than legal penalties, which I believe there can, then there can be duty–right relations other than those enforced by law.
89 Cf. Hohfeld, *Fundamental Legal Conceptions*, especially pp. 50–60.
90 Jonas finds this 'formal' concept of responsibility inadequate because, he says, it is retroactively oriented to punishment or compensation, and because it supplies no orientation to the *bonum humanum*; thus he favours a more moral concept of public responsibility whose 'eminent paradigms' would be fathers or statesmen whose sense of responsibility spurs them to an *opus supererogationis* (*The Imperative of Responsibility*, chapter 4). As regards the first point, removal from office, so that another will be installed, is not really a retroactive sanction so much as the institution's way of seeing that its own norms are preserved. As regards the second point, I think it is important that social institutions have norms which have been agreed on democratically by their members rather than by a patriarch, however beneficent.
91 I have in mind a symmetry with Shue's characterization of a right as involving 'a rationally justified demand for social guarantees against standard threats' (*Basic Rights*, p. 17). In practice this might mean, for example, that fiscal measures be applied to discourage certain types of contract or to provide funds for compensation of their adverse social effects. In more extreme circumstances certain types of contract could be made illegal: there are, after all, certain restrictions already imposed by public law on freedom of contract (e.g. hiring killers, selling drugs or arms).
92 See Hohfeld, *Fundamental Legal Conceptions*, especially pp. 60–4.
93 H.L.A. Hart has drawn out the importance of immunities: 'The chief . . . employment of this notion of an immunity from adverse legal change which we may call an "immunity right" is to characterize distinctively the position of individuals protected from such adverse change by constitutional limitations' limiting the powers of the legislature 'to make (or unmake) the ordinary law, where to do so would deny to individuals certain freedoms and benefits now regarded as essentials of human well-being, such as freedom of speech and of association, freedom from arbitrary arrest, security of life and person, education, and equality of treatment in certain respects' ('Bentham on Legal Rights', pp. 198–9.)
94 Cf. Seyla Benhabib, 'Obligation, Contract and Exchange'.
95 Benton, *Natural Relations*, p. 180.

Chapter 5 Ecological Politics

1 The classic manifesto which has set the standard for green parties world-wide is that of *die Grünen*, 1983.

2 It could be significant, though, that the slogan itself was coined by Herbert Gruhl in his struggle against the left within the German Greens in their formative period (cf. Werner Hülsberg, *The German Greens*, chapter 6). It has most often been deployed since by those who wished to resist any leftward tendency within greens.

3 See e.g. Robert C. Paehlke, *Environmentalism and the Future of Progressive Politics*, chapter 7; Arne Naess, 'Notes on the Politics of the Deep Ecology Movement'.

4 Paehlke, *Environmentalism and the Future of Progressive Politics*, locates various influential writers in relation to the traditional ideological spectrum, but broadly supports this view; for a contrasting view of ecological politics see Anna Bramwell, *Ecology in the 20th Century*.

5 C.B. Macpherson, *The Life and Times of Liberal Democracy*, p. 1.

6 Quoted in Andrew Dobson, *Green Political Thought*, p. 89.

7 Ibid., p. 172.

8 Paehlke, *Environmentalism and the Future of Progressive Politics*, pp. 191–2.

9 Dobson, *Green Political Thought*, p. 84.

10 Cf. e.g. Robyn Eckersley, *Environmentalism and Political Theory*, p. 24, who offers decidedly faint praise for liberalism.

11 Keekok Lee, *Social Philosophy and Ecological Scarcity*, p. 245.

12 Martin Ryle, *Ecology and Socialism*, p. 73.

13 Quoted in Dobson, *Green Political Thought*, p. 189.

14 Ibid., pp. 189–90.

15 See Tim Hayward, 'Ecosocialism: Utopian and Scientific'.

16 For other reasons, see e.g. Ryle, *Ecology and Socialism*; James O'Connor, 'Socialism and Ecology'; Rudolf Bahro, *Socialism and Survival*; Raymond Williams, 'Socialism and Ecology'. The journal *Capitalism, Nature, Socialism* was established as a forum for discussion of this question.

17 Hans Magnus Enzensberger, 'A Critique of Political Ecology'.

18 Cf. Bahro, *Socialism and Survival*.

19 Weston quoted in Dobson, *Green Political Thought*, p. 178.

20 Ryle, *Ecology and Socialism*, p. 12.

21 Robert E. Goodin, *Green Political Theory*, especially chapter 4.

22 Ibid., p. 159.

23 Ibid., p. 163.

24 See Hülsberg, *The German Greens*. Along with *Realos* and *Fundis*, two other main factions are ecosocialists and ecolibertarians: see Wolfram Bickerich, *SPD und Grüne*, for arguments from each quarter.

25 See Goodin, *Green Political Theory*, chapter 2 for the details of his theory of value. I have not included a separate discussion of his theory in this book, but the account of values given in chapters 2 and 3 amounts to what I believe is a comprehensive alternative to it.

26 Ibid., p. 87.

27 Goodin himself admits his claim would be hard, if not impossible, to prove since he would have to show his theory of value to be the only thread that could possibly be running through all the planks of the green political programme. He therefore opts to proceed more impressionistically, elaborating his claim by means of examples.

Unfortunately, however, the main example he chooses scarcely provides clear support even for a modest reading of his claim. The example concerns green attitudes to animals: Goodin remarks that greens are generally concerned less with the rights or welfare of individual animals than with threats posed to whole species. On the basis of this opposition he thinks to set out the virtue of his theory (p. 90). What he has done, though, is assign greens to the camp of environmentalists as opposed to the camp of animal concern. Aside from its dubious relation to any actual evidence about greens' beliefs, I think it is anyway highly tenuous even as a statement of what they should consistently believe: for not only *do* many greens care about animal welfare and rights, their caring could be shown to derive from just the sort of concern for nature that Goodin himself prescribes. Indeed, it can well be argued (as we saw in the previous chapter that it is by animal liberationists) that reasons favouring the natural environment over particular animals can be reduced to less green and more anthropocentric premises. To the extent that there are anomalies here, Goodin's green theory of value does not suffice to resolve them, and does not yield unequivocal guidance. It therefore does nothing to prevent piecemeal borrowing.

28 This distinction is from Habermas: for a concise statement see *Moral Consciousness and Communicative Action*, p. 58; its implications are further explored in section 5.3. Relatedly, Offe has shown differences between monological and dialogical models of coordination, emphasizing how collective action can depend on learning and refining interests (Claus Offe and Helmut Wiesenthal, 'Two Logics of Collective Action').

29 Goodin, *Green Political Theory*, p. 168.

30 Ibid.

31 Dobson, *Green Political Thought*, p. 205.

32 For an overview of the range, see Boris Frankel, *The Post-Industrial Utopians*.

33 This description is a summary of Goodin, *Green Political Theory*, pp. 149–50.

34 Kropotkin's *Mutual Aid*, in particular, is frequently referred to as a seminal tract in this connection.

35 Eckersley, *Environmentalism and Political Theory*, p. 145.

36 Murray Bookchin, *Ecology and Revolutionary Thought*, p. 14.

37 Ibid.

38 Quoted in Goodin, *Green Political Theory*, p. 149n.

39 From ibid., p. 150.

40 Sale quoted in Dobson, *Green Political Thought*, p. 119.

41 Ibid.

42 Ibid.

43 Cf. John S. Dryzek, 'Ecology and Discursive Democracy'.

44 Cf. Dryzek, *Rational Ecology*, chapter 8.

45 Quoted in Hülsberg, *The German Greens*, p. 78.

46 Joachim Hirsch, 'Die Grünen: Zwischen Fundamentalopposition und Realpolitik', p. 11.

47 Hülsberg, *The German Greens*, p. 123.

48 Goodin, *Green Political Theory*, pp. 144–6.

49 Ibid., p. 142.

50 Ibid., p. 144.

51 Dobson, *Green Political Thought*, p. 135.

52 This is the conclusion Rudolf Bahro came to: see Bahro's resignation speech, *Building the Green Movement*, pp. 210–11.

53 E.F. Schumacher, *Small is Beautiful*, pp. 249–50.

54 See Bill Devall, *Simple in Means, Rich in Ends*.

55 Arne Naess, *Ecology, Community and Lifestyle*, p. 89.

56 Dobson, *Green Political Thought*, p. 140.
57 Naess, *Ecology, Community and Lifestyle*, p. 91.
58 Dobson, *Green Political Thought*, p. 141.
59 Ibid., pp. 142–3.
60 Ibid., p. 146.
61 Quoted in Frankel, *The Post-Industrial Utopians*, p. 140.
62 Eckersley, *Environmentalism and Political Theory*, p. 165.
63 Naess, *Ecology, Community and Lifestyle*, p. 159.
64 Gorz quoted in Frankel, *The Post-Industrial Utopians*, p. 59.
65 Dobson, *Green Political Thought*, p. 124.
66 Paehlke in Eckersley, *Environmentalism and Political Theory*, p. 174.
67 Cf. Anthony Arblaster, *Democracy*.
68 Quoted in Dobson, *Green Political Thought*, p. 122.
69 P. Kemp and D. Wall, *A Green Manifesto for the 1990s* p. 177.
70 Despite the high standards of political morality professed by green spokespersons, there is a disconcerting tendency of some to make a radical distinction between what they, as deep Greens, really think and can say in conversation with likeminded people, and what they will say in public contexts to the uninitiated, who are expected at best to grasp a shallow message which is not merely simplified but qualitatively different. This tendency, as manifest in Jonathon Porritt's *Seeing Green* for instance, has been remarked on by Dobson, *Green Political Thought*, p. 20. I should therefore emphasize that when I speak of overcoming oppositions between reformists and radicals, this condescending, one-way transmission of diluted messages is *not* what I mean. What I envisage is a dialogical exchange of the best possible information, which would also allow the views of the 'private ecologist' to have an airing from which they might benefit. In this regard, J.S. Mill's arguments for freedom of thought and discussion remain a benchmark of good sense.
71 Cf. Joseph Schumpeter, *Capitalism, Socialism and Democracy*.
72 Offe and Wiesenthal, 'Two Logics of Collective Action'.
73 Cf. e.g. Will Kymlicka, *Contemporary Political Philosophy*, chapter 6; also the critical discussion in Seyla Benhabib, *Situating the Self*, chapter 3, especially pp. 96ff on legitimacy and the requirement of neutrality as a constraint in liberalism.
74 Benhabib, *Situating the Self*, p. 100.
75 Cf. H. Marcuse, 'Repressive Tolerance'.
76 Benhabib, *Situating the Self*, pp. 100–1.
77 Ibid., p. 104.
78 Ibid., p. 105.
79 Ibid., p. 98.
80 Dryzek, 'Ecology and Discursive Democracy', p. 38.
81 Ibid, p. 39.
82 Ibid.
83 Ibid.
84 Andrew Dobson, 'Critical Theory and Green Politics', p. 98.
85 Horkheimer quoted in ibid., pp. 201–2.
86 Horkheimer quoted in ibid., p. 202.
87 Barbara Holland-Cunz, 'Eco-Feminist Philosophy: Interview', pp. 76–7.
88 It is one of the key concepts elaborated in Ernst Bloch, *Das Prinzip Hoffnung*.
89 John Ely, 'Marxism and Green Politics in West Germany', p. 36.
90 Karl Marx, 'Letter to Ruge', pp. 207–8.
91 See e.g. Ernst Bloch, 'Marx, aufrechter Gang, konkrete Utopie'.
92 Seyla Benhabib, *Critique, Norm, and Utopia*, p. 35.

93 Steven Lukes, 'Marxism and Utopianism', p. 158.
94 Ibid., p. 159.
95 Benhabib, *Critique, Norm, and Utopia*, p. 329.
96 Ibid., p. 13.
97 Ibid., my emphasis.
98 Ibid.
99 Ibid., p. 352.

Afterword: Ecological Enlightenment

1 Arne Naess, 'Notes on the Politics of the Deep Ecology Movement', p. 180.

Bibliography

Acot, Pascal, *Storia dell'ecologia*, Lucarini, Rome, 1989; trans. from the French, *Histoire de l'écologie*, Presse Universitaire de France, Paris, 1988.

Aiken, William, 'Human Rights in an Ecological Era', *Environmental Values*, 1, 3 (1992), pp. 191–203.

Alford, C. Fred, *Science and the Revenge of Nature*, University Presses of Florida, Tampa/Gainsville, 1985.

Altvater, Elmar, 'Ecological and Economic Modalities of Time and Space', *Capitalism, Nature, Socialism*, 3 (1989), pp. 59–70.

Anderson, Victor, *Alternative Economic Indicators*, Routledge, London, 1990.

Apel, Karl-Otto, 'The Problem of a Macroethic of Responsibility to the Future', *Man and World*, 20 (1987), pp. 3–40.

Apel, Karl-Otto, 'The Ecological Crisis as a Problem for Discourse Ethics', in *Ecology and Ethics*, ed. Audun Øfsti, Tapir Trykk, Trondheim, 1992.

Arblaster, Anthony, *Democracy*, Open University Press, Milton Keynes, 1987.

Arnaud, A.J. and Kingdom, E., *Women's Rights and the Rights of Man*, Aberdeen University Press, Aberdeen, 1990.

Atkinson, Adrian, *Principles of Political Ecology*, Belhaven Press, London, 1991.

Attfield, Robin, 'The Good of Trees', *Journal of Value Inquiry*, 15 (1981), pp. 35–54.

Attfield, Robin, 'Western Traditions and Environmental Ethics', in *Environment Philosophy*, eds R. Elliott and A. Gare, Open University, Milton Keynes, 1983.

Attfield, Robin, *A Theory of Value and Obligation*, Croom Helm, London, New York and Sydney, 1987.

Attfield, Robin, *The Ethics of Environmental Concern*, 2nd edn, The University of Georgia Press, Athens and London, 1991.

Attfield, Robin, 'Sylvan, Fox and Deep Ecology: A View from the Continental Shelf', *Environmental Values*, 2, 1 (1993), pp. 21–32.

Attfield, Robin, 'The Comprehensive Ecology Movement', in *Environment Philosophy: Principles and Prospects*, Avebury, Aldershot, 1994.

Attfield, Robin and Belsey, Andrew (eds), *Philosophy and the Natural Environment*, Cambridge University Press, Cambridge, 1994.

Attfield, Robin and Dell, Katharine (eds), *Values, Conflict and the Environment*, Ian Ramsey Centre, Oxford, and Centre for Applied Ethics, Cardiff, 1989.

Bahro, Rudolf, *The Alternative in Eastern Europe*, trans. D. Fernbach, Verso, London, 1978.

Bahro, Rudolf, *Socialism and Survival*, trans. D. Fernbach, with an introduction by E.P. Thompson, Heretic Books, London, 1978.

Bahro, Rudolf, *From Red to Green*, Verso, London, 1984.

Bahro, Rudolf, *Building the Green Movement*, trans. Mary Tyler, Heretic Books, London, 1986.

Bahro, Rudolf and Vester, Michael, 'Seven Taboos and a Perspective', *Telos*, 51 (1982), pp. 45–52.

Balbus, Isaac, 'A Neo-Hegelian, Feminist, Psychoanalytic Perspective on Ecology', *Telos*, 52 (1982), pp. 140–55.

Balibar, E., 'Irrationalism and Marxism', *New Left Review*, 107 (1977), pp. 3–18.

Bangone, Gianfranco et al., *Gli ordini del caos*, Manifestolibri, Rome, 1991.

Banks, Ronald (ed.), *Costing the Earth*, Shepheard-Waldwyn/CIT, London, 1989.

Bartolommei, Sergio, *Etica e ambiente*, Guerini, Milan, 1989.

Bateson, Gregory, *Steps to an Ecology of Mind*, Ballantine Books, New York, 1972.

Bateson, Gregory, *Mind and Nature: A Necessary Unity*, Bantam Books, New York, 1980.

Baudrillard, Jean, *The Mirror of Production*, trans. with introduction by Mark Poster, Telos Press, St Louis, 1975.

Beckenbach, Frank, 'Social Costs in Modern Capitalism', *Capitalism, Nature, Socialism*, 3 (1989), pp. 72–91.

Becker, Egon, 'Natur als Politik?', in *Grüne Politik: Eine Standortbestimmung*, ed. Thomas Kluge, Fischer, Frankfurt, 1984.

Beechey, Veronica, *Unequal Work*, Verso, London, 1987.

Benhabib, Seyla, 'Modernity and the Aporias of Critical Theory', *Telos*, 49 (1981), pp. 39–59.

Benhabib, Seyla, 'The Methodological Illusions of Modern Political Theory: The Case of Rawls and Habermas', *Neue Hefte für Philosophie*, 21 (1982), pp. 47–74.

Benhabib, Seyla, 'Obligation, Contract and Exchange: On the Significance of Hegel's Abstract Right', in *The State and Civil Society*, vol. 2, ed. Z.A. Pelczynski, Cambridge University Press, Cambridge, 1984.

Benhabib, Seyla, 'The Generalized and the Concrete Other: The Kohlberg–Gilligan Controversy and Feminist Theory', *Praxis International*, 5, 4 (1986), pp. 402–24; reprinted in Seyla Benhabib, *Situating the Self*, Polity Press, Cambridge, 1992.

Benhabib, Seyla, *Critique, Norm and Utopia: A Study of the Foundations of Critical Theory*, Columbia University Press, New York, 1986.

Benhabib, Seyla, *Situating the Self: Gender, Community and Postmodernism in Contemporary Ethics*, Polity Press, Cambridge, 1992.

Benhabib, Seyla and Cornell, Drucilla, 'Beyond the Politics of Gender', in *Feminism as Critique: Essays on the Politics of Gender in Late-Capitalist Societies*, eds Seyla Benhabib and Drucilla Cornell, Polity Press, Cambridge, 1987.

Bentham, Jeremy, *Introduction to the Principles of Morals and Legislation*, chapters I–V in *Utilitarianism*, ed. M. Warnock, Collins, London, 1962.

Benton, Ted, 'Humanism = Speciesism? Marx on Humans and Animals', *Radical Philosophy*, 50 (1988), pp. 4–18; reprinted in *Socialism, Feminism and Philosophy*, eds Sean Sayers and Peter Osborne, Routledge, London, 1990.

Benton, Ted, 'Marxism and Natural Limits: An Ecological Critique and Reconstruction', *New Left Review*, 178 (1989), pp. 51–86.

Benton, Ted, 'On the Limits of Malleability', *Capitalism, Nature, Socialism*, 4 (1990), pp. 68–71.

Benton, Ted, 'The Malthusian Challenge: Ecology, Natural Limits and Human Emancipation', in *Socialism and the Limits of Liberalism*, ed. P. Osborne, Verso, London, 1991.

Benton, Ted, 'Ecology, Socialism and the Mastery of Nature: A Reply to Reiner Grundmann', *New Left Review*, 194 (1992), pp. 55–74.

Benton, Ted, 'Animal Wrongs and Rights: Prolegomena to a Debate', *Capitalism, Nature, Socialism*, 10 (1992), pp. 79–82.

Benton, Ted, *Natural Relations: Ecology, Animal Rights and Social Justice*, Verso, London and New York, 1993.

Berlin, Isaiah, 'Two Concepts of Liberty', in *Liberty*, ed. David Miller, Oxford University Press, Oxford, 1991.

Bernstein, Richard J., 'Heidegger on Humanism', *Praxis International*, 5, 2 (1985), pp. 95–114.

Bhaskar, Roy, *The Possibility of Naturalism: A Philosophical Critique of the Contemporary Human Sciences*, Harvester, Brighton, 1979.

Bhaskar, Roy, *Reclaiming Reality: A Critical Introduction to Contemporary Philosophy*, Verso, London, 1989.

Bickerich, Wolfram (ed.), *SPD und Grüne: Das neue Bündnis?*, Spiegel Verlag, Hamburg, 1985.

Birch, Charles and Cobb, John B., *The Liberation of Life: From the Cell to the Community*, Cambridge University Press, Cambridge, 1981.

Blackstone, W.T. (ed.), *Philosophy and Environmental Crisis*, University of Georgia Press, Athens, 1974.

Bloch, Ernst, *Das Prinzip Hoffnung*, three volumes, Suhrkamp, Frankfurt, 1959.

Bloch, Ernst, *Naturrecht und menschliche Würde*, Suhrkamp, Frankfurt, 1961.

Bloch, Ernst, 'Marx, aufrechter Gang, konkrete Utopie', in *Uber Karl Marx*, Suhrkamp, Frankfurt, 1968.

Blumenberg, Hans, *The Legitimacy of the Modern Age*, trans. R.M. Wallace, MIT Press, Cambridge, MA and London, 1983.

Bocchi, Gianluca, Ceruti, Mauro and Morin, Edgar, *Turbare il futuro: un nuovo inizio per la civiltà planetaria*, Moretti and Vitali, Bergamo, 1990.

Böhme, Gernot and Schramm, Engelbert (eds), *Soziale Naturwissenschaft: Wege zu einer Erweiterung der Ökologie*, Fischer, Frankfurt, 1985.

Bookchin, Murray, *Ecology and Revolutionary Thought*, with an introduction by Howard Hawkins, Green Program Project, Vermont, undated (first published in 1964).

Bookchin, Murray, *Toward an Ecological Society*, Black Rose Books, Montreal, 1980.

Bookchin, Murray, *The Ecology of Freedom*, Cheshire Books, Palo Alto, California, 1982.

Bookchin, Murray, 'Finding the Subject: Notes on Whitebook and Habermas Ltd.', *Telos*, 52 (1982), pp. 78–98.

Bookchin, Murray, 'Social Ecology versus "Deep Ecology": A Challenge for the Ecology Movement', *Green Perspectives*, 4/5 (1987), the newsletter of the Green Program Project.

Bramwell, Anna, *Ecology in the 20th Century: A History*, Yale University Press, New Haven, 1989.

Brandt, W., *North–South: A Programme for Survival*, Pan, London, 1980.

Brennan, Andrew, *Thinking about Nature: An Investigation of Nature, Value and Ecology*, Routledge, London, 1988.

Bryson, Valerie, *Feminist Political Theory: An Introduction*, Macmillan, London, 1992.

Callicott, J. Baird, 'Elements of an Environmental Ethic: Moral Considerability and the Biotic Community', *Environmental Ethics*, 1 (1979), pp. 71–81.

Callicott, J. Baird, 'Animal Liberation: A Triangular Affair', *Environmental Ethics*, 2 (1980), pp. 311–38.

Callicott, J. Baird, 'Hume's *Is/Ought* Dichotomy and the Relation of Ecology to Leopold's Land Ethic', *Environmental Ethics*, 4 (1982), pp. 163–74.

Callicott, J. Baird, 'Traditional American Indian and Traditional Western European Attitudes towards Nature', in *Environmental Philosophy*, eds R. Elliot and A. Gare, Open University Press, Milton Keynes, 1983.

Callicott, J. Baird, 'Intrinsic Value, Quantum Theory and Environmental Ethics', *Environmental Ethics*, 7 (1985), pp. 257–75.

Callicott, J. Baird, 'The Metaphysical Implications of Ecology' *Environmental Ethics*, 8 (1986), pp. 301–16.

Callicott, J. Baird, 'The Case against Moral Pluralism', *Environmental Ethics*, 12 (1990), pp. 99–124.

Caney, Simon, 'Liberalism and Communitarianism: A Misconceived Debate', *Political Studies*, XL, 2 (1992), pp. 273–89.

Capra, Fritjof, *The Turning Point*, Fontana, London, 1983.

Capra, Fritjof and Spretnak, Charlene, *Green Politics*, Hutchinson, London, 1984.

Carver, Terrell, 'Marx's Commodity Fetishism', *Inquiry*, 18 (1975), pp. 39–63.

Cassano, Franco, 'Il diritto e il suo rovescio', *Democrazia e Diritto*, 2–3 (1988), pp. 31–41.

Cassirer, Ernst, *Rousseau, Kant, Goethe: Two Essays*, Princeton University Press, Princeton, 1945.

Cassirer, Ernst, *The Philosophy of the Enlightenment*, trans. F.C.A. Koelln and J.P. Pettegrove, Princeton University Press, Princeton, 1951.

Castoriadis, Cornelius, 'From Marx to Aristotle, from Aristotle to Us', *Social Research*, 45, (1978), pp. 667–738.

Cini, Marcello, 'Science and Sustainable Society', *Capitalism, Nature, Socialism*, 7 (1991), pp. 39–54.

Clark, Lorenne M.G. and Lange, Lynda (eds), *The Sexism of Social and Political Theory*, University of Toronto Press, Toronto, 1979.

Cohen, G.A., 'Freedom, Justice, and Capitalism', *New Left Review*, 126 (1981), pp. 3–16.

Cohen, G.A., 'Capitalism, Freedom, and the Proletariat', in *Liberty*, ed. David Miller, Oxford University Press, Oxford, 1991.

Cohen, Jean L., *Class and Civil Society: The Limits of Marxian Critical Theory*, Martin Robertson, Oxford, 1982.

Collard, Andrée, *Rape of the Wild: Man's Violence against Animals and the Earth*, Women's Press, London, 1988.

Collingwood, R.G., *The Idea of Nature*, Oxford University Press, Oxford, 1945.

Court, Thijs de la, *Beyond Brundtland: Green Development in the 1990s*, Zed Books, London, 1990.

Cramer, Jacqueline and Daele, Wolfgang van den, 'Is Ecology an "Alternative" Natural Science?', *Synthese*, 65 (1985), pp. 347–75.

Cranston, Maurice, 'Human Rights, Real and Supposed', in *Political Theory and the Rights of Man*, ed. D.D. Raphael, Indiana University Press, Bloomington, 1967.

Daly, Herman (ed.), *Toward a Steady-State Economy*, W.H. Freeman, San Francisco, 1973.

Daly, Herman, *Steady-State Economics*, W.H. Freeman, San Francisco, 1977.

Daly, Herman (ed.), *Economics, Ecology, Ethics*, W.H. Freeman, San Francisco, 1980.

Daly, Herman E. and Cobb, John B., *For the Common Good: Redirecting the Economy toward Community, the Environment, and a Sustainable Future*, Green Print, London, 1990.

Deléage, Jean-Paul, 'Eco-Marxist Critique of Political Economy', *Capitalism, Nature, Socialism*, 3 (1989), pp. 15–31.

Delphy, Christine and Leonard, Diana, *Familiar Exploitation: A New Analysis of Marriage in Contemporary Western Societies*, Polity Press, Cambridge, 1992.

Demirovic, Alex, 'Ecological Crisis and the Future of Democracy', *Capitalism, Nature, Socialism*, 2 (1989), pp. 40–61.

Devall, Bill, *Simple in Means, Rich in Ends: Practising Deep Ecology*, Green Print, London, 1990.

Dickens, Peter, *Society and Nature: Towards a Green Social Theory*, Harvester Wheatsheaf, Hemel Hempstead, 1992.

Die Grünen, The Program of the Green Party of the Federal Republic of Germany, Bonn, 1983.

Dobson, Andrew, *Green Political Thought*, Unwin Hyman, London, 1990.

Dobson, Andrew, 'Critical Theory and Green Politics', in *The Politics of Nature*, eds A. Dobson and P. Lucardie, Routledge, London, 1993.

Dobson, Andrew and Lucardie, Paul (eds), *The Politics of Nature*, Routledge, London, 1993.

Douglas, Mary, *Purity and Danger*, Routledge, London, 1991.

Douglas, Mary and Wildavsky, Aaron, *Risk and Culture: An Essay on the Selection of Technological and Environmental Dangers*, University of California Press, London, 1983.

Doyal, Len and Gough, Ian, *A Theory of Human Need*, Macmillan, London, 1991.

Dryzek, John S., *Rational Ecology: Environment and Political Economy*, Blackwell, Oxford, 1987.

Dryzek, John S., 'Green Reason: Communicative Ethics for the Biosphere', *Environmental Ethics*, 12 (1990), pp. 195–210.

Dryzek, John S., 'Ecology and Discursive Democracy: Beyond Liberal Capitalism and the Administrative State', *Capitalism, Nature, Socialism*, 10 (1992), pp. 18–42.

Easlea, Brian, *Liberation and the Aims of Science: An Essay on Obstacles to the Building of a Beautiful World*, Chatto and Windus, London, 1973.

Easlea, Brian, *Science and Sexual Oppression: Patriarchy's Confrontation with Women and Nature*, Weidenfeld and Nicholson, London, 1981.

Eckersley, Robyn, *Environmentalism and Political Theory*, UCL Press, London, 1992.

Eckersley, Robyn, 'Free Market Environmentalism: Friend or Foe?', *Environmental Politics*, 2 (1993), pp. 1–19.

Eder, Klaus, 'A New Social Movement?', *Telos*, 52 (1982), pp. 5–20.

Eder, Klaus, *Die Vergesellschaftung der Natur: Studien zur sozialen Evolution der praktischen Vernunft*, Suhrkamp, Frankfurt, 1988.

Ehrenfeld, David, *The Arrogance of Humanism*, Oxford University Press, Oxford, 1978.

Ehrlich, Paul R., *The Population Bomb*, Pan/Ballantine, London, 1971.

Ekins, Paul (ed.), *The Living Economy*, Routledge and Kegan Paul, London, 1986.

Elkington, John and Burke, Tom, *The Green Capitalists*, Victor Gollancz, London, 1989.

Elliot, Robert, 'Ecology and the Ethics of Environmental Restoration', in *Philosophy and the Natural Environment*, eds Robin Attfield and Andrew Belsey, Cambridge University Press, Cambridge, 1994.

Elliot, Robert and Gare, Aaron (eds), *Environmental Philosophy*, Open University, Milton Keynes, 1983.

Ely, John, 'Marxism and Green Politics in West Germany', *Thesis 11*, 13 (1986), pp. 22–38.

Ely, John, 'Ernst Bloch and the Second Contradiction of Capitalism', *Capitalism, Nature, Socialism*, 2 (1989), pp. 93–107.

Ely, John, 'An Ecological Ethic? Left Aristotelian Marxism versus the Aristotelian Right', *Capitalism, Nature, Socialism*, 2 (1989) pp. 143–54.

Ely, John, 'Green Politics and the Revolution in Eastern Europe?', *Capitalism, Nature, Socialism*, 4 (1990), pp. 77–97.

Engels, Frederick, 'Introduction to the Dialectics of Nature', in *Selected Works*, K. Marx and F. Engels, Lawrence and Wishart, London, 1968.

Engels, Frederick, 'The Origin of the Family, Private Property and the State', in *Selected Works*, K. Marx and F. Engels, Lawrence and Wishart, London, 1968.

Engels, Frederick, 'Socialism: Utopian and Scientific', in *Selected Works*, K. Marx and F. Engels, Lawrence and Wishart, London, 1968.

Enzensberger, Hans Magnus, 'A Critique of Political Ecology', *New Left Review*, 84 (1974), pp. 3–31.

Evans, Judith et al., *Feminism and Political Theory*, Sage, Beverley Hills, California, 1986.

Faber, Daniel and O'Connor, James, 'The Struggle for Nature: Environmental Crisis and the Crisis of Environmentalism', *Capitalism, Nature, Socialism*, 2 (1989), pp. 12–39.

Feinberg, Joel, 'The Rights of Animals and Unborn Generations', in *Philosophy and Environmental Crisis*, ed. W.T. Blackstone, University of Georgia Press, Athens, 1974.

Ferguson, Ann and Folbre, Nancy, 'The Unhappy Marriage of Patriarchy and Capitalism', in *Women and Revolution*, ed. L. Sargent, South End Press, Boston, 1981.

Foucault, Michel, *Discipline and Punish*, Penguin, Harmondsworth, 1979.

Fox, Warwick, 'Approching Deep Ecology: A Response to Richard Sylvan's Critique of Deep Ecology', Environmental Studies Occasional Paper 20, University of Tasmania, 1989.

Frankel, Boris, *The Post-Industrial Utopians*, Polity Press, Cambridge, 1987.

Frankena, William K., 'Ethics and the Environment', in *Ethics and Problems of the 21st Century*, eds K.E. Goodpaster and K.M. Sayre, Notre Dame University Press, Notre Dame and London, 1979.

Friedman, Marilyn, 'Feminism and Modern Friendship: Dislocating the Community', in *Feminism and Political Theory*, ed. Cass R. Sunstein, University of Chicago Press, Chicago and London, 1990.

Fromm, Erich, *Man for Himself: An Inquiry into the Psychology of Ethics*, Holt, Rinehart and Winston, New York, 1947.

Fromm, Erich, *To Have or To Be*, Abacus, London, 1979.

Gandhi, Mahatma, *Towards Non-Violent Socialism*, Navajivan Press, Ahmedabad, 1951.

Garner, Robert, *Animals, Politics and Morality*, Manchester University Press, Manchester, 1993.

Gay, Peter, *The Enlightenment: An Interpretation*, vol. 1, *The Rise of Modern Paganism*, vol. 2, *The Science of Freedom*, Weidenfield and Nicholson, London, 1967 and 1970.

George, Susan, *How the Other Half Dies: The Real Reasons for World Hunger*, Penguin, Harmondsworth, 1977.

George, Susan, *Ill Fares the Land*, Writers and Readers, London, 1984.

George, Susan, *A Fate Worse than Debt*, Penguin, Harmondsworth, 1988.

Georgescu-Roegen, Nicholas, *The Entropy Law and the Economic Process*, Harvard University Press, Cambridge, MA, 1971.

Georgescu-Roegen, Nicholas, *Energy and Economic Myths: Institutional and Analytical Economic Essays*, Pergamon Press, Oxford, 1976.

Geras, Norman, 'Essence and Appearance: Aspects of Fetishism in Marx's *Capital*', *New Left Review*, 65 (1975), pp. 69–85.

Gilligan, Carol, *In a Different Voice: Psychological Theory and Women's Development*, Harvard University Press, Cambridge, MA, 1982.

Glacken, C.J., *Traces on the Rhodian Shore*, University of California Press, Berkeley, 1967.

Goldman, Michael and O'Connor, James, 'Ideologies of Environmental Crisis: Technology and its Discontents', *Capitalism, Nature, Socialism*, 1 (1988), pp. 91–106.

Golley, F.B., 'Deep Ecology from the Perspective of Environmental Science', *Environmental Ethics*, 9 (1987), pp. 45–55.

Goodin, Robert E., *Green Political Theory*, Polity Press, Cambridge, 1992.

Goodpaster, Kenneth E., 'On Being Morally Considerable', *The Journal of Philosophy*, LXXV, 6 (1978), pp. 308–25.

Goodpaster, Kenneth E., 'From Egoism to Environmentalism', in *Ethics and Problems of the 21st Century*, eds K.E. Goodpaster and K.M. Sayre, Notre Dame University Press, Notre Dame and London, 1979.

Gorz, André, *Ecology as Politics*, South End Press, Boston, 1980.

Gorz, André, *Farewell to the Working Class: An Essay on Post-Industrial Socialism*, trans. Michael Sonenscher, Pluto Press, London, 1982.

Gorz, André, *Paths to Paradise: On the Liberation from Work*, trans. Malcolm Imrie, Pluto Press, London, 1985.

Gorz, André, *Critique of Economic Reason*, Verso, London, 1989.

Griffin, Susan, *Woman and Nature*, Women's Press, London, 1984.

Grove-White, Robin and O'Donovan, Oliver, 'An Alternative Approach', in *Values, Conflict and the Environment*, eds R. Attfield and K. Dell, Ian Ramsey Centre, Oxford and Centre for Applied Ethics, Cardiff, 1989.

Grundmann, Reiner, 'The Ecological Challenge to Marxism', *New Left Review*, 187 (1991), pp. 103–20.

Habermas, Jürgen, *Towards a Rational Society: Student Protest, Science, and Politics*, trans. J.J. Shapiro, Beacon Press, Boston, 1970.

Habermas, Jürgen, *Theory and Practice*, trans. John Viertel, Heinemann, London, 1974.

Habermas, Jürgen, 'The Public Sphere: An Encyclopaedia Article', *New German Critique*, 3 (1974), pp. 49–55.

Habermas, Jürgen, *Legitimation Crisis*, trans. Thomas McCarthy, Heinemann, London, 1976.

Habermas, Jürgen, *Communication and the Evolution of Society*, trans. Thomas McCarthy, Heinemann, London, 1979.

Habermas, Jürgen, 'New Social Movements', *Telos*, 49 (1981), pp. 33–7.

Habermas, Jürgen, 'A Reply to My Critics', in *Habermas: Critical Debates*, eds J.B. Thompson and D. Held, Macmillan, London, 1982.

Habermas, Jürgen, 'The Entwinement of Myth and Enlightenment: Rereading *Dialectic of Enlightenment*', *New German Critique*, 26 (1982), pp. 13–30.

Habermas, Jürgen, *The Theory of Communicative Action*, vol. 1, trans. Thomas McCarthy, Heinemann, London, 1984.

Habermas, Jürgen, *Autonomy and Solidarity: Interviews*, ed. Peter Dews, Verso, London, 1986.

Habermas, Jürgen, *Moral Consciousness and Communicative Action*, trans. Christian Lenhardt and Shierry Weber Nicholson, Polity Press, Cambridge, 1990.

Habermas, Jürgen, *Erläuterungen zur Diskursethik*, Suhrkamp Verlag, Frankfurt, 1991.

Hampson, Norman, *The Enlightenment*, Penguin, Harmondsworth, 1968.

Hardin, Garrett, 'The Tragedy of the Commons', *Science*, 162 (1968), pp. 1243–8; reprinted in Garrett Hardin, *Exploring New Ethics for Survival*, Viking, New York, 1972.

Hardin, Garrett, 'Lifeboat Ethics: The Case against Helping the Poor', in *World Hunger and Moral Obligation*, eds William Aiken and Hugh La Follette, Prentice-Hall, Englewood Cliffs, NJ, 1977.

Hart, H.L.A., 'Are There Any Natural Rights?', *Philosophical Review*, LXIV (1955), pp. 175–91; reprinted in *Theories of Rights*, ed. J. Waldron, Oxford University Press, Oxford, 1984.

Hart, H.L.A., 'Bentham on Legal Rights', in *Oxford Essays in Jurisprudence*, ed. A.W.B. Simpson, Oxford University Press, Oxford, 1973.

Hartmann, Heidi, 'The Unhappy Marriage of Marxism and Feminism: Toward a More Progressive Union', in *Women and Revolution*, ed. L. Sargent, South End Press, Boston, 1981; published in UK as *The Unhappy Marriage of Marxism and Feminism*, Pluto Press, London, 1986.

Harvey, David, 'The Nature of Environment: The Dialectics of Social and Environmental Change', *The Socialist Register*, 1993, eds, R. Miliband and L. Panitch, Merlin Press, London, pp. 1–51.

Hayward, Tim, 'Ecosocialism: Utopian and Scientific', *Radical Philosophy*, 56 (1990), pp. 2–14.

Hayward, Tim, 'Ecology and Human Emancipation', *Radical Philosophy*, 62 (1992), pp. 3–13.

Hayward, Tim, 'The Meaning of Political Ecology', *Radical Philosophy*, 66 (1994), pp. 11–20.

Hayward, Tim, 'Kant and the Moral Considerability of Non-Rational Beings', in *Philosophy and the Natural Environment*, eds, Robin Attfield and Andrew Belsey, Cambridge University Press, Cambridge, 1994.

Hegel, G.W.F., *Phenomenology of Spirit*, trans. A.V. Miller, Clarendon Press, Oxford, 1977.

Heidegger, Martin, *Being and Time*, trans. J. Macquarrie and E. Robinson, Harper and Row, New York, 1962.

Heidegger, Martin, 'Letter on Humanism', in *Basic Writings*, ed. D.F. Krell, Harper and Row, New York, 1977.

Held, David, *Introduction to Critical Theory: Horkheimer to Habermas*, Hutchinson, London, 1980.

Heller, Agnes, *The Theory of Need in Marx*, St Martin's Press, New York, 1976.

Henderson, Hazel, *Creating Alternative Futures*, Berkley Windhover, New York, 1978.

Henderson, Hazel, *The Politics of the Solar Age: Alternatives to Economics*, Anchor/Doubleday, New York, 1981.

Hirsch, Fred, *Social Limits to Growth*, Routledge and Kegan Paul, London, 1977.

Hirsch, Joachim, 'Die Grünen: Zwischen Fundamentalopposition und Realpolitik', *Grüne Hessen-zeitung*, no. 9/10 (December/January 1982/3), pp. 8–11.

Hohendahl, Peter Uwe, 'Critical Theory, Public Sphere and Culture. Jürgen Habermas and his Critics', *New German Critique*, 16 (1979), pp. 89–118.

Hohfeld, Wesley N., *Fundamental Legal Conceptions*, Yale University Press, New Haven, 1919.

Holland, Alan, 'Natural Capital', in *Philosophy and the Natural Environment*, eds. Robin Attfield and Andrew Belsey, Cambridge University Press, Cambridge, 1994.

Holland-Cunz, Barbara, 'Eco-Feminist Philosophy': an interview by Valerie Kuletz, *Capitalism, Nature, Socialism*, 10 (1992), pp. 63–78.

Horkheimer, Max, *Critical Theory: Selected Essays*, trans. M.J. O'Connell et al., Herder and Herder, New York, 1972.

Horkheimer, Max, *The Eclipse of Reason*, Seabury Press, New York, 1974.

Horkheimer, Max and Adorno, Theodor A., *Dialektik der Aufklärung*, Fischer, Frankfurt, 1969; trans. John Cumming, *Dialectic of Enlightenment*, Verso, London, 1979.

Hudson, Wayne, *The Marxist Philosophy of Ernst Bloch*, Macmillan, London, 1982.

Hull, David L., *Philosophy of Biological Science*, Prentice-Hall, Englewood Cliffs and London, 1974.

Hülsberg, Werner, *The German Greens: A Social and Political Profile*, trans. Gus Fagan, Verso, London, 1988.

Illich, Ivan, *Tools for Conviviality*, Calder and Boyers, London, 1973.

Illich, Ivan, *Towards a History of Needs*, Pantheon, New York, 1978.

Illich, Ivan, *Shadow Work*, Marion Boyars, London, 1981.

Ilting, Karl–Heinz, 'Naturrecht', encyclopaedia article in *Geschichtliche Grundbegriffe*, Klett, Stuttgart, 1984.

Jacobelli, Jader (ed.), *Il pensiero verde tra utopia e realismo*, Laterza, Bari, 1989.

Jacobs, Michael, 'Growth Can Be Green', *New Ground*, Winter/Spring 1989, pp. 5–6.

Jamieson, Dale, 'Global Environmental Justice', in *Philosophy and the Natural Environment*, eds Robin Attfield and Andrew Belsey, Cambridge University Press, Cambridge, 1994.

Johnson, David K. and Johnson, Kathleen R., 'Humans Must Be So Lucky: Moral Prejudice, Speciesism and Animal Liberation', *Capitalism, Nature, Socialism*, 10 (1992), pp. 83–109.

Johnson, Edward, 'Animal Liberation versus the Land Ethic', *Environmental Ethics*, 3 (1981), pp. 265–73.

Johnson, Lawrence E., *A Morally Deep World: An Essay on Moral Significance and Environmental Ethics*, Cambridge University Press, Cambridge, 1991.

Johnston, R.J., *Environmental Problems: Nature, Economy and State*, Belhaven Press, London and New York, 1989.

Jonas, Hans, *The Phenomenon of Life: Toward a Philosophical Biology*, Harper and Row, New York, 1966.

Jonas, Hans, *The Imperative of Responsibility: In Search of an Ethics for the Technological Age*, University of Chicago Press, Chicago and London, 1984.

Jones, Alwyn, 'From Fragmentation to Wholeness: a Green Approach to Science and Society', *The Ecologist*, 17, 6 (part 1), 18, 1 (part 2) (1987–8).

Kant, Immanuel, *Critique of Pure Reason*, trans. Norman Kemp Smith, Macmillan, London, 1933.

Kant, Immanuel, *Groundwork of the Metaphysic of Morals*, trans. H.J. Paton as *The Moral Law*, Hutchinson, London, 1948.

Kant, Immanuel, *Critique of Judgment*, trans. James C. Meredith, in *The Philosophy of Kant: Immanuel Kant's Moral and Political Writings*, ed. Carl J. Friedrich, Random House, New York, 1949.

Kant, Immanuel, *Lectures on Ethics*, trans. L. Infield, Harper and Row, New York, 1963.

Kant, Immanuel, *The Doctrine of Virtue*, trans. Mary Gregor, Harper and Row, New York, 1964.

Kant, Immanuel, 'An Answer to the Question: What Is Enlightenment?', trans. Ted Humphrey, in *Perpetual Peace and Other Essays*, ed. Ted Humphrey, Hackett, Indianapolis and Cambridge, 1983.

Keat, Russell, 'Liberal Rights and Socialism', in *Contemporary Political Philosophy*, ed. Keith Graham, Cambridge University Press, Cambridge, 1982.

Kelly, Petra, *Fighting for Hope*, trans. Marianne Howarth and with an introduction by Heinrich Boll, Chatto and Windus, London, 1984.

Kemp, Penny and Wall, Derek, *A Green Manifesto for the 1990s*, Penguin, Harmondsworth, 1990.

Kleinig, John, 'Human Rights, Legal Rights and Social Change', in *Human Rights*, eds Eugene Kamenka and Alice Ehr-Soon Tay, Edward Arnold, London, 1978.

Kluge, Thomas (ed.), *Grüne Politik: Der Stand einer Auseinandersetzung*, Fischer, Frankfurt, 1984.

Kortian, Garbis, *Metacritique: The Philosophical Argument of Jürgen Habermas*, trans. John Raffan with an introductory essay by Charles Taylor and Alan Montefiore, Cambridge University Press, Cambridge, 1980.

Kropotkin, P., *Mutual Aid: A Factor in Evolution*, Porter Sargent, Boston, 1914.

Kuhn, Thomas S., *The Structure of Scientific Revolutions*, 2nd edn, enlarged, University of Chicago Press, Chicago and London, 1970.

Kukathas, Chandran and Pettit, Philip, *Rawls: A Theory of Justice and its Critics*, Polity Press, Cambridge, 1990.

Kymlicka, Will, *Contemporary Political Philosophy: An Introduction*, Clarendon Press, Oxford, 1990.

Laclau, Ernesto and Mouffe, Chantal, *Hegemony and Socialist Strategy: Towards a Radical Democratic Politics*, Verso, London, 1985.

Lee, Donald C., 'Towards a Marxian Ecological Ethic', *Environmental Ethics*, 4 (1982), pp. 339 43.

Lee, Keekok, *Social Philosophy and Ecological Scarcity*, Routledge, London, 1989.

Leiss, William, *The Domination of Nature*, George Braziller, New York, 1972.

Leiss, William, *Under Technology's Thumb*, McGill-Queen's University Press, Montreal, 1990.

Leopold, Aldo, 'The Land Ethic', in Aldo Leopold, *A Sand County Almanac*, Oxford University Press, Oxford, 1949.

Levins, Richard and Lewontin, Richard, 'Dialectics and Reductionism in Ecology', *Synthese*, 43, 1 (1980), pp. 47–78.

Lewontin, Richard and Levins, Richard, 'Animals Have a Complex Nature', *Capitalism, Nature, Socialism*, 4 (1990), pp. 63–7.

Lichtman, Richard, 'The Production of Human Nature by Means of Human Nature', *Capitalism, Nature, Socialism*, 4 (1990), pp. 13–51.

Lichtman, Richard, 'Response to Comments', *Capitalism, Nature, Socialism*, 4 (1990), pp. 72–5.

Lloyd, Genevieve, *The Man of Reason: 'Male' and 'Female' in Western Philosophy*, Methuen, London, 1984.

Locke, John, *Two Treatises of Government*, Dent, London, 1924.

Lovelock, J.E., *Gaia: A New Look at Life on Earth*, Oxford University Press, Oxford, 1979.

Lukes, Steven, *Power: A Radical View*, Macmillan, London, 1974.

Lukes, Steven, 'Can a Marxist Believe in Human Rights?', *Praxis International*, 1, 4 (1982), pp. 334–45.

Lukes, Steven, 'Marxism and Utopianism', in *Utopias*, eds Peter Alexander and Roger Gill, Duckworth, London, 1984.

Lyotard, Jean-François, *The Postmodern Condition*, trans. G. Bennington and B. Manumi, University of Minnesota Press, Minneapolis, 1984.

MacIntyre, Alasdair, *After Virtue: A Study in Moral Theory*, Duckworth, London, 1981.

Macpherson, C.B., *The Political Theory of Possessive Individualism*, Oxford University Press, Oxford, 1962.

Macpherson, C.B., 'Capitalism and the Changing Concept of Property', in *Feudalism, Capitalism and Beyond*, eds E. Kamenka and R.S. Neale, Edward Arnold, London, 1975.

Macpherson, C.B., *The Life and Times of Liberal Democracy*, Oxford University Press, Oxford, 1977.

Macpherson, C.B., *The Rise and Fall of Economic Justice and Other Essays*, Oxford University Press, Oxford, 1987.

Marcuse, Herbert, *Reason and Revolution: Hegel and the Rise of Social Theory*, 2nd edn with supplementary chapter, Routledge and Kegan Paul, London, 1955.

Marcuse, Herbert, *Eros and Civilization: A Philosophical Inquiry into Freud*, Routledge and Kegan Paul, 1956.

Marcuse, Herbert, *One-Dimensional Man: Studies in the Ideology of Advanced Industrial Society*, Beacon Press, Boston, 1964.

Marcuse, Herbert, 'Repressive Tolerance', in R.P. Wolff, B. Moore and H. Marcuse, *A Critique of Pure Tolerance*, Beacon Press, Boston, 1965.

Marietta, Don E., 'The Interrelationship of Ecological Science and Environmental Ethics', *Environmental Ethics*, 2 (1979), pp. 195–207.

Martinez-Alier, Juan, 'Ecological Economics and Eco-Socialism', *Capitalism, Nature, Socialism*, 2 (1989), pp. 109–22.

Martinez-Alier, Juan, *Ecological Economics: Energy, Environment and Society*, with Klaus Schlüpmann, paperback edn with new introduction, Blackwell, Oxford, 1990.

Marx, Karl, *Capital*, vol. 1, ed. F. Engels, trans. S. Moore and E. Aveling, Lawrence and Wishart, London, 1970.

Marx, Karl, *Grundrisse*, trans. M. Nicolaus, Penguin, Harmondsworth, 1973.

Marx, Karl, 'A Contribution to the Critique of Hegel's Philosophy of Right,' in *Early Writings*, ed. Lucio Colletti, trans. R. Livingstone and G. Benton, Penguin, Harmondsworth, 1975.

Marx, Karl, *Early Writings*, ed. Lucio Colletti, trans. R. Livingstone and G. Benton, Penguin, Harmondsworth, 1975.

Marx, Karl, 'On the Jewish Question', in *Early Writings*, ed. Lucio Colletti, trans. R. Livingstone and G. Benton, Penguin, Harmondsworth, 1975.

Marx, Karl, 'Letter to Ruge', in *Early Writings*, ed. Lucio Colletti, trans. R. Livingstone and G. Benton, Penguin, Harmondsworth, 1975.

Marx, Karl, 'Economic and Philosophical Manuscripts (1844)', in *Early Writings*, ed. Lucio Colletti, trans. R. Livingstone and G. Benton, Penguin, Harmondsworth, 1975.

Marx, Karl and Engels, Frederick, *Selected Works*, in one volume, Lawrence and Wishart, London, 1968.

Marx, Karl and Engels, Frederick, *The German Ideology*, ed. C.J. Arthur, Lawrence and Wishart, London, 1977.

Mathews, Freya, *The Ecological Self*, Routledge, London, 1991.

McBurney, Stuart, *Ecology into Economics Won't Go*, Green Books, Bideford, 1990.

McCarthy, Thomas, *The Critical Theory of Jürgen Habermas*, MIT Press, Cambridge, MA, 1978.

McCarthy, Thomas, 'Reflections on Rationalization', in *Habermas and Modernity*, ed. R. Bernstein, MIT Press, Massachusetts, 1985.

McCloskey, H.J., *Ecological Ethics and Politics*, Rowman and Littlefield, Totowa, 1983.

McIntosh, Robert P., 'The Background and Some Current Problems of Theoretical Ecology', *Synthèse*, 43, 1 (1980), pp. 195–255.

McIntosh, Robert P., *The Background of Ecology: Concept and Theory*, Cambridge University Press, Cambridge, 1985.

Meadows, Donella H., Meadows, Dennis L., Randers, Jørgen and Behrens, William W. III, *The Limits to Growth*, a report for the Club of Rome's Project on the Predicament of Mankind, Pan, London, 1974.

Mellor, Mary, 'Eco-Feminism and Eco-Socialism: Dilemmas of Essentialism and Materialism', *Capitalism, Nature, Socialism*, 10 (1992), pp. 43–62.

Merchant, Carolyn, *The Death of Nature: Women, Ecology and the Scientific Revolution*, Wildwood House, London, 1982.

Merchant, Carolyn, *Ecological Revolutions: Nature, Gender and Science in New England*, University of North Carolina Press, Chapel Hill and London, 1989.

Mewes, Horst, 'The West German Green Party', *New German Critique*, 28 (1983), pp. 51–85.

Midgley, Mary, *Beasts and Man: The Roots of Human Nature*, Harvester, Hassocks, 1979.

Midgley, Mary, *Animals and Why They Matter*, Penguin, Harmondsworth, 1983.

Midgley, Mary, 'A Problem of Concern', in *Animal Welfare and The Environment*, ed. Richard D. Ryder, Duckworth/RSPCA, London, 1992.

Mulhall, S. and Swift, A., *Liberals and Communitarians: An Introduction*, Blackwell, Oxford, 1992.

Murphy, J.G., *Kant: The Philosophy of Right*, Macmillan, London, 1970.

Naess, Arne, 'The Shallow and the Deep, Long-Range Ecology Movement', *Inquiry*, 16 (1973), pp. 95–100.

Naess, Arne, 'A Defense of the Deep Ecology Movement', *Environmental Ethics*, 6 (1984), pp. 265–70.

Naess, Arne, *Ecology, Community and Lifestyle*, trans. and ed. David Rothenberg, Cambridge University Press, Cambridge, 1989.

Naess, Arne, 'Notes on the Politics of the Deep Ecology Movement', in *Sustaining Gaia: Contributions to Another World View*, ed. Frank Fisher, Clayton, Victoria, 1987.

Nanda, B.R., *Mahatma Gandhi: A Biography*, Allen and Unwin, London, 1965.

Nebbia, Giorgio, 'La bioeconomia: somiglianze e diversità fra fatti economici e fatti biologici', *Rassegna Economica*, 52,3 (1988), pp. 521–44.

Nebbia, Giorgio, *La società dei rifiuti*, Edipuglia, Bari, 1990.

Nicholson, Linda, 'Feminism and Marx: Integrating Kinship with the Economic', in *Feminism as Critique*, eds S. Benhabib and D. Cornell, Polity Press, Cambridge, 1987.

Norton, Bryan G., 'Environmental Ethics and Nonhuman Rights', *Environmental Ethics*, 4 (1982), pp. 17–36.

Norton, Bryan G., 'Environmental Ethics and the Rights of Future Generations', *Environmental Ethics*, 4 (1982), pp. 319–37.

Norton, Bryan G., 'Environmental Ethics and Weak Anthropocentrism', *Environmental Ethics*, 6 (1984), pp. 133–48.

Norton, Bryan G., 'Intergenerational Equity and Environmental Decisions: A Model Using Rawls's Veil of Ignorance', *Ecological Economics*, 1 (1989) pp. 137–59.

Nozick, Robert, *Anarchy, State and Utopia*, Blackwell, Oxford, 1974.

O'Brien, Mary, 'Reproducing Marxist Man', in *The Sexism of Social and Political Theory*, eds L. Clark and L. Lange, University of Toronto Press, Toronto, 1979.

O'Connor, James, 'Capitalism, Nature, Socialism: A Theoretical Introduction', *Capitalism, Nature, Socialism*, 1 (1988), pp. 11–38.

O'Connor, James, 'Uneven and Combined Development and Ecological Crisis: A Theoretical Introduction', *Race and Class*, 30, 3 (1989), pp. 1–11.

O'Connor,.James, 'Political Economy of Ecology of Socialism and Capitalism', *Capitalism, Nature, Socialism*, 3 (1989), pp. 93–107.

O'Connor, James, 'Global Interdependency and Ecological Socialism', transcript of speech given at Unità festival, Genoa, August 1989.

O'Connor, James, 'Ideologies of Human Nature', *Capitalism, Nature, Socialism*, 4 (1990), pp. 1–9.

O'Connor, James, 'Socialism and Ecology', *Capitalism, Nature, Socialism*, 8 (1991), pp. 1–12.

O'Connor, Martin, 'Codependency and Indeterminacy: A Critique of the Theory of Production', *Capitalism, Nature, Socialism*, 3 (1989), pp. 33–57.

Odum, Eugene P., *Ecology and Our Endangered Life-Support Systems*, Sinauer Associates, Sunderland, MA, 1989.

Offe, Claus, *Contradictions of the Welfare State*, ed. John Keane, Hutchinson, London, 1984.

Offe, Claus and Wiesenthal, Helmut, 'Two Logics of Collective Action', in Claus Offe, *Disorganized Capitalism*, ed. John Keane, Polity Press, Cambridge, 1985; originally published in M. Zeitlin (ed.), *Political Power and Social Theory*, 1 (1980), pp. 67–115.

Olson, Mancur Jr, *The Logic of Collective Action*, Harvard University Press, Cambridge, MA, 1965.

O'Neill, John, 'The Varieties of Intrinsic Value', *Monist*, 75 (1992), pp. 119–37.

O'Neill, John, *Ecology, Policy and Politics: Human Well-Being and the Natural World*, Routledge, London, 1993.

O'Neill, Onora, *Faces of Hunger: An Essay on Poverty, Justice and Development*, Allen and Unwin, London, 1986.

O'Neill, Onora, *Constructions of Reason: Explorations of Kant's Practical Philosophy*, Cambridge University Press, Cambridge, 1989.

Ophuls, William, *Ecology and the Politics of Scarcity*, W.H. Freeman, San Francisco, 1977.

O'Riordan, T., *Environmentalism*, 2nd edn, Pion, London, 1981.

Osborne, Peter (ed.), *Socialism and the Limits of Liberalism*, Verso, London, 1991.

Paehlke, Robert C., *Environmentalism and the Future of Progressive Politics*, Yale University Press, New Haven and London, 1989.

Pantham, Thomas, 'Thinking with Mahatma Gandhi: Beyond Liberal Democracy', *Political Theory*, 112 (1983), pp. 165–88.

Parsons, Howard L., *Marx and Engels on Ecology*, Greenwood Press, Westwood, CT and London, 1977.

Partridge, Ernest, 'On the Rights of Future Generations', in *Upstream/Downstream*, ed. D. Scherer, Temple University Press, Philadelphia, 1990.

Pashukanis, Evgeny B., *Law and Marxism: A General Theory*, trans. B. Einhorn, ed. Chris Arthur, Ink Links, London, 1978.

Passmore, John, *Man's Responsibility for Nature*, Duckworth, London, 1974; 2nd edn, corrected with new preface and appendix, 1980.

Pateman, Carole, *Participation and Democratic Theory*, Cambridge University Press, Cambridge, 1970.

Pateman, Trevor, *Language Truth and Politics*, 2nd edn, Jean Stroud, Lewes, 1980.

Pearce, David et al., *Blueprint for a Green Economy*, Earthscan, London, 1989.

Pearce, David et al., *Blueprint 2: Greening the World Economy*, Earthscan, London, 1991.

Pepper, David, *The Roots of Modern Environmentalism*, Croom Helm, London, 1984.

Plant, Judith (ed.), *Healing the Wounds: The Promise of Ecofeminism*, Green Print, London, 1989.

Plumwood, Val, 'Ecofeminism: An Overview and Discussion of Positions and Arguments', *Australasian Journal of Philosophy*, 64, supplement (1986), pp. 120–38.

Polanyi, Karl, *The Great Transformation*, Beacon Press, Boston, 1967.

Pollis, Adamantia and Schwab, Peter (eds), *Human Rights: Cultural and Ideological Perspectives*, Praeger, New York, 1980.

Porritt, Jonathon, *Seeing Green: The Politics of Ecology Explained*, Blackwell, Oxford, 1984.

Prasad, M., *Social Philosophy of Mahatma Gandhi*, Vishwavidyalaya Prakashan Gorakhpur, India, 1958.

Raphael, D.D., 'Human Rights, Old and New', in *Political Theory and the Rights of Man*, ed. D.D. Raphael, Indiana University Press, Bloomington, 1967.

Ratner, Carl, 'Socio-historical Psychology and Human Nature', *Capitalism, Nature, Socialism*, 4 (1990), pp. 52–62.

Rawls, John, 'Justice as Fairness', in *Philosophy, Politics and Society*, second series, eds Peter Laslett and W.G. Runciman, Blackwell, Oxford, 1962.

Rawls, John, 'Distributive Justice', in *Philosophy, Politics, and Society*, third series, eds Peter Laslett and W.G. Runciman, Blackwell, Oxford, 1967.

Rawls, John, *A Theory of Justice*, Oxford University Press, Oxford, 1971.

Redclift, Michael, *Development and the Environmental Crisis: Red or Green Alternatives?*, Methuen, London, 1984.

Redclift, Michael, *Sustainable Development: Exploring the Contradictions*, Methuen, London, 1987.

Rée, Jonathan, *Descartes*, Allen Lane, London, 1974.

Regan, Tom, 'The Nature and Possibility of an Environmental Ethic', *Environmental Ethics*, 3 (1981), pp. 16–31.

Regan, Tom, *The Case for Animal Rights*, Routledge, London, 1988.

Regan, Tom, 'Animal Rights: What's in a Name?', in *Animal Welfare and the Environment*, ed. Richard D. Ryder, Duckworth/RSPCA, London, 1992.

Rolston, Holmes III, 'Is There an Ecological Ethic?', *Ethics*, 92 (1975), pp. 93–109.

Rolston, Holmes III, 'Are Values in Nature Subjective or Objective?', *Environmental Ethics*, 4 (1982), pp. 125–51.

Rose, Gillian, *Hegel contra Sociology*, Athlone, London, 1981.

Rose, Steven, Critical Discussion of Johnson and Johnson, *Capitalism, Nature, Socialism*, 10 (1992), pp. 117–20.

Roszak, Theodore, *Person/Planet*, Granada, St Albans, 1981.

Rousseau, Jean Jacques, *The Social Contract and Discourses*, trans. with introduction G.D.H. Cole, Dent, London, 1973.

Routley (now Sylvan), Richard and Routley (now Plumwood), Val, 'Against the Inevitability of Human Chauvinism', in *Ethics and Problems of the 21st Century*, eds K.E.

Goodpaster and K.M. Sayre, Notre Dame University Press, Notre Dame and London, 1979.

Ruse, Michael (ed.), *Philosophy of Biology*, Macmillan, New York and London, 1989.

Ryder, Richard D. (ed.), *Animal Welfare and the Environment*, Duckworth/RSPCA, London, 1992.

Ryle, Martin, *Ecology and Socialism*, Radius, London, 1988.

Sachs, Wolfgang, 'Development: A Guide to the Ruins', *The New Internationalist*, 232 (June 1992), pp. 4–27.

Sachs, Wolfgang, 'The Discovery of Poverty', *New Internationalist*, 232 (1992), pp. 7–9.

Sahlins, Marshall, *Stone Age Economics*, Routledge, London, 1988.

Sale, Kirkpatrick, *Human Scale*, Secker and Warburg, London, 1980.

Salleh, Ariel, 'Discussion: Eco-Socialism/Eco-Feminism', *Capitalism, Nature, Socialism*, 6 (1991), pp. 129–34.

Saloman, M. et al., 'Appel de Heidelberg aux chefs d'états et de gouvernements présents à la conférence de Rio de Janiero', in *Environmental Values*, 1 (1992), p. 190.

Sandel, Michael J., *Liberalism and the Limits of Justice*, Cambridge University Press, Cambridge, 1982.

Sargent, Lydia (ed.), *Women and Revolution*, South End Press, Boston, 1981; published in UK as *The Unhappy Marriage of Marxism and Feminism*, Pluto Press, London, 1986.

Scherer, Donald, 'Anthropocentrism, Atomism, and Environmental Ethics', *Environmental Ethics*, 4 (1982), pp. 115–23.

Schmidt, Alfred, *The Concept of Nature in Marx*, New Left Books, London, 1971.

Schouls, Peter A., *Descartes and the Enlightenment*, Edinburgh University Press, Edinburgh, 1989.

Schumacher, E.F., *Small is Beautiful*, Abacus, London, 1974.

Schumacher, E.F., *A Guide for the Perplexed*, Abaçus, London, 1978.

Schumpeter, Joseph, *Capitalism, Socialism and Democracy*, 3rd edn, Allen and Unwin, London, 1950.

Schwarz, Walter and Dorothy, *Breaking Through: Theory and Practice of Wholistic Living*, Green Books, Bideford, 1987.

Shanley, Mary Lyndon and Pateman, Carole (eds), *Feminist Interpretations and Political Theory*, Polity Press, Cambridge, 1990.

Shiva, Vandana, *Staying Alive: Women, Ecology and Development*, Zed Books, London, 1988.

Shiva, Vandana, 'Recovering the Real Meaning of Sustainability', transcript of paper given at Ecosvillupo conference, Siena, November 1989.

Shue, Henry, *Basic Rights: Subsistence, Affluence, and US Foreign Policy*, Princeton University Press, New Jersey, 1980.

Silvestrini, Vittorio, *Ristrutturazione ecologica della civiltà: Il Comunismo verso il terzo millennio*, CUEN, Naples, 1990.

Simberloff, D., 'A Succession of Paradigms in Ecology: Essentialism to Materialism and Probabilism', *Synthese*, 43 (1980), pp. 2–29.

Singer, Peter, *Animal Liberation: A New Ethic for Our Treatment of Animals*, Jonathan Cape, London, 1976.

Singer, Peter, 'Not for Humans Only: The Place of Nonhumans in Environmental Issues', in *Ethics and Problems of the 21st Century*, eds K.E. Goodpaster and K.M. Sayre, Notre Dame University Press, Notre Dame and London, 1979.

Skolimowski, Henryk, *Eco-Philosophy*, Marion Boyars, London, 1981.

Smuts, J.C., *Holism and Evolution*, Macmillan, New York, 1926.

Snoeyenbos, Milton H., 'A Critique of Ehrenfeld's Views on Humanism and the Environment', *Environmental Ethics*, 3 (1981), pp. 231–5.

Sontheimer, Sally (ed.), *Women and the Environment: A Reader: Crisis and Development in the Third World*, Earthscan, London, 1991.

Soper, Kate, *On Human Needs*, Harvester, Brighton, 1981.

Soper, Kate, *Humanism and Anti-Humanism*, Open Court, La Salle, Illinois, 1986.

Soper, Kate, 'Feminism, Humanism and Postmodernism', *Radical Philosophy*, 55 (1990), pp. 11–17.

Soper, Kate, 'Greening Prometheus: Marxism and Ecology', in *Socialism and the Limits of Liberalism*, ed. Peter Osborne, Verso, London, 1991.

Soper, Kate, 'Discussion: Eco-Feminism and Eco-Socialism', *Capitalism, Nature, Socialism*, 11 (1992), pp. 111–14.

Stone, Christopher D., 'Should Trees Have Standing?', *Southern California Law Review*, 45 (1972), pp. 450–501.

Sunstein, Cass R. (ed.), *Feminism and Political Theory*, University of Chicago Press, Chicago and London, 1990.

Sylvan, Richard, 'A Critique of Deep Ecology', *Radical Philosophy*, 40 (1985) pp. 2–12; 41 (1985), pp. 10–22.

Szelenyi, Ivan, 'Whose Alternative?', *New German Critique*, 20 (1981), pp. 117–34.

Tadić, Ljubomir, 'The Marxist Critique of Right in the Philosophy of Ernst Bloch', *Praxis International*, 1, 4 (1982), pp. 422–9.

Tallert, Harry, *Eine Grüne Gegenrevolution: Aspekte der ökologistischen Bewegung*, Ullstein, Frankfurt, 1980.

Taylor, Charles, *Hegel and Modern Society*, Cambridge University Press, Cambridge, 1979.

Taylor, Charles and Montefiore, Alan, 'From an Analytic Perspective', an introductory essay to Garbis Kortian, *Metacritique*, trans. John Raffan, Cambridge University Press, Cambridge, 1980.

Taylor, Paul W., 'The Ethics of Respect for Nature', *Environmental Ethics*, 3 (1981), pp. 197–218.

Taylor, Paul W., 'In Defense of Biocentrism', *Environmental Ethics*, 5 (1983), pp. 237–43.

Thomas, Keith, *Man and the Natural World*, Penguin, Harmondsworth, 1983.

Thompson, E.P., 'Notes on Exterminism', *New Left Review*, 121 (1980), pp. 3–31.

Thompson, Janna, 'Preservation of Wilderness and the Good Life', in *Environmental Philosophy*, eds. R. Elliott and A. Gare, Open University Milton Keynes, 1983.

Thompson, Janna, 'A Refutation of Environmental Ethics', *Environmental Ethics*, 12, 2 (1990), pp. 147–60.

Thompson, John B. and Held, David (eds), *Habermas: Critical Debates*, Macmillan, London, 1982.

Thomson, Judith Jarvis, *The Realm of Rights*, Harvard University Press, Cambridge, MA and London, 1990.

Touraine, Alain, *The Voice and the Eye: An Analysis of Social Movements*, trans. Alan Duff, Cambridge University Press, Cambridge, 1981.

Trainer, Ted, *Developed to Death: Rethinking Third World Development*, Green Print, London, 1989.

Turner, Frederick W. III, *The Portable North American Indian Reader*, Penguin, Harmondsworth, 1977.

Waldron, Jeremy, *Nonsense upon Stilts: Bentham, Burke and Marx on the Rights of Man*, Methuen, London, 1987.

Wall, Derek, *Getting There: Steps to a Green Society*, Green Print, London, 1990.

Walzer, Michael, *Spheres of Justice: A Defence of Pluralism and Equality*, Blackwell, Oxford, 1983.

Waring, Marilyn, *Counting for Nothing: What Men Value and What Women are Worth*, Allen and Unwin Port Nicholson Press, Wellington, NZ, 1988.

Warnock, G.J., *The Object of Morality*, Methuen, New York, 1971.

Webster, John, 'Husbandry Regained: Animals in Sustainable Agriculture', in *Animal Welfare and the Environment*, ed. Richard Ryder, Duckworth/RSPCA, London, 1992.

Weizsacker, Ernst von, 'Economic Measures in Environmental Policy Making', transcript of paper given at Ecosvillupo conference, Siena, November 1989.

Wellmer, Albrecht, *Critical Theory of Society*, trans. John Cumming, Seabury Press, New York, 1974.

White, Lynn Jr, *Medieval Technology and Social Change*, Clarendon Press, Oxford, 1962.

White, Stephen K., *The Recent Work of Jürgen Habermas*, Cambridge University Press, Cambridge, 1988.

Whitebook, Joel, 'The Problem of Nature in Habermas', *Telos*, 40 (1970), pp. 41–69.

Whitebook, Joel, 'Saving the Subject: Modernity and the Problem of the Autonomous Individual', *Telos*, 50 (winter 1981/2), pp. 79–102.

Williams, Raymond, *Socialism and Ecology*, SERA Pamphlet, 1982; reprinted in *Resources of Hope*, Verso, London, 1989.

Wolter, Ulf (ed.), *Rudolf Bahro: Critical Responses*, M.E. Sharpe, White Plains, NY, 1980.

World Commission on Environment and Development (WCED), *Our Common Future*, chair Gro Harlem Brundtland, Oxford University Press, Oxford, 1987.

Worster, D., *Nature's Economy: A History of Ecological Ideas*, Cambridge University Press, Cambridge, 1985.

Young, Iris, 'Beyond the Unhappy Marriage: A Critique of Dual Systems Theory', in *Women and Revolution*, ed. Lydia Sargent, South End Press, Boston, 1981; published in UK as *The Unhappy Marriage of Marxism and Feminism*, Pluto Press, London, 1986.

Zudeick, Peter, *Der Hintern des Teufels*, Elster, Moos and Baden-Baden, 1985.

Index